the executed god

the executed god

The Way of the Cross in Lockdown America

mark lewis taylor

fortress press
minneapolis

THE EXECUTED GOD

The Way of the Cross in Lockdown America

Cover photo: *I'm Going Home,* photograph of gas chamber in Santa Fe, New Mexico, copyright © David Michael Kennedy, Santa Fe, New Mexico, U.S.A. Used by permission.
Cover and interior design: Beth Wright

Library of Congress Cataloging-in-Publication Data

Taylor, Mark L. (Mark Lewis), date-
The executed God : the way of the cross in lockdown America / Mark Lewis Taylor.
p. cm.
Includes bibliographical references and index.
ISBN 0-8006-3283-4 (alk. paper)
1. Punishment—Religious aspects—Christianity. 2. Imprisonment—Religious aspects—Christianity. 3. Capital punishment—Religious aspects—Christianity. 4. Criminal justice, Administration of—United States. 5. Christianity and justice—United States. I. Title.

HV8687 .T38 2001
364.6'0973—dc21

2001018775

The paper used in this publication meets the minimum requirements of American National Standard for Information Sciences—Permanence of Paper for Printed Library Materials, ANSI Z329.48–1984.

Manufactured in the U.S.A. AF1–3283
05 04 03 02 01 1 2 3 4 5 6 7 8 9 10

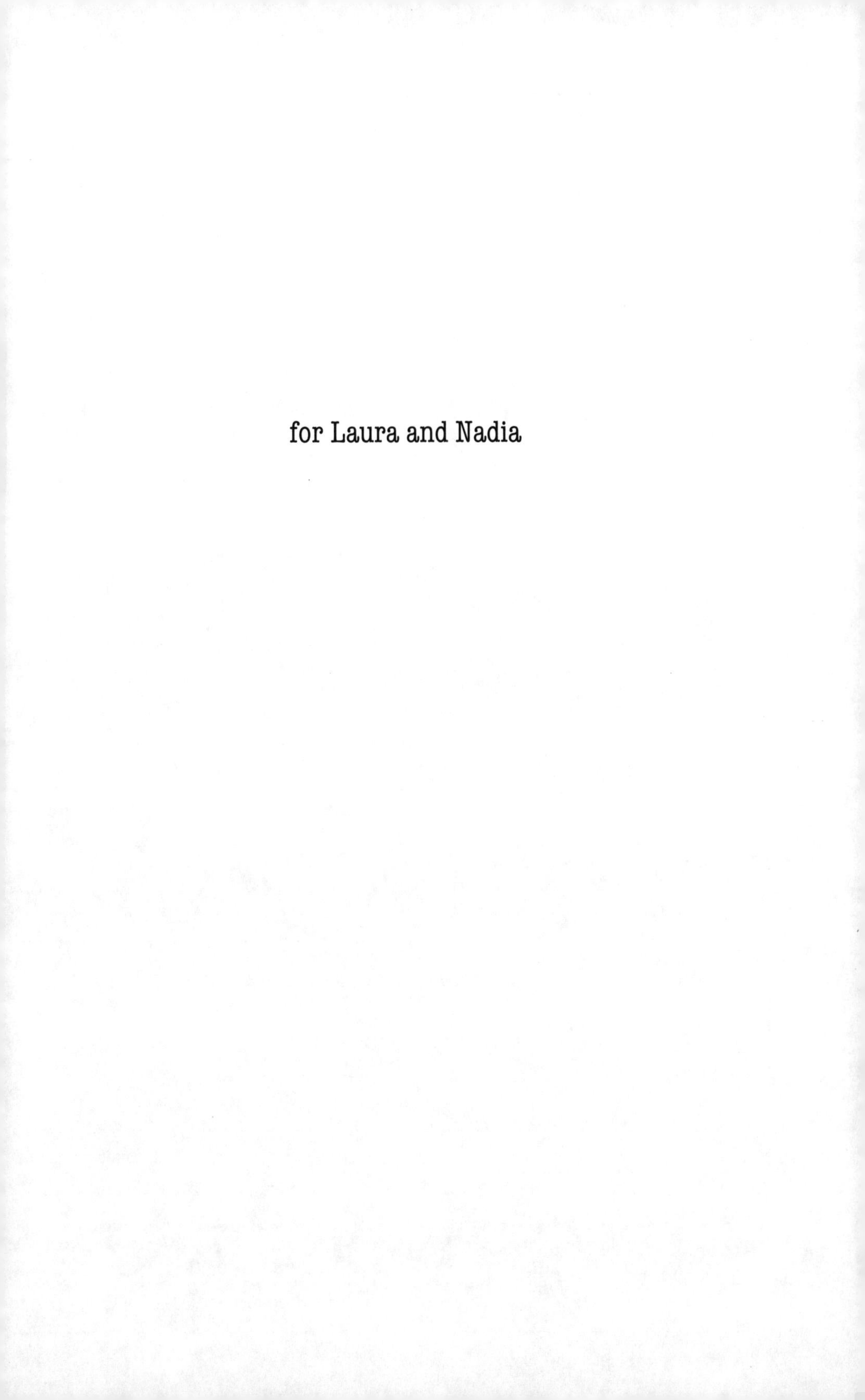

for Laura and Nadia

In this [prison] room, which was called the meeting-room, Nekhlyudov was startled by the sight of a large picture of the crucifixion. "What's that here for?" he thought, his mind involuntarily connecting the subject of the picture with liberation and not with imprisonment.

—Leo Tolstoy, *Resurrection*

contents

preface

> Isn't it odd that Christendom—that huge body of humankind that claims spiritual descent from the Jewish carpenter of Nazareth—claims to pray to and adore a being who was prisoner of Roman power, an inmate of the empire's death row? That the one it considers the personification of the Creator of the Universe was tortured, humiliated, beaten, and crucified on a barren scrap of land on the imperial periphery, at Golgotha, the place of the skull? That the majority of its adherents strenuously support the state's execution of thousands of imprisoned citizens? That the overwhelming majority of its judges, prosecutors, and lawyers—those who condemn, prosecute, and sell out the condemned—claim to be followers of the fettered, spat-upon, naked God?
>
> —Mumia Abu-Jamal, *Death Blossoms: Reflections from a Prisoner of Conscience*

Is it a contradiction that Christians pray to and adore their imprisoned and executed God while supporting or tolerating the execution and imprisonment of so many today? The United States is now on a lockdown craze, and many confessing Christians have played a key part in building it up. Termed *lockdown America* in a recent book by Christian Parenti,[1] this nation now incarcerates more than two million citizens. The massive number now confined—70 percent of whom are people of color—is nearly quadruple the figure of 1980, being "the largest and most frenetic correctional buildup of any country in the history of the world."[2]

Mumia Abu-Jamal is one of these imprisoned two million, and one of the thirty-seven hundred locked down on death row (usually for twenty-two or twenty-three hours per day), awaiting execution. He is fighting for his life and for a new trial, aided in this by Amnesty International, branches of both the National Association for the Advancement of Colored People (NAACP) and the American Civil Liberties Union (ACLU), and by a worldwide movement.[3] In 1999 and 2000 alone, while Abu-Jamal waits and fights for his own life, nearly two hundred people were marched down prison corridors for execution, often with the approval of Christian chaplains and U.S. Christians.

Is Abu-Jamal right? Is there not only something "odd" but perhaps also something hollow, inconsistent, wrong in Christians supporting the imprisoning and executing apparatus of lockdown America while claiming to be followers of a "fettered, spat-upon, naked God"?

Is there not a contradiction when in 2001 a new U.S. president, George W. Bush, confesses Christian belief, attends church, and seeks the blessings of Christian leaders, while proudly announcing his support of executions, overseeing more than 150 of them during his term as governor of Texas?

Not only was Jesus, the "Lord" and "founder" of what came to be called Christianity, executed (after arrest, flogging, torture, and a forced march), but Christians' first prophet, John the Baptist, was also imprisoned and executed. Its first missionaries, Paul and Peter, were imprisoned and executed, the first beheaded, the second crucified. Early followers of Jesus were pitched against empire, often fell out of safe positions in the system, or were disloyal to it. They suffered Rome's punitive regime, living at the edge of prison, in and out of jails, risking torture and execution.[4] Isn't it odd, indeed, that Christians today are so accepting of the punitive regime that is lockdown America?

Many Christian defenders of lockdown America would say, in response to Abu-Jamal, that it is not odd at all. First, Rome was an unjust imperial power that early Christians had to resist, whereas the U.S. system today is not an unjust entity; hence, detentions and executions in America are more justifiable. Second, the defenders might say, the early Christian community should not be likened to the criminal element we see in our prisons and death rows today. Christians should help and approve the locking up and executing of the criminal element today, who are so different from early Christians.

I will show in this book that these defenders are wrong on both their points. First of all, lockdown America today is significantly like the punitive regime of imperial Rome in the early Christian context. There are, to be sure, significant differences, and no easy equations of the two regimes can be made. Some of the most recent and best analyses of empire, however, confirm that the official powers at work in the United States today (often transnational ones working with national and local politicians) are similar to the unjust processes that the first-century Roman empire used against Christians.[5]

As to the second point made by Abu-Jamal's critics, or at least those of them who view early followers of Jesus as nice, noncriminalized people, we need to remember that members of early Jesus movements were much closer to the alleged and actual criminal element than most people think. They were not pure and holy, in the sense of being separate from those whom Rome and Roman society deemed the criminal element. In fact, what Protestant theologian Karl Barth termed "the first Christian community" consisted of the executed Jesus in his relation to common criminals (the thieves alongside of whom he was crucified) and in relation to those convicted of sedition and rebellion.[6]

It is the solidarity of the executed Jesus with the other imprisoned and other executed ones that makes up the "first certain Christian community." The first community *was* this criminal element, all three, Jesus and the criminals, hanging together—"exposed to the same public abuse, to the same interminable pain, to the same slow and irrevocable death throes."[7] Even though Barth emphasizes the importance of this criminal identity taken on in the process of Jesus' crucifixion, he fails to take with theological seriousness the politically seditious character of that identity. What later became Christian community and church was birthed, as this book will argue, from a communal identity that could be labeled both criminal and seditious.[8] The Pauls and Peters, the disciples whom many presume to be Jesus' first community, were not present at the time of execution. These can only "get in line behind the two criminals who were already first, and up there in front, with Jesus on Golgotha."[9]

Abu-Jamal's query stands, then, as not only appropriate but also as a prophetic critique that challenges communities calling themselves Christian. This book will develop an argument that I see as a positive implication of his critique, though he himself does not make it. The overall argument of this book is that remembering the executed Jesus and enacting what I will call his *way of the cross,* are crucial for mobilizing effective resistance to lockdown America today and to the Christendoms that are complicit with it.

The book has a (perhaps) startling culmination. By its end, I am calling Christians to work with all faiths and people of conscience to dismantle the police function as we know it, to terminate our nation's dependency on prisons, and to end the practice of capital punishment. The "executed God," as I will argue throughout the book, is a most needed force for reorienting Christians in the United States to these daring acts of transformation.

The executed Jesus of Nazareth is not in himself some executed God, as readers might first think from this book's title. No, the God who is executed, suffering imperial, state-sanctioned crucifixion, is presented in this book as a whole life force, a greater power, if you will, that is made up of three dynamics that were crucial to Jesus' way of the cross: (1) being politically adversarial to religiously backed imperial power, (2) performing creative and dramatic instances of resistance to imperial power, and (3) organizing movements that can continue resistance and flourish even after imperial executioners do their worst. The executed God is a force of life that is greater than all imperial powers and thus can foment the resistance and hope that all suffering peoples need.

This executed God, the life force that can endure, resist, and flourish in these ways, comes into view when we remember that Jesus on the cross images not just some general death, upon which many traditional notions might be projected (for example, deliverance from guilt and sin, forgiveness, the exemplification of love, and so on). No, Jesus on the cross is best viewed as what that event concretely was, an imperial execution. When understood and interpreted as that kind of death, as it will be in this book, it has a most needed, transformative effect for suffering peoples today.

Christianity's executed God can be understood as catalyzing people's actions to resist and transform lockdown America—with its locked down two million in prisons and its locked up thousands on death row, U.S.A. The transformation needs also to address the way many neighborhoods today are locked down by police surveillance and sweeps. People today are lifting up their cries, as out of some new oppressed Egypt, against an epidemic of police brutality and racial profiling. Even the normally cautious human rights organization Amnesty International charges the United States with violating its own citizens' human rights with a pattern of unchecked police brutality.

If Christians do not act on their solidarity with criminalized populations and locked-down communities, and within a U.S. system more like first-century imperial Rome than we often admit, they still may suffer the indignities of today's punitive regime. This is because lockdown America has become a labyrinthine maze of control that can touch almost all of us in some way. Hundreds of billions of taxpayer dollars stream from the collected wages of our labor into building up the nation's new apparatus of discipline. Millions of U.S. citizens are also enticed today to derive their wages from lockdown America—not only guards, executioners, and prison administrators but also food preparers, social workers, psychologists, chaplains, and, in addition, the many whole communities whose economies are thought to benefit from the presence of a prison in their area.[10] The U.S. political economy of prison industries and execution protocols is giving rise to a whole bureaucracy of punishment and discipline in civil society, which now threatens the freedom of us all.

Amid lockdown America, Abu-Jamal's meditation on the oddness of Christians supporting a state power that imprisons and executes can prompt us to discover and rediscover the power for liberating change that lies along Jesus' way of the cross. Indeed, as Tolstoy's character ruminates in the quote at the front of this book, the crucifixion *can* be connected with liberation, and not just with imprisonment and death penalties.

I write not just out of an altruistic or paternalist concern for the imprisoned and executed other. This work is also offered for all of us whose lives, I believe, are diminished and threatened by our support or toleration of lockdown America. I therefore write with a strong regard for the victims of crime and for the humanity of prison guards, police, executioners, and for all their families. While this book has a primary regard for those who suffer by being kept and terrorized in lockdown America, many of the keepers, who come from all backgrounds and ethnicities in multicultural America, are also people seeking to survive. They attempt to make a living, to wrestle with their own demons (psychic and social), to forge their own growth.

To these keepers, and to all who are complicit with them, this book is an invitation to come out, to acknowledge the systemic failure of so-called criminal justice and law enforcement institutions in this country, to expose not only the occasional imperfections but also the lies that attach to our maintaining the current approaches. The criminal justice system today brutalizes the humanity of those who work to service it.[11] Not only are we tormenting offenders, we are weakening the same social fabric we think supports us all. Lockdown America's rates of incarceration and execution, especially with their racially skewed profiles, are creating more victims of crime and so dishonoring the memory of the many victims who have already suffered.

Many critics outside of Christianity have been repulsed by the church and its long history of imperial pretension, conquest, racist and sexist practice, and more. The efforts of these critics for life and justice in resistance to lockdown America often show more nobility of spirit, love, and justice than do those of many in Christendom. To them I want to say, Yes, let us fight against all oppressive Christendoms and struggle against the repressions of our era, but let us note, too, that Christian remembrance of the executed Jesus, one of thousands crucified by repressive state powers in the first century, is an important resource for Christians who enter the struggle for justice that all people of conscience must wage. Lockdown America is building up a political theatrics of terror, a way of ruling through spectacles that create fear and disseminate regimentation and compliance with growing state powers. I will be proposing that the way of the cross is a Christian resource for creating an alternative to a political theatrics of terror. It is a way to practice a theatrics of *counter*terror, to develop people's own capacity to create movements and alternative dramas (and spectacles) that free the public from fear of, and dominance by, state power.

As in Jesus' day, allowing again for key differences, there is in our day an empire into whose theater of death Christians must walk. "Empires," writes politics professor Michael Doyle, "are relationships of political control by some political societies over the effective sovereignty of other political societies."[12] That imperial phenomenon is very much alive today.

The United States, contrary to many of its citizens' expectations, is not an anti-imperial force. To the contrary, it is the key and privileged player in supporting the imperial ways of a transnational, global empire that services primarily the wealthier nations and the elites in poorer countries.[13] The substance of imperialism, reminds journalist Felix Greene, is "economic exploitation of other peoples buttressed by military and political domination."[14] There is a domestic theatrics of terror within the U.S. industrial state that is part of our nation's participation internationally in the military and political defense of a global empire marked by gross economic inequality. The fusion of our nation's punishment regime at home with a military regime abroad was dramatically signaled in 2001 by the rise of George W. Bush from chief executioner among U.S. governors to chief executive commanding the U.S. military forces that guard transnational business interests. This is empire nearly as real and as vicious as that of Rome. A new millennium has dawned with a superpower presence of the United States that founds what many have called a *Pax Americana* (the imposed ordered peace of America). We might dare to hope that this will drive Christians to embrace the Jesus whose life and death challenged, in his time, the *Pax Romana* (the imposed ordered peace of Rome).

Please do not mistake this critique of Christendom, or the book's critique of today's theater of terror, as a mere rhetoric of denunciation and doom. I do seek to expose a systematic theatrics of terror at work today. This, however, is intrinsic to rhetoric that calls us to resistance, to the practice of a theatrics of counterterror. The very notion of the executed God is a solely gruesome notion only if we forget what it means. Its meaning is that the God of life not only suffered, but also endured and somehow surprisingly continues an effective resistance to executing state powers. I refuse to make sacred any execution—that of Jesus or of anyone else. But along the way of this executed one we can learn of a way that guards the sacredness of life, that resists, challenges, and flourishes amid the terror of executing systems. No, this work is no rhetoric of doom and denunciation. It may be, instead, more than we usually dare to hope. The way of the cross in today's theatrics of terror, in lockdown America, is a way *through* the terrorizing powers toward a restored humanity and civic order. My theological approach is different from Tolstoy's, but in the spirit of his nineteenth-century work, *Resurrection,* this volume will seek to connect the gruesome torture-death of crucifixion "not with imprisonment" but "with liberation."[15]

introduction: The Executed God

> If the concept of God has any validity or any use, it can only be to make us larger, freer and more loving. If God cannot do this, then it is time we got rid of Him.
>
> —James Baldwin, *The Fire Next Time*

To consider the executed God and the spiritual practice that it entails will demand some important preparatory work. Christians have written a great deal on the notion of Jesus' crucifixion and death. What new turn is taken when we emphasize today, as this book does, that Jesus' death was an execution?

I will begin by acknowledging the ways some traditional theologians have spoken of Jesus' death as disclosing a crucified God and will then suggest the difference it makes to speak of an executed God. This is the concept of God I will be developing throughout the book, as disclosed in the way of the cross. In Baldwin's terms, this concept of an executed God can help make us "larger, freer and more loving,"[1] especially when we confront imperial power today. Such a concept is a gift to be welcomed.

The phrase *executed God* links the state-sanctioned killing of Jesus to God, then forces us to ask what precisely we mean by that three-letter term, *God.* After clarifying how that term functions in the phrase, I will suggest that we allow to die some alternative but all too common views of God (other gods, as I call them). These are the concepts of which, to recall Baldwin again, we do well to rid ourselves. These concepts, many of them quite prevalent in the established religions, are not gifts but constructs that reinforce exploitative power.

Let us begin by acknowledging the debt we owe to theological discourses that have used the concept of the crucified God.

The Crucified God

Jürgen Moltmann's important book *The Crucified God* reminds us just how central the fact of Jesus' crucifixion is to Christian faith in the God of life. Moltmann and many others have reminded us that the God of Jesus Christ—though risen and living, powerful, grace-full, liberating and reconciling, salvific, if you will—is the one who was also crucified. Jesus' crucifixion, interpreted by Moltmann as "the power of God as grace amongst the rejected" provokes the idea that some transformative power has come through Jesus' poverty, lowliness, and abandonment to others who are similarly "the poor, lowly, and abandoned."[2]

What does it mean to use the expression *the crucified God?* In short, it is to take the many meanings carried by the term *God*—of ultimacy, power, mystery, transcendence, love, justice, being, life—and to focus all this in the passion and death of the concrete Jesus of Nazareth who met his ignoble end. Talk of the crucified God links all of the basically positive meanings of God to the ignoble end of a Jesus who died on an instrument of torture amid Roman empire.

You will find in this book no extensive speculating on just how it might be that God was in Jesus or precise descriptions of how one usually seen to be so beyond, transcendent, all powerful, and all good could be in a human figure and nailed to a cross. You will not find here the complex discussions of christological dogma, about how two natures (divine and human) come together. Christian talk about the crucified God has not persisted, primarily, because of some convincing science or rational explanation of how God became man, became this crucified Nazarene.

It has usually been enough for Christians to believe and say that the life of love and justice they most need, a veritable power of God with and for them, somehow emerged from the life and teachings of this crucified Jesus. Oral testimonies and written narratives about a crucified Jesus, whose life was bound up with God, were kept alive and developed by communities variously called the Jesus movement or the early Christian movement. For this movement, first and foremost a variant of Judaism, the reality of God was focused around remembrance of this one who had been crucified. *The crucified God* is a phrase that keeps that focus to the fore.

As Moltmann and others have pointed out, there has often been a risk that such a way of focusing our talk about God, around such a crucified one, will lead to a glorification of suffering. The risk is that suffering, weakness, and being exploited are all sacralized. Suffering is made so holy by talk of a crucified God that, for some minds, glorying in one's own weakness seems in itself a kind of worship of God.

The results of the pieties that worship suffering have been quietism, acceptance of suffering (for self and others), and in the extreme, a kind of sacralizing of destructive sadomasochistic impulses. Torturers during the Argentine Dirty War of the 1970s and 1980s, for example, told their victims, "We are going to make you Christ," and actually seemed to cloak themselves in the mantle of holiness because they were applying torture to victims, "putting them to the cross."[3]

Even though this sacralization of suffering can be found in the past and present of Christianity in both subtle and blatant forms, it is not a necessary feature of thought about the crucified God. At its best, the expression *crucified God* reminds us that the power of all life, God, faces and suffers some of the worst that a creature can endure and emerges with newfound power, strength, and hope. What is sacralized or made holy is not suffering but the facing and endurance of suffering with hope and life.

A God believed to be entangled in crucifixion is an antidote to pieties and theologies that would seek their God above the earth and its suffering peoples. The crucified God takes believers on a journey into earth, into its pain and suffering, and finds in that journey not the holiness of pain but the wonder of life's power to persist and transform. The way of the crucified God seeks God in earth's humanity, which has been abandoned, rejected, and despised, the people who know life amid their struggle.

From Crucified to Executed

To speak of Jesus, Christianity's revelatory figure, as executed adds something distinctive. A crucifixion, of course, was an execution, a horrific one, involving public display of the victim in a slow and agonizing death. Over centuries of Christian discourse, however, *crucified* has tended to signify largely Jesus' general experience of suffering and death. Then, the death of Jesus is often fitted into some other larger theological schema, some overall plan of God for all the living and all the dead. Within this broadened schema, the focus tends to shift away from the fact of his experience of one of Rome's most distinctive kinds of execution, to a supposedly more sublime plan of God. By shifting to a divine plan above or behind the concrete world of executions, traditional Christology risked presenting a God who does not suffer at all. Latin American liberation theologian Jon Sobrino was right to term this an act of "abstraction" from the concrete world of Jesus of Nazareth.[4] The horrors of crucifixion as execution unfortunately then retreat to the background of Christian reflection and faith.

The phrase *the executed God* reminds us that the God who was bound up with the life of Jesus of Nazareth was exposed to material conditions so malignant that he was executed. Jesus did not die accidentally. He did not expire as the culmination of any long disease. He died no death when his life was full of years and maturity. Nor can we say that Jesus possessed, in E. P. Sanders' language, some "will to die" in order to make a "redemptive death."[5] No, he was put to death. He was captured by armed agents; he was confined (however briefly on the way to a quick execution), was ridiculed and whipped (perhaps also sexually abused and assaulted[6]); he was driven on a forced march to his place of death. There, he was done in by executioners.

Comedian Dick Gregory once said, with an enlightening twinkle in his eye, that if Christians understood the meaning of Jesus' cross, they would wear around their necks and hang from their earlobes little electric chairs. I think he's right. The fact that his suggestion seems morbid and that many of us persist in hanging a silver or gilded cross from our bodies suggest we have lost touch with this ugly dimension of execution.

It is time to confess forthrightly that in Jesus of Nazareth, God suffered not just death but execution: a state-sanctioned execution supported by religious officials. To call Jesus' death execution is to renew our awareness of the official terror that crucifixion was. Jesus' life, as bound up with God's life, receives its distinctive stamp because of the way he suffered state-sanctioned killing.

Christianity, defined by this Jesus, is not just about a crucified one who deals with death in general. No, in spite of all pious abstractions, in spite of any polite liberal faiths, the faith in this Jesus is about a founder who wrestled with and suffered crucifixion as an execution by an imperial power. Christians who confess that the presence or reign of God was uniquely given with Jesus' presence, who hold that God was somehow in Jesus, or who say, as many do, that Jesus was or is God come face to face in this Jesus with the executed God. By our own tradition's logic, we are compelled to face and to meditate on the God who entered into Rome's and Palestine's state-sanctioned theatrics of terror. We are challenged to say how it is that from within such a theater of violence, new life was born for him, and for other crucified peoples who suffer the terrors of imperial force.

Jesus of Nazareth and the Executed God

As is true for many Christians, I have already been using the words *Jesus* or *the executed Jesus* as interchangeable with *God.* This is, of course, consistent with a long classical tradition in Christianity that confessed Jesus of Nazareth to be God. This interchangeability is especially suggested in the phrase that is also this book's title, *the executed God.* Even if I have promised to avoid many of the christological discourses (metaphysical, philosophical, doctrinal) about how this Jesus could be held to be God, I do need to say more about how this term, *God,* functions in this book.

I must confess to a certain personal reticence in using the term *God* at all. God-talk has often served as a reservoir of easy answers and stock solutions. Theologian though I be, and one who writes this book abounding in God-talk, I feel the human situation—the mass death sentence we all live under; the terrorizing systems of slavery, genocide, and holocaust—and I often hearken more to the counsel of an Albert Camus than to that of many churches and their easy God-talk. Camus counseled not so much atheism as a good healthy blasphemy, one marked by "denouncing God as the father of death who provokes our outrage."[7] In this section and throughout the Introduction, therefore, I seek to identify the helpful work that is done by the term *God* and at the same time set aside certain other uses that are less helpful, which only compound the outrage.

To begin with, it is still necessary (though, perhaps, by now tedious and obvious) to begin by noting that God is not a kingly and whiskered fellow ruling over the universe. We risk the tedious and obvious in pointing this out, because the critique of such anthropomorphic thinking has long been made both by classical theology (recall St. Thomas Aquinas, "God is . . . being itself."[8]) and most forcefully, by contemporary womanist and feminist theologians. Readers of popular science fiction works have readily adapted ideas of God to those of the force (as in *Star Wars* scenarios). Other sources in popular literature make similar moves. "I believe God is everything," says Alice Walker's character Shug in the popular novel and film, *The Color Purple*. "And when you can feel that, and be happy to feel that, you've found It."[9]

Although popular imaginations show these tendencies to hold very fluid God-concepts, it is still necessary to point out the limitations of the kingly, whiskered fellow since males with authority (usually Caucasian heads of families, their presidents, and generals) are still influential as ready-to-hand images (especially in children's eyes) for forging visions of God. Moreover, the still powerful Christendoms, the organized and official churches of many lands, still do not challenge the God who flourishes in our minds as some kind of male authority figure writ large. Even Jesus of Nazareth, especially when rendered with Caucasian features, has been pressed into service of those visions of God that are tempted to see the deity as a kingly, male (usually white) individual.

This book's notion of the executed God presupposes readers' growth beyond male authority figures as the best models for thinking about God. The very term, *God,* invites experimentation. British philosopher of religion Ian Ramsey reminded us that *God,* that three-letter word, is a rather astounding integrator word. It is astounding because it does so much work, linguistically and conceptually. It brings together (integrates) so many of our thoughts, especially as we push the limits of our lives, trying to develop insights about our world by stretching language and awareness to the furthest horizons of our experience. Since those horizons are foggy regions of great mystery, our language about them will usually be "odd"—not the ordinary vernacular but a language in which we embrace myth, legend, fiction, and stories in order to grapple with what is most important to us.[10] Even if the practices of religious faith are disruptive, resistant, and revolutionary in effect, the God-concept functions to integrate and mobilize the language and symbols necessary to those practices.[11]

In post–World War I Germany, theologian Paul Tillich tried to get the hearers of his sermons to think of God in these new, broader, and less anthropomorphic ways. Acknowledging that the word might not have much meaning for his traumatized German listeners, he suggested to them another way to approach the term *God:* "Translate it and speak of the depth of your life and the source of your ultimate concern and of what you take seriously without reservation." In one's ultimate concern, he noted, God is "the name of this infinite and inexhaustible depth and ground of all being."[12]

In this book, when I embrace approvingly the word *God,* it will be in this sense, as a term that names the mysterious source of what is ultimately significant. It is a way to name that which is ultimately satisfying, ultimately fulfilling, a source of the power to make justice and love, to find meaning and hope.

This generalist understanding of God can also be noted in some of contemporary U.S. society's popular contexts, for example, in the twelve-step movements (as in Alcoholics Anonymous [AA] and Narcotics Anonymous [NA]), in which members speak of a higher power. The phrase rarely means an anthropomorphically rendered male authority figure, though the frequent references to the higher power as "He" suggest that the kingly, whiskered fellow can also haunt the world of AA and NA conversations. The real force of the phrase, however, is to invoke a greater power, a force that can be found for delivering substance abusers from other powers that hold them in their addictions, in their suffering and oppression.

Similarly, in this book, I will speak of God as that greater power: greater than all the forces of executing and imprisoning authorities, greater than all the powers coalescing in lockdown America, indeed, greater than all those arrayed in the global, megastate empire catalyzed by U.S. military power and the international polis of *Pax Americana.*[13]

The book will also, however, expand the notion of God as greater power in two other directions. I will envision God as also deeper power and as wider power. These notions of depth and breadth of power are no mere supplements to the idea of greatness; rather, the greatness of the power of God emerges in the ways it is also deep and wide.

I speak of God as naming a power emerging from the very nature of things, thus a deeper power. The power that will be greater than lockdown America is a power breaking from within the deepest resources of life and its vitality. The political forces stronger than lockdown America are not just marshaled by critique or by admonitions to comply with a new, higher or greater moral demand. It is also a matter of discerning and attuning ourselves to the power that already pulses in the universe, in all things. There is, thus, an earthiness about the political power that can enable our overcoming of lockdown America. Life's own vital forces—flowing through bodies, land, wind, and all creation—are resources for catalyzing political efforts. Powerful change that somehow taps this vitality of life is what I refer to as the deeper power.

I also speak of God as wider power, as naming what is resident in the complex social and political movements of diverse peoples. The power that is great and deep is also wide, in the sense of dispersed throughout a full diaspora of peoples hungering for empowerment amid oppression. God's power is, here, sociopersonal, sociopolitical, and socioeconomic. The greater power of God moves throughout a breadth of peoples' movements, their coalitions, their networking, their continual efforts to organize resistance and new structures.

It is this greater, deeper, and wider power that the word *God* names across the pages of this book. It is this kind of force, or array of forces, that I will invoke when considering the way of the cross, the way of the executed Jesus.

Such an understanding of God means that the phrase *the executed God* cannot be identical with the discrete ego or historical person Jesus of Nazareth. The greater, deeper, and wider forces named God are more appropriately ascribed to an entire way of the cross—a way taken by Jesus, highlighted powerfully by his individual life and death, but a way that is more complex and more expansive than can be contained in Jesus or in any individual life. Even if as Christians we confess Jesus' execution on the cross to especially disclose the meaning of the way of the cross, what is disclosed about God's power along that way is always more complex, more elaborate, and more extensive than what can be seen in Jesus' individual life.

Thus, the God who is the executed God affirmed by this book corresponds less to Jesus' body and life and more to an entire way of the cross in which Jesus participated. As the book's title and subtitle show, the executed God stands in apposition to the way of the cross, not in apposition to Jesus. The greater, deeper, and wider power for overcoming lockdown America is known, then, amid a practice, along a way that has distinctive properties that I unfold in the book's final chapters (Chapters 3, 4, and 5). It would be premature to unfold the features of this way now. We will need to present in more detail the oppressive configuration we are up against today, the contours of this oppressive order called lockdown America (Chapters 1 and 2).

Before setting about that descriptive task, we now need to comment on how the executed God is related to other views of God, to other ultimate concerns, to other gods, if you will. We must examine these so we can let them go.

The Executed God and the Death of Our Gods

The notion of the executed God, if seriously embraced and lived, means the loss of certain long-standing modes of belief in God. Some of our dearest gods die, we might say, when we allow ourselves to meditate on the executed God.

To be sure, the gods looked for apart from world struggle, apart from concrete suffering, these die. The gods that keep us talking about small problems, about worlds of clean churches and safe spaces, these are put to death. When we turn to Jesus of Nazareth, whose life and work was defined by participation in material conditions that led to torture and death, then we have to let go of other kinds of gods whose allure is still strong in some quarters today.

I have in mind three particular gods that die when we stand before the kind of executed God that emerges in this book. They are gods with a long history and whose legacy is still fierce and strong in the new millennium dominated by an empire dependent upon the U.S. superpower. Permit me, then, to celebrate the demise of three deities: the god of political domination, the god of religious respectability, and the god of revolutionary purism. I am not saying that these gods are now dead, but that if we were fully to embrace the way of the executed God that I try to present in this volume, then we would let go of these gods. We would let them die.

The God of Political Domination

To value the executed God is to let go of the god of political domination. This means not the death of all respect for political organizations that shape social life and define the basic rights and duties of citizenry. The god of political domination is the one that lives in imperial modes of control, like the state-sanctioned apparatus that came to issue a death warrant on Jesus of Nazareth. The apparatus that worked the execution of Jesus was part of a highly developed imperial machine that demanded utmost respect and administered power over many nations and peoples. Under its Caesar Augustus, proclaimed "savior" just prior to Jesus' birth, the Roman empire crossed its threshold into maximum effectiveness.[14] Slightly later, the Rome of Pontius Pilate and Caesar Tiberius, together with their lackey kings of Palestine, still worked this apparatus of imperial control.

Jesus died the victim of executioners with imperial power. There is an inescapable opposition between the life and death of Jesus, and imperial power. To embrace and love the executed God is to be in resistance to empire. To be a follower of the executed Jesus of Nazareth is to venture down a road without having a place in systems of imperial control. It is to be on the suffering side of empire, but in spite of that it is also to work resistance and even victory amid imperial pretension and practice.

Christians working in the United States are accustomed to seeing themselves as abiding at the heart of a democratic system. Imperial power, tyranny, domination—these, allegedly, are traits of some other system. I will be arguing in this book, however, that the United States today anchors an imposed and ordered peace, a *Pax Americana,* as real and effective as was the *Pax Romana,* the ordered peace of the Roman Caesars. To be sure, there are spaces of freedom, processes of representation, and legacies of democratic practice, but there is still imperial power exercised by U.S. power holders in coordination with transcontinental powers.

Moreover, within the U.S. superpower, there is, increasingly, a subjugation of its citizenry to forces of transnational empire, and thus that citizenry comes under the control of state-sanctioned prisons, death penalties, and paramilitary policing. As U.S. military force and aerial bombardment back the process of economic globalization, so the power to jail and execute grows in the United States.

Christian acceptance and compliance with this country as unrivaled superpower is a de facto worship of the god of political domination. One of the reasons we see few Christians speaking of the executed God, following Jesus understood in that sense, is that they would then be situated on the underside of today's imperial practice. Many Christians do not desire to live on that underside. Many cannot even see, or refuse to see, that underside of imperial power. Instead, they have made a god of U.S. political domination, and they adjust their spiritual life to the landscape shaped by the United States. It is precisely this god, however, that dies when the executed God comes to orient our living and practice.

The God of Religious Respectability

So also does the god of religious respectability die, when the executed God claims our allegiance. Jesus died as victim of a political punishment reserved for criminals and insurrectionaries. His state-sanctioned execution, however, was the work not only of the politically powerful but also of the religiously powerful. State power, especially in Judea, centered around the temple-state, which fused elites of Rome with political and religious leaders.[15] Religious leaders provoked, connived with, and supported Rome's imperial concerns in order to execute Jesus.

Even when Pontius Pilate seemed reluctant to execute Jesus, perhaps not really thinking that Jesus was that much of a threat to imperial power,[16] priestly elites wishing to kill him stood ready to wed their faith to imperial politics. The Gospel of John (19:15) gives expression to this readiness, when it records Pilate exclaiming, "Shall I crucify your king?" The chief priests confess, "We have no king but the emperor." As John Dominic Crossan points out, this is anti-Jewish propaganda, but it also exemplifies tendencies of religious authorities to support imperial power.[17]

Jesus died, then, not only as rebel in an imperial and politicized context. He also died as a blasphemer in the eyes of the religious establishment.[18] The way of the executed God entails being not only on the underside of imperial power but also on the downside of established religious leaders who work in concert with the imperial hegemony. Rome did have its own imperial theology that often put it into conflict with the theology of Jewish priestly elites, but those elites also often stood ready to build their respectability and power through connections with imperial Rome.

Why had Jesus been rejected by these religious leaders? It was not simply because Jesus embraced some critique of all religion and ritual. He and the movement he spawned remained full of God-talk and spiritual practices that most would consider deeply religious in character. Nor did he give voice to an anti-Jewish polemic, as has Christian anti-Semitic discourse that rants about the Jews having killed Jesus. By no means. The Jewish Jesus never renounced his heritage, and the Jesus movement remained largely a variant of Judaism throughout the first century.

No, it was a religious elite, seeking to defend its power and respectability, that brought him into opposition with the religious system of his day. He was a blasphemer in the eyes of the powerful guardians of his people's law. He located himself, his ministry, his teaching, his dining, drinking, and eating—all, among the nonelites. He was open to elite worlds, even invited some of them, such as Nicodemus and the rich young ruler, to join him in a comprehensive ministry among and for nonelites. Moreover, he interpreted the very presence of God (the reign of God) to be with, for, and among the alienated, the ground-down poor, the stigmatized sinners. Using more traditional language, Jürgen Moltmann summarizes: "The source of the contradiction [to religious and legalistic elitism] is that he, a human being who was powerless, should anticipate the power of God as grace amongst the rejected and the powerless. . . . through his very poverty, lowliness and abandonment, the kingdom, the righteousness and the grace of God, come to the poor, lowly, and abandoned."[19] If we cast our lot with Jesus, and the way of an executed God, we see die the aspirations for religious power and respectability. The god of religious respectability dies with that of political domination.

Welcome this. Today, as the hegemony of the U.S. superpower has risen, so also has a way of achieving religious respectability by accommodating religious practice to class and political domination. The Christian right is just one example, given its vigorous role during the presidency of Ronald Reagan in the 1980s, in making common cause with his anticommunist rhetoric and military spending. The Christian right also played an important role in relation to the 1994 Republican movement, the Contract with America, which scaled back social services on so many fronts. Jerry Falwell's Moral Majority, as well as nation-loving U.S. patriot-evangelists, and formulators of the dominion theology movement—all these are obvious examples of religious cooperation with political power in the United States.[20]

Among other Christian groups, however, there is a kind of religious practice that also reinforces political domination. It is a kind of liberal Christian faith—enlightened, urbane, philosophical, sometimes culturally astute, which yet eschews political controversy and conflict. It is difficult to find a political dimension at all to this kind of liberal preaching and practice. Here, there is silence, for example, about the rise and abuse of the U.S. superpower and its hegemony. Often there is silence, too, about U.S. actions abroad that violate human rights or those that do so within our own borders. Political consciousness among progressive Christians in the age of empire often gets reduced to organizing charity and philanthropy, in themselves fine but hardly sufficient. The respectable denominations may wince but still leave essentially unchallenged the concluding line of every president's speech, "May God bless America."

In fact, to raise questions about the United States' right to be the superpower with a quasi-religious aura, to wield its fist of military might, to enact policies that concentrate wealth in an ever smaller elite, or to build up lockdown America—all this is rarely taken up by good Christian liberals. To be sure, there may be an occasional critical comment, a prophetic posture struck from some safe place, but this usually entails no real threat to the political order of things, no loss of religious respectability.

The way of the executed God, however, which entails locating oneself among the alienated or among movements of diverse people consigned to an underclass, will often entail loss of religious respectability. Especially if one lives and organizes or participates in movements among such as these, religious power in an imperial milieu will consider you to be one without respect, without power. To follow the executed God today is to let die the god of religious respectability. We cannot serve the executed God and the god of religious respectability.

The God of Revolutionary Purism

If political and religious hegemonies cannot win the outright loyalty of their citizens or produce accommodation to imperial ways, then they resort to provoking subordinated peoples into revolutionary actions that are easily beaten down and controlled. Those of us who resist exploitative power, those who have let die the gods of political domination and religious respectability, need to beware lest we resort to modes of "resistance and revolution" that only allow dominant powers to reproduce themselves.

I use the phrase *revolutionary purism* for those modes of resistance that are provoked and ultimately, for all their talk of resistance and revolution, only end up reinforcing (often unintentionally) the very imperialist powers they claim to resist. These modes exist on both the political right and left. To embrace the executed God, is to let die also the gods of revolutionary purism. Let me mention just two forms of this revolutionary purism.

There is, first, the longing for conflagration, that is, the searching and working for an event of overthrow that is thought to come as a purge of all things oppressive, as the end of all domination through a decisive battle. This often takes the form of hoping for that mass uprising, the unleashing of revolutionary fervor to burn away all that grinds down and weighs heavily upon the poor and downtrodden.

This "conflagrationalism," if you will, is tempting. Indeed, there are examples in our own lifetimes of revolutionary change through social tumult and a dramatic ending of old orders: Fidel Castro's coming to power in Cuba in 1959, ending there the corrupt, U.S.-backed regime of Fulgencio Bautista; the 1979 emergence of the Sandinistas in Nicaragua who sent the last of the Somoza family dictatorship into exile; the overthrow of Ferdinand Marcos in the Philippines of 1986, which brought Corazon Aquino to power.

These were necessary and valuable events, changes worth welcoming in spite of the flaws of the successor regimes. I confess to having my own dreams of revolutionary conflagration and dreams of perfecting the events of dramatic uprising and overthrow. Yet to make of these an idol (to make a god of this moment of social change), to make them the sole focus of efforts to resist imperial structures of our day, is to overlook other important factors crucial to lasting revolutionary change. What are these additional factors that obsessing on conflagration can sometimes gloss over?

First, these events of political conflagration can often be short-lived. They emerge as a kind of catharsis in an oppressive system. Catharsis can be welcome, but once the pressure is released, acted out dramatically in the streets, in the overthrow of the old, then often the old can return. It can return in new ways and with new faces but return nevertheless.

Second, even if the conflagration does result in a changed order that develops new and more emancipatory modes of organization that have staying power (as in the cases of Cuba, Nicaragua, and the Philippines), this is often because of painstaking and often unseen organizing going on below the surface of dramatic events, that is, day-to-day networking and coalition-building, protracted struggle. This is carried out by many actors, with and without fame, who create conditions for conflagration and conditions for something new to be in place afterward. To focus only on conflagration, to make a god of this one revolutionary moment, can gloss over this important reality.

Third, the commitment to political conflagration—whether as mass uprising, decisive battle, or some other mode—often commits subordinated peoples to a strategy that can rebound upon them and set them further back.

The conflagrational strategies masquerade in a certain revolutionary purity, as the very notion of purging the old order indicates. Yet, by themselves, such strategies can result in the further crushing of the already downtrodden. To focus on the final battle or conflagration is often a luxury of the already strong. The weak need their own weapons of strength to forge the revolution for which they dream. These weapons will be far more subtle and more complex than simply taking aim at some decisive battle.[21]

At the time of the Passover in the year Jesus was executed, expectation of conflagration seems to have been high as Jesus entered Jerusalem.[22] His ministry, then, apparently raised enough commotion that finally Pilate was pressured into the crucifixion that ended his life. When Pilate did so, the conflagration that would purge Jewish lands of imperial Roman power and elite control slid from view. This god of revolutionary purism died. Similarly, the executed God will leave us wondering about how to forge revolution when we let go of this mode of purism.

There is another form of revolutionary purism that we must assess, "oppositionalism." To be sure, I will present the way of the executed God in lockdown America as an adversarial practice. There is no real resistance and revolutionary change amid religio-political oppression without strategies and postures of opposition. What is problematic, however, is a kind of oppositionalism that refuses to engage the resources of oppressing cultures because of a concern to be pure, to be free of every vestige and remnant of the elements of dominator cultures.

Sometimes this purity is maintained by invoking Audre Lorde's well-known dictum: "You cannot destroy the master's house with the master's tools."[23] The context of this expression, however, suggests that her intent was to remind readers that the sources of resisting and criticizing the master's world come from outside his house. It is too simplistic a reading to interpret the words of this revolutionary sister to mean that no tools, no equipment, or no resources of the oppressor's world can be used for revolutionary change.

In fact, real resistance and revolutionary change is dialectical, that is, it engages and interacts with the very order it wishes to end or change. Real revolutionary change may use the standing order's language, technology, and media. It may even have to get its hands dirty with big capital and things like the credit cards and bank accounts of the twenty-first-century market economy. Grassroots radicals mobilizing change by use of the Internet and the World Wide Web, first organized by the U.S. Department of Defense,[24] exemplify this mode of resistance. Some activists have had to use the master's arms, that is, guns and ammunition. How to do that and not be pushed down the road of that other mode of revolutionary purism, conflagrationalism, is the challenge of any who find themselves forced to use these ugly tools of change.

One value of letting go of this revolutionary purism and of remembering that we often use the same tools to bring about different ends is that we are reminded of the common humanity that extends across the boundary between oppressor and oppressed. I am not one who contends that the oppressor-oppressed dichotomy has no place. It does: there does exist a world of oppressing cultures (classes, military personnel, security forces, intelligence officials, political leaders, and so on) that can be distinguished from oppressed groups. There are victims and executioners. That being granted, even if the oppressing groups are criticized as vicious (the beast, as some in revolutionary movements call it), even then, a common humanity persists. It is crucial for revolutionary change to remember this common humanity when mounting fierce resistance to oppressing powers. It is for this reason that the Jesus who went the way of the executed God articulated and practiced a love ethic that included love of the enemy. This love is no capitulation to the enemy; it is a strategy of revolutionary change that uses adversarial drama, as we shall see, in order to rival the enemy's powers.

Recognizing this common humanity, seeking some way to love enemies even while resisting them, is to allow to die that form of revolutionary purism marked by a facile oppositionalism. The way of the executed God will be adversarial, but it is not oppositionalist in the ways I have here mentioned.

This facile oppositionalism is also problematic because it is so easily made impotent by the disguised and serpentine ways empire works today. As Richard Hardt and Antonio Negri show in their book *Empire,* imperial control creates racist and class-based suffering through very complex deceptions, ones that often offer to embrace, affirm, and include the very ones who end up being systematically excluded. The purism that thinks only in terms of opposition and binary terms of resistance will not forge a resistance complex enough to engage effectively today's complex and multiform strategies of imperial control.[25]

There are no doubt other forms of revolutionary purism, in addition to the conflagrationalism and oppositionalism I have discussed here. There is, for example, a kind of avant-garde elitism that exalts cadres of revolutionary and organizing elites, that often looks down on the messier democratic mode of consensual politics and on the organizing potential of what is often called the lumpen proletariat.[26] Another form of revolutionary purism might be found in that kind of idealism that seeks to organize the ideal socialist state, which can yield, and has often yielded, a mode of bureaucratic tyranny. This is often as in need of overthrow as is many a capitalist hegemony.[27] The state socialisms of Eastern Europe that fell in the latter decades of the twentieth century are key examples of such tyrannies of a bureaucratic elite.

The way of the executed God seeks a mode of revolutionary practice that emerges as revolutionary but that lets go of all the purist gods of our revolutionary consciousness. It does not let go of the dreams and real work for revolutionary change amid political and religious domination. It does let go, however, of the way of purity in things of revolution, the kind of purity proclaimed by some revolutionaries or that defenders of imperial control think revolutionaries should practice. The way of the executed God relinquishes that kind of purity, even in the revolutionary domain. The death of the god of revolutionary purism is as necessary as that of the gods of political domination and religious respectability. So what is left for the follower of the executed God?

Arguing for a Theatrics of Counterterror: Way of the Cross, Way of the Book

Once these gods die, a Christian spiritual practice emerges that is full of political and revolutionary meaning. Remembrance of the executed God sets Christians on a way of the cross that is a journey of resistance to imperial power and of flourishing within and in spite of it. The way of this book is to point readers down that way of the cross through lockdown America, which is also a new way of experiencing the triumph of God. By book's end, I will have given this latter phrase a distinctive twist by discussing the triumph as a pageant of empowerment, one that invokes and evokes God as a creative power that is greater, deeper, and wider than oppressing powers that grind so many down today.

Revering and following the executed God places Christian practice at the center of imperial power's theater of terror, and from within it Christian practice constructs a theatrics of counterterror. I will clarify this notion of *theatrics* more below; for now, consider it a dramatic mode of public action. Through a distinctive kind of drama, followers of the way of the executed Jesus counter and renounce all terror and so gain leverage and political effect for countering the ways of established political terror.

In the first century, people's efforts to survive and counter the terror of imperial power gave rise to, among other development, movements of resistance and hope that followed Jesus. Such an effort is needed now, in the twenty-first century, for generating movements that help us survive and counter the terror of imperial power at work today.

Part One of this book is devoted to displaying the theater of terror that we face today. I discuss it as lockdown America. Chapter 1 not only details the nearly unprecedented rise of the prison industry, with its stricter policing and sentencing and more routine executions, but also shows how all these unite to create a political theatrics of terror, functioning to control and contain new groups of disenfranchised people that are generated by recent forms of economic and racist exploitation.

Chapter 2 will conclude Part One with an account of why lockdown America has emerged and the function of this lockdown within the larger global role assumed today by the United States as the so-called world's only superpower. The whole of Part One is necessary for understanding the need for the way of the executed God. Many of us, Christian or not, need to face the reality of lockdown America and nurture our understanding of why it has grown so virulently in our midst.

Part Two takes up directly the way of hope and life that attends the way of the executed God. Situated as we may be amid a political theatrics of terror, Christians and many people of spirit following the way of the executed God can practice and are practicing a theatrics of counterterror. I will here devote three chapters to unfolding the major qualities of a Christian theatrics of counterterror, showing how the symbol of the executed God gives rise to a Christian adversarial practice (Chapter 3), to dramatic action (Chapter 4), and to kinetic responses that yield organized movements for revitalizing and revolutionary change (Chapter 5).

Together, these final chapters yield a new understanding of the Christian way of the cross in today's American contexts. As will become clear, this is not so much a matter of carrying or bearing one's cross as it is a matter of wielding the cross for liberating change. Nothing less can be demanded of Christians who truly revere and know their founding figure, their executed but living Jesus, who work in the way of their "fettered, spat-upon, naked God."[28]

part one

The Theatrics of Terror

We are all trapped in the terrible jaws of something shaking the life out of us.

—John Edgar Wideman, *Philadelphia Fire*

1. lockdown america: A Theater of Terror

> Short-term terror or revulsion are more powerful than long-term wisdom or self-interest.
>
> —Molly, prison educator, Rikers Island, in Jonathan Kozol, *Amazing Grace*

In my own church in Trenton, New Jersey, Tamika rises, with all of her thirteen years of age, to share a concern before the adults go to their "Prayers of the People" during Sunday morning worship. "We had a hard week in school," she says. "For two days we were on lockdown." Her metaphor of *lockdown* was applied to her classmates' being denied study hall privileges, but it is derived from the world of prison life.

Out of the Mouths of Babes and . . .

Today's children and youth routinely use the metaphors of prison life to portray their own lives outside of prison. Twelve-year-old Jeremiah, interviewed by Jonathan Kozol for his 1995 book, *Amazing Grace: The Lives of Children and the Conscience of a Nation,* contrasted his own poor community (Bronx, New York) with the more northern and wealthier one of Riverdale.

"Life in Riverdale is opened up," observed Jeremiah. "Where we live, it's locked down."[1] When asked by Kozol to elaborate, Jeremiah and his friends pointed to city parks they can't play in, schools without learning where the police teach them how to walk the halls, libraries they see but cannot go into because the buildings are locked down and falling apart, shopping malls they can't get into because they cannot get past security vigilance, Bloomingdale stores in Manhattan at Christmastime that chase them away because they look African American, Latino/a, or poor.[2]

Then there is the homeless street poet that Kozol encountered in a Bronx city park, who, amid his own life of struggle dared language to interpret the whole metropolis. "I see New York as a symbolic city. These buildings are our concrete prisons piled up like Babel. A Satanic technology surrounds us. What we see is apparatus not humanity."[3] Whether from the mouths of youth or of homeless elders, today's prison-speak is not just the result of metaphorical dexterity or poetic license. It is rooted in the material, economic, political, and social conditions of our times. The Bronx children interviewed by Kozol, for example, live across from Rikers Island in the East River. Rikers is the largest penal institution in the world. Ninety-two percent of its caged people are African American or Hispanic. People in the Bronx community and elsewhere have family members cycling in and out, know friends who have been, are, or will be there, as either inmates or employees.

New York City spends $58,000 annually on each caged adult, according to 1994 statistics, $70,000 for each juvenile.[4] This is ten times what the city spends on each child in its public schools. In trying to justify these expenditures, an educational administrator at Rikers (we will call her Molly) explains why this happens. Her blunt words speak more truth than perhaps she knew, and she points the way toward real understanding of why this country is building prisons and why its system of punishment works as it does. "Without this island [Rikers], the attractive lives some of us lead in the nice sections of New York would simply not be possible. If you want to get your outcasts out of sight, first you need a ghetto and then you need a prison to take pressure off the ghetto. . . . Short-term terror and revulsion are more powerful than long-term wisdom or self-interest."[5] Molly's words are not just those of some twisted staff member caught speaking out of place. They are, in fact, a window onto the dynamics that are driving our nation's use of prisons and the ready use of the death penalty that is applied in the prison house. Quite frankly, this administrator is revealing a hard truth: "short-term terror and revulsion" are now necessary as modes of control, essential modes of governance.

We see here the commitment to employ that which terrorizes and repels, and does so powerfully, in order to have an effect of keeping certain people in place or moving them from one place to another. All of this is to commit those with governing powers to a show, a spectacle that displays power and creates motivating terror. This is to engage in "theatrics," the official orchestration of security forces and disciplinary practices.

The very buildup of prisons, a veritable archipelago of incarcerating institutions in the United States is one sign of this theatrics of terror. To be sure, the buildup is usually justified in high moral terms as a way to fight crime, to give just desserts to those who have violated the rules by which society decides to learn. But the scale of buildup, nearly unprecedented in both size and rate of growth, suggests that creating a spectacle of terror is the primary aim. We thus have the spectacle of Gulag America.

Gulag America

The United States of America has become, in Christian Parenti's words, "Big House Nation." Prisons are growing in numbers held and are big business. Over two million people are in prison.[6] The figure may be 7.5 million by early in the twenty-first century, according to the National Criminal Justice Commission's report of 1996.[7] Another three million are doing time today in an outer prison of regimented society, under care of the court system, exposed to unannounced visits from parole and probation officers, mandatory urine tests, home detention, or the invisible tether of electronic bracelets.[8] Just since 1980, the prison population has nearly quadrupled, constituting "the largest and most frenetic correctional build-up of any country in the history of the world."[9]

Millions more are connected to the incarceration system from the outside. (Michel Foucault has reminded us that in societies that organize massively for incarcerating citizens, "there is no outside" for anyone.[10]) Many outsiders make their living directly or indirectly off the economic stimuli provided to communities by the lockup craze. Administrators at Rikers Island tout themselves as a "huge employment opportunity" for the South Bronx. While caging their inmates, Rikers employs ten thousand people, eight thousand as guards.[11]

Small towns in economic slump regularly seek recovery by organizing to host a big prison. Crescent City, California, for example, organized to get the $277.5 million Pelican Bay State Prison, a maximum security institution with space-age security measures and elaborate technologies for isolating prisoners. Crescent City also got population growth, new garbage contracts, a battery of counseling offices and services (including prison chaplains, of course), an Ace Hardware, a new area hospital, a ninety thousand square foot K-Mart, and jobs.[12] Similar benefits have come to areas like parts of New York state, where new prisons host New York City's sentenced youth. "The City is subsidizing us by producing these criminals," said one resident of Romulus, New York.[13]

Parenti reports that yearly expenses from the correction industry are between $20 and $35 billion annually, with "more than 523,000 full-time employees working in American corrections—more than in any Fortune 500 company except General Motors."[14] More than $7 billion annually has been spent on prison construction in the 1990s.

In 1996 alone, twenty-six federal and ninety-six state prisons were begun. The National Criminal Justice Commission report found that nearly 5 percent of rural population growth between 1980 and 1990 was due to the transfer of prisoners to the country, "captured in the cities and exiled to the new carceral arcadia."[15]

Convention center hotels play host to "Prison Expo" conventions. The American Correctional Association held one of these in Nashville in 1996, with "more than 600 booths touting the very latest in prison innovation and technology to more than 5,000 conventioneers."[16] The *New York Times* article on the convention, titled, "Utmost Constraint and How to Exercise It," discusses the buying-spree culture among those who have to keep up with lockdown America's frenetic pace of incarceration.

"For the warden who has run out of room," says the article, "there are temporary cells at $40,000 a piece. For hard-to-handle inmates, there is the latest in restraining chairs, ballistic batons, and plastic handcuffs. And for those who simply prefer to delegate, there are companies that do it all, from designing cellblocks to determining staffing, from setting up a dispensary to beefing up security."[17] All this remarkable investment and growth in burgeoning penal institutions is what justifies the frequently used language of "prison-industrial complex."[18]

This phenomenal growth of the prison industry, a Gulag America, is often seen as justified because it allegedly reduces violent crime. As columnist Tom Wicker has documented, however, the decline of crime is not even roughly equivalent to the massive prison buildup. In fact, the buildup is due more to locking up people for more minor offenses, which has little to do with the rise or fall of incidents of violent crime.[19]

Some cultural observers have said that drug crimes, which have played a special role in swelling the prison numbers, are violent offenses because of their link to the whole chain of social events that yield violence. Committing a drug offense, however, is far from always being a prelude to committing acts of direct violence. Moreover, many acts of "white collar crime" also yield violent consequences, and yet these acts do not lead to quick imprisonment. Many, with assistance from family and community services, have addressed their drug use and abuse problems without setting off into violent actions. In fact, white affluent youth, especially, get all kinds of help and tolerance when they develop drug problems, while others, especially the racially stigmatized poor, get hustled off to jail. It is cynical and self-defeating to declare all drug offenders violent and at the same time withdraw from them the resources needed to redress the problems that create drug use.

It should also be remembered that crimes of outright violence are themselves not best fought with simple imprisonment. Violent offenses showed signs of abating even prior to the draconian sentencing guidelines and the prison industry of the 1980s.[20] No, Big House Nation cannot be justified as the necessary means of violent crime reduction. To really understand the phenomenon of Gulag America, we must explore more deeply its function to sustain social terror.

Theatrics of Terror: Six Dimensions

As Molly, the administrator at Rikers Island, put it, "short-term terror and revulsion" are necessary. Just precisely what purpose, what necessity they serve, will be discussed in the next chapter. In this chapter we describe this situation of terror and revulsion. The incarcerating institutions that make up a gulag, and the punitive measures relating to it (more intensive policing, near routine use of the death penalty, stricter sentencing laws), make up a house of horrors, a structure for the practice of a political theatrics of terror. Let me explain this in terms of six dimensions.

Time: Devourer of Flesh and Spirit

There is, first of all, the way prisons transform the human experience of time. The prison should be seen as a kind of theater in which time is turned into a weapon of terror. It can also be wielded by authorities—lengthened, shaped by routine—and thus is an important aspect of the criminal justice system's theatrics of terror.

In most theatrical performances, in the interaction between the play, players, and audience, there is an experience of time transformed. Perhaps, there is a suspension of ordinary time, a creation of a new time that enables a particular insight, often another kind of experience.[21]

In the prison theater, time is transformed in a particularly new and destructive way. There is not simply a loss of time, nor is this just some more intense form of being sent to your room for time out. It is time out, and so time is lost, with mothers and fathers, aunts and uncles missing out seeing children grow into adulthood. Mumia Abu-Jamal, a resident on Pennsylvania's death row since 1982, observes about prison time, that "Once loving relationships wither into yesterday's dust. Relatives die, their loss mourned in silent loneliness. Times, temperaments, mores change, and the caged move to outdated rhythms."[22] Yet beyond this lost time and lost experience there is a more crucial transformation. Time is a kind of agent that does things to the one passing through it. Many a prisoner will give voice to this idea by saying, "You don't do time; time does you."

Time's agency becomes most vicious when it is routinized, when institutions organize time with a certain practical effect in mind. The routinization of time is a transformation cultivated by prison authorities and designed to make every day like every other. In this experience, paradoxically, time acts even to deaden one's sense of time. As Abu-Jamal says in an essay titled "Killing Time," intentionally constructed regimens yield a hypnotic sameness. Time in prison then becomes "a thick dull mallet that pounds consciousness into a coma."[23] As mallet, time acts to yield a kind of spirit death. "The mind-numbing, soul-killing savage sameness that makes each day an echo of the day before, with neither thought nor hope of growth, makes prison the abode of Spirit death that it is for over a million men and women now held in U.S. hell holes."[24]

Time as the devourer of flesh and life is borne witness to by countless others. There is the poem by Ojibwe Sioux political prisoner Leonard Peltier, imprisoned for twenty-three years in federal prisons for killing two FBI agents. (The prosecutor actually has admitted that he does not know who the real killer is.[25]) Twenty-three years have given him this viewpoint on time as agent in the prison.

> Doing time creates a
> demented darkness of my
> own imagination . . .
>
> Doing time does this thing
> to you. But, of course, you
> don't do time.
>
> You do without it. Or
> rather, time does you.
>
> Time is a cannibal that
> devours the flesh of your
> years
> day by day, bite by bite.[26]

The Bitter Gall of Injustice

Terror and revulsion can also be found in the sense of injustice known by many during the time of their confinement. Many citizens today simply dismiss prisoners' sense of injustice as just so much self-justification and evasion of personal responsibility.[27] It is more complex than that, and to understand the bitter gall of injustice as a terror that afflicts prisoners and all of us, we need to think more deliberately about prisoners' sense of injustice. Return to Mumia Abu-Jamal and Leonard Peltier.

Both Abu-Jamal and Peltier are two well-known figures who have claimed they are innocent of the charges for which they were sentenced. Both prisoners have supporters who either concur that they are innocent or believe their guilt has not been established by means of fair judicial process. Both are at the center of strong movements pressing for their release or new trial.[28]

The movements for Abu-Jamal and Peltier have not arisen simply because of the particulars of their cases, crucial as these are. No, the vigor of these movements lies in the fact that Abu-Jamal and Peltier are moving reminders of how many others are in prison not simply because of crimes committed but because they were on the wrong side of certain political powers, on the downside of educational opportunity, on the underside of access to wealth.

Abu-Jamal and Peltier can garner impressive support because what has befallen them can, or has, befallen many others.

I have participated in both movements, and what is striking to me is the way such participation takes one into discovery of so many others who carry the burden of being incarcerated unjustly. Other activist colleagues and I find our desks stacked high with letters detailing the lives of folk unfairly treated by the courts and by authorities whose carelessness or guile has contributed to shackling some unfortunate souls.

The skeptic will say that everyone says they didn't do it, that especially the criminally-minded regularly find it hard to admit their own wrongdoing, their own responsibility. It is easier to complain about life's unfairness or that of someone else.

This is a callous and self-justifying skepticism that overlooks just how easy it is to fall down the road to prison as a result of others' unfair practices and vicious action, or because of the vicissitudes of navigating poverty and racism. Let us grant for a minute, however, some truth in our skeptic's charge about prisoners' complaints.

The bitter gall of injustice that circulates in the beings of the confined may not be due to the purity or innocence of the prisoner. Maybe he or she did some crime. Maybe they do bear the burden of responsibility for their crimes. The bitter gall, however, is due to their sense that the punishment of incarceration is somehow out of proportion to the wrong done.

Remember, incarceration is not just time out from society. It is being done to by time. It is, in Peltier's language, to have one's flesh devoured bite by bite. In Abu-Jamal's language it is a "Spirit death" worked by a "pounding mallet." The bitter gall of injustice is created not so much by the sheer awareness that one is a confined innocent but by the sense that this spirit death is more than should be borne by the one who has committed a violation.

One inmate in the system who is doing life for burglary, known only as John J., bursts out in lament, "I admit that I have a serious drug problem and am no angel—but I am *not* an animal that needs to be locked up for the rest of his life."[29]

John J.'s situation of having a drug problem and now doing life for burglary raises the question of who is being incarcerated today and for what. Politicians and pundits who justify the lockdown craze often argue that we are ridding our streets and neighborhoods of violent offenders and feared superpredators. Actually, only 29 percent of all prison admissions are for violent offenses such as rape, murder, kidnapping, robbery, and assault. The other 71 percent are for various nonviolent crimes: 31 percent for property offenses such as fraud, burglary, auto theft, and larceny; another 30 percent for drug offenses such as possession and trafficking; then 9 more percent for public order offenses like drunk driving and arms possession.[30]

Consequently, the majority of the burgeoning number of our citizens exposed to spirit death are not perpetrators of violent crime. Again, I am not diminishing the seriousness of many of these crimes at this point, or of the need to take responsibility for one's actions instead of blaming other people or other forces. I am saying that the violence of spirit death and of the dull mallet of time, together with all the other modes of prison violence worked on one's body and soul, all this creates or exacerbates a bitter gall of injustice. To have that gall poured into one by the realities of confinement is part of the terror in the theater of Gulag America. In most cases of the confined, whether one is guilty or not of the charges for which one is confined, the terror is greater than the error. The bitter gall and resentment circulate and maim within, especially for those whose nonviolent crimes are being met with forced spirit death.

A few of the confined will tap the grandeur of mind and spirit to fight off this spirit death and guard their humanity. Many others, though, will descend into the hellhole of prison to become a hell-making force. Then the gall of their personal resentment and rancor works suffering for us all, in and outside the prison gates. Many families of the imprisoned have lamented, "He came out of prison worse than when he went in." In part, that is due to the bitter gall of injustice, the suffering that does not reform but tends to deform. The bile of resentment from this can make the terrorized inmate into a new terrorizing force.

The bitter gall of injustice, arising from lack of fit between one's fault and the forced travail of spirit death becomes all the more a terrorizing assault when compounded by other unjust practices that characterize prison systems. To these we now turn.

The Prison Spectacle Brought to You in Living Color

The theatrics of terror in Big House Nation offer up a spectacle in living color. Our U.S. prisons are implicated in America's long-standing, cruel sickness of white supremacy. Poor people of color, especially African Americans, are the majority of residents in the U.S. carceral archipelago. Those who live the prison life are those from communities of color: African American, Hispanic, Asian, Native American. Over 70 percent of persons in the prison population are minorities or (poor) people of color.[31]

The situation for the African American communities has reached a special stage of crisis. Figures for the year 2000 estimate that one out of ten black men are in prison.[32] One-third of all African American men aged eighteen to thirty-four are under the supervision of the criminal justice system: in jail or prison or probation, parole or court supervision.[33] In Baltimore, Maryland, as early as 1992, over one-half (56 percent) of all African American men between the ages of eighteen and thirty-five were "under some form of criminal justice supervision on any given day."[34] The majority of all women in prison are women of color, a majority that is significant because the number of women incarcerated in the United States has tripled since 1985, and is "ten times the number of women imprisoned in Spain, England, France, Scotland, Germany and Italy combined."[35]

At present, although African Americans make up only 13 percent of this country's population, "half of all prisoners are Black," according to Christian Parenti.[36] Tom Wicker reports that 41 percent of the imprisoned are black. Whoever has it right, both figures display a striking disproportion between the percent of African Americans in prison and that of blacks in the U.S. population. The disparity is so great, as the National Criminal Justice Commission report has noted, that cumulative racial bias at all points of the criminal justice system must now be seen as the major cause of the disparity in our prisons.[37]

That racial bias is the cause of the striking racial disparity in U.S. prisons has been a claim that many American citizens have been unable or unwilling to accept. Criticisms of this cumulative racial bias are often interpreted by others as just so much special pleading and justification, as if the critics were saying that African Americans can never receive fair treatment in today's system. This is not the argument. Catastrophic effects of racism in the criminal justice system can and do coexist with the realities of guilt and occasional fair treatment. Mumia Abu-Jamal has tried to find words to summarize the phenomenon accurately. Wrestling with the fact that 60 percent of Pennsylvania's death row inmates are black, although blacks make up only 9 percent of the state's population, he writes:

> Does this mean that African-Americans are somehow innocents, subjected to a setup by state officials? Not especially. What it does suggest is that state actors, at all stages of the criminal justice system, including slating at the police station, arraignment at the judicial office, pretrial, trial, and sentencing stage before a court, treat African-American defendants with a special vengeance not experienced by white defendants.[38]

This is cumulative bias. Without claiming that African Americans are always innocent and without denying that African Americans can sometimes get a fair break from the system, this cumulative bias must be acknowledged. It accounts for the fact that in our prisons today, for every one white, there are seven African Americans, and that young black males in their late twenties, according to the Bureau of Justice statistics, are incarcerated at a rate of about ten times that of white males.[39]

This phenomenon of cumulative racial bias, described by Abu-Jamal, which almost every African American can feel in his or her bones when navigating the authority system in this country, has been confirmed by study after study. In 1988, the *Harvard Law Review*, one of the most authoritative legal periodicals, undertook a comprehensive examination of racial bias throughout the U.S. system. In a study of over 150 pages, the examination concluded that "there is evidence that discrimination exists against African-Americans at almost every stage of the criminal justice process."[40] Numerous other studies can be cited to make similar conclusions.[41]

The National Criminal Justice Commission report minces no words in also warning that we risk social catastrophe, first for African American communities but ultimately for the whole nation. We are on a "treacherous course," only deepening the entrenched racial injustice that often has torn the country apart. If cumulative racial bias continues to afflict our criminal process as it does today, yielding the same rates of unfair incarceration, a shocking picture of the United States emerges. I cite the National Criminal Justice Commission report of 1996, if for no other reason than it has been roundly ignored by mainstream media outlets. If present rates continue

> almost two out of three of all young African-American men nationwide between the ages of 18 and 34 will be in prison by the year 2020. For young Hispanic men in the same age range, one out of four will be in prison in the year 2020. If the growth were to continue uninterrupted at the present annual rate of increase, 4.5 million African-American men and 2.4 million Hispanic men will be incarcerated in 2020—a prison population of minority men about five times as large as the prison population of all races combined today.[42]

Today, virtually everyone in inner-city minority communities lives with knowledge of family in the prisons. Children often visit prisons to see loved ones more often than they have school field trips. Talk on the street is often about a kind of new age slavery, with predominantly black populations caged and housed in the prisons. Rappers from the worlds of contemporary hip-hop refer to the big prisons as the new slave galleons of our time. This street talk about slavery today is not pure hyperbole, given that, after the abolition of slavery, prisons became the major institutions in the United States for continuing racist regulation of black life and labor. Slavery is not just an institution that can be dismantled; it has been a viciously resurgent curse taking ever new forms that mix forced labor, confinement, and white supremacist opprobrium.[43]

With this racial disparity in prison incarceration, we are moving "closer to a racial abyss that has little to do with the creation of a safe society."[44] Gulag America is a special terror to black and Hispanic communities, and increasingly for other minorities too. Whatever the degree of guilt of any African American, for whatever crime, being forced to deal daily with life in the cages created by cumulative racial bias is an acutely painful experience of today's theatrics of terror.

The racial disparity is ultimately a blight upon all U.S. residents, whatever their ethnicity. In America, generally, fault and blame, transgression and punishability have regularly been marked by the black body, the isolated, controlled, and attacked black body. Today's blackenization, if you will, of the prisons only exacerbates racist proclivities in nonblack Americans to associate black people with wrong. At the same time that blacks are disproportionately sent to prison, all citizens of other colors further stoke their racist fear of blacks as criminals. It is a vicious circle: blacks are confined together en masse, and so blackness and transgression get yoked together in America's racist, collective mind, yielding tendencies to send still more blacks to the prison house, swelling its racialized composition even more. Their terror in the Big House is presented as the terrible reminder of what all the rest of us must not become but could become if we fall down the road of transgression. Within the confines of this subtle but scurrilous, racist logic, being white and being law-abiding become nearly synonymous in many minds. Not only are we thereby creating conditions of rage in minority communities that could sometime break this country apart again, affluent white America and its supporters are constructing cages for their own lives, often shrinking behind the walls of gated communities and security systems that are devised to ward off the masses.

The prisons' terror in living color yields new racially stigmatized hordes in warehouses of Gulag America. These impose suffering, above all, for the confined, but they are also an affront to the dignity of any citizen of conscience.

Terror and a Culture of Rape

The prison world is also one of sexual violation. The theater of terror is inscribed into the very bodies of the confined. In my state, mid-Jersey talk shows are replete with nervous titters about prison rape. Prison cinema gives its own glimpses of the violation. What is often overlooked is that prison culture is a systematically maintained and nurtured rape culture. Rape happens in prison not just because there are a few predatory individuals. The system, ever more draconian in its abilities to control the body, could control predatory individuals if it chose to as a matter of policy.

Rape does not occur in our burgeoning prisons simply because the denial of human contact in prison is made worse today by greater restrictions on conjugal visits and healthy human interaction with family and friends. Nor is it only because of the deprivation of heterosexual interchange in prison environments. It is mainly because guards and supervisors use the practice and threat of rape to divide and subdue the imprisoned population, which otherwise would be unmanageable. In other words, guards and supervisors connive with a thriving "sex chattel" system in which many men are made "female" sexual slaves, "punks" to other men.[45] Moreover, guards and supervisors themselves use powers over the imprisoned for their own sexual gratification, especially male guards supervising females.[46]

In the men-on-men violence of prison rape, there is more than simply great suffering for the direct victims. There is also something like a ritual practice that continues the denigration of women and so afflicts the entire society. Better said, the already existing exploitation of women in the wider society is, in the prisons, honed into a destructive weapon where some men "make women" out of other men, and where the women "made" become brutalized objects, punks. The terror of prison rape, therefore, can be seen as the creation and manufacture of ever more brutal men, who brutalize each other while strengthening the whole culture that brutalizes women.

> So the sexualized "other" is manufactured with almost Fordist regularity, on the conveyor belt of absolute sadism and homicidal violence. . . . Sex slaves [in prison] are used as prostitutes, domestics and "wives." They are forced to provide all the sexual, manual, and emotional services that men in a sexist society normally extract from women.[47]

There is a complex cycle of terror here. It runs from sexist society to prison life between men (and between male guards and confined women), and then runs back out to reinforce more brutal practices on the outside. Rape as terror for the bodies of the confined, terrorizes also the whole body politic.

Parenti suggests that there are "roughly 200,000 male inmates in America raped every year, and many of them raped daily." A movement in the prisons, called Stop Prisoner Rape, puts the figure at 290,000, noting that most studies of prison rape do not look at those who pair off for protection or the high incidents of juvenile rape in most facilities.[48]

The systematic and officially sanctioned dimensions of rape are dramatized by an account by Dr. James Gilligan, a doctor and psychiatrist working in the Massachusetts Department of Corrections.

> In one prison holding close to 700 inmates, one of the prison administrators, who was in a position to know, informed me that, out of that total number, probably no more than half a dozen men failed to engage in some form or other of regular sexual encounter with other men. How did he know that? Because in that prison an "observation gallery" overlooks every cell in the three tiers of its maximum-security wing so that the correction officers can observe what goes on within each and every cell.[49]

The use of this sexual terror to divide and control the inmate population is just one such use of violence against confined bodies for purposes of administration and control. It is well known that supervisors and guards work also with gangs internal to the prison system and use and encourage ethnically constituted tensions to exacerbate conflict between groups (such as the Aryan Brotherhood, the Black Guerrilla Family, Mexican Mafia, Bloods and Crips, and so on)—all with the aim of keeping the big house a veritable "Balkans in a box."[50]

The average citizen, with little familiarity of daily practice in prisons, may find it hard to believe that a systematically nurtured and tolerated rape culture exists. To be sure, no administrative guidelines in correctional institutions' manuals suggest or allow for the practice. Many, if not most, supervisors, guards, and other prison personnel present themselves as good citizens trying to do a tough job. At the heart of many a barbaric system, there have often persisted majorities that most would call basically kind. At the level of daily practice, however, rape thrives and functions positively for those who are the keepers of the confined. From a functional point of view, at least, a rape culture has become a kind of de facto family value in prison institutions, thriving among the fraternity of guards, wardens, and supervisors. Needless to say, this makes for an institutionalized dysfunctional family in the extreme.

The often hidden maintenance of prison rape comes to the surface occasionally. Cases of unruly inmates or ideologically unpopular prisoners who are deliberately placed in cells with known prison rapists as punishment, with some "booty bandit" used to terrorize the general population are well known. One of these "booty bandits" was routinely moved around by guards into cells with "fresh fish," or new inmates, in order to control potential disobedience or simply to express the power of the guards. When one inmate complained, he reported that guards answered him, "Welcome to Shirley [the name of the State Prison, in Massachusetts]. Toughen up, punk."[51] Prison systems of Massachusetts, Louisiana, and California are just a few that have been exposed as having penitentiary staff and administrators who set up, watch, and profit from the rape of prisoners.[52]

I must introduce a more positive point in this section, since the extent of this problem may leave some readers in shock and despair. This terror against the prisoners' bodies reveals to what desperate lengths officials in the system will go to control its confined. The administrative use of rape culture, and officials' dependency upon it, also destroys the pretense of prison officials that their prison work contributes to some higher moral and social virtue. If prison order can be maintained only by such terrorizing scandal, by the cycling and recycling of terrorizing brutality, then the prison system itself is revealed to be not just administratively imperfect but just as morally bankrupt (perhaps more so) as those it claims need confining. Consequently, the movements against prisoner rape, once the systematic practice is exposed, have the capacity to destroy the moral justification for prisons. We will then be well on our way to supporting the No More Prisons! movement that I will describe in this book's final chapter. We can then also dare to pray for, dream, and work for what chaplain Lee Griffith calls "the fall of the prison."[53] Once that justification is stripped from the repertoire of political authorities, we have an opportunity to press social and political leaders to devise other ways for dealing with the traumatized persons of our society, alternatives to the terror we now impose upon them, upon their families, and ultimately upon all of us.

But I rush ahead. Instead of presenting alternatives, let me present two other dimensions of terror in Big House Nation.

Paramilitary Policing and the Neighborhood Spectacle

As the United States feeds more of its citizens to the big house, the country has come to live with, and often under, high-tech, well-equipped police forces. Regimentation within prisons goes hand in glove with a general social regimentation outside. The spread of more vigorous and extensive police forces is a key example. These forces know how to wield technology and drama to control neighborhoods. They fuse them into dramatic actions, into neighborhood spectacles that further contribute to the political theatrics of terror. If we recall the words of Molly of Rikers Island, we see that they, too, resort to "terror and short-term revulsion." This is another dimension of the theatrics of terror.

The power of dramatic short-term terror for controlling populations has been chillingly displayed in other countries, whose security forces have been funded and trained by U.S. largesse.[54] This was illustrated in Argentina for all the Americas to see, during a five-year period in the late 1970s and early 1980s known as the Dirty War.[55] Argentina, long touted as one of the more civilized, European-like countries of Latin America, is still recovering from the horror.

Beginning in 1976, more than twelve thousand Argentine citizens (perhaps as many as thirty thousand)[56] were sacrificed by a military junta obsessed with eliminating all vestiges of leftist guerrilla movements. "First we'll kill all the subversives," announced the junta. "Then we'll kill the collaborators. Then the sympathizers. Then the undecided. And finally, we'll kill the indifferent."[57]

Mass abductions of all kinds of citizens were carried out in broad daylight and in the middle of the night. These were carefully staged police and military raids, and were regularly followed by ritualized torture carried out in 170 clandestine jails and by execution through shooting at the edge of mass graves or by dropping victims from helicopters into the ocean far from the Argentine coast.[58]

The horror, known but unknown at the time, lurked at the edge of all Argentina's consciousness. The very spectacle of force, the entrancing and awesome show, helped create acceptance of repressive paramilitary tactics. The typical neighborhood spectacle consisted of circling helicopters lighting up the night, streets closed to traffic, guns everywhere, uniformed officials taking charge. There was little secrecy to the raids. Not only were citizens silent out of fear and powerlessness, but in the light of spectacle grew the refrain, well "*Algo habrán hecho*" ("They must have done something").[59] The state's torturers then carved, hacked, and probed with the electric *picana,* (a coiling rod of torture) the bodies of the abducted innocent, often strapped to tables in detention centers, in what they called the "theater of operations."[60]

Torturers targeted especially the bonds of intimacy in families, so that young children were tortured in front of their parents, parents in front of their children, husbands and wives in front of one another in modes of eroticized violence. Physicians were regularly on hand to check appropriate voltage levels, so as to torture young children without killing them.[61] "They must have done something."

In the United States today, we have not reached the situation of Argentina under its junta of the 1970s and 1980s. Unfortunately, though, enough of the same dynamics of security operations are present in the United States that Americans need to admit the possibility of a low intensity version of the Argentine Dirty War being played out here. Two dynamics are of special concern.

The first dynamic reminiscent of the Argentine situation is the link between today's police forces and U.S. military traditions of operation.[62] The currently well equipped police forces in the United States are the result of applying military styles of dramatic enforcement to U.S. neighborhoods and streets. Police imbibe and propagate a kind of military or paramilitary approach to fighting crime in public spaces. When funding started to flow into police forces in cities like Philadelphia, New York, and Los Angeles in the 1960s and 1970s through large monetary grants, there also grew up a rhetoric in American law enforcement that saw itself as employing counterinsurgency techniques like those deemed necessary to fight revolutionaries in Southeast Asia, Africa, and Latin America.

I was once stopped for speeding in suburban New Jersey and then had my car thoroughly searched while I was instructed to keep standing and facing away from my car. After finding nothing, the policeman muttered, "Sorry for the inconvenience, but this is a high reconnaissance zone."

High reconnaissance zone? Where does that discourse come from? I wondered. It was as if I wasn't supposed to complain about the inconvenience of this thorough search because it was an official military operation.

Parenti cites one instructor from the U.S. Army War College whose recommendations found their way into *Police Chief* magazine.[63] In it, he touted the "value of an effective police organization—both civil and military—in maintaining law and order, whether in California, Pennsylvania, Mississippi, or the rice paddies and jungles of Vietnam."[64] Perhaps the most visible symbol of this militarization of the police is the use of the helicopter in urban so-called counterinsurgency and reconnaissance work. Bell and Hughes manufacturers, which supply helicopters to counterinsurgency efforts across the globe, were selling 120 a year to U.S. police forces by 1972. In 1985, a helicopter dropped a military explosive on the MOVE family headquarters in a standoff with police, killing eleven adults and children, and destroying some sixty blocks in West Philadelphia.[65] As helicopters were used increasingly, "they helped create an urban panopticon, where citizens internalized the police gaze and made the effects of state power constant even when its application was sporadic."[66]

There is also a second element linking the U.S. situation to scenes of terror like that known in Argentina's Dirty War: the authorities' reliance on dramatic spectacle as a technique to control neighborhood populations. In the late 1980s, for example, massive and dramatic raids and sweeps by U.S. city police forces began a war on users of drugs. Among these were Operation Sting in Miami (1986) tallying nearly twenty-six hundred arrests; Operation Snow Ball in Orange County, California (1986); Operation Clean Sweep in Washington, D.C. (1987) involving twenty-eight thousand arrests, catching up fourteen hundred adolescents who were apprehended for minor dealing and possession; Operation Pressure Point in New York City (1987), wherein police once a week conducted sweeps, stings, and "buy busts," cooperating with federal agents.[67]

Perhaps most famous was Operation Hammer in Los Angeles (1988), in which fourteen thousand people, "mostly young Black men—were arrested and booked in mobile command centers during a massive paramilitary occupation of south LA's de-industrialized ghettos."[68] More black youth were arrested here than at any time since the 1965 Watts Rebellion. "Kids are humiliatingly forced to "kiss the sidewalk" or spread-eagle against police cruisers while officers check their names against computerized files of gang members. . . . The kids are processed in mobile booking centers, mostly for trivial offenses like delinquent parking tickets or curfew violations. Hundreds more, uncharged, have their names and addresses entered into the electronic gang roster for future surveillance."[69]

As impressive as the simple number of arrests might be, it is the drama and spectacle of these inner-city actions that is most important. The aim is to create a sense of drama, of total surveillance. As one sergeant of a California

SWAT team said about sweeps, "They see our big gray SWAT bus, and the weapons, and they know we mean business."[70] The logic of enforcement is clear, knowing the seriousness of police plans is rooted in a spectacular seeing.

In 2000, I was taking a friend home to the Bronx, New York, late one night. While we were stopped at a traffic light, a police squad car came out of nowhere, raced straight toward me with bright lights ablaze for what I was sure would be a head-on crash. Instead, the squad car stopped on a dime, his front bumper just inches from mine. Two other squad cars converged from right and left sides, policemen tumbled out to grab a driver out of the car behind us. All then sped off from our briefly illuminated night. We were not the target of the police action, but we both felt spectacularly dazed and ruled.

Spectacular, paramilitary-style policing continued into 1999 and 2000, often used against peaceful protestors. In November 1999, for example, hundreds were arrested by helmeted police ("robocops," as some called them) in Seattle, Washington, during protest actions against the meetings of the World Trade Organization. In April 2000, five hundred people were arrested (and later released) by Washington, D.C., police in a preemptive strike against peaceful demonstrators at meetings of the International Monetary Fund and the World Bank. Similar police tactics were in play against demonstrators at the Republican and Democratic Conventions in August 2000.[71]

The interest in what Christian Parenti and others have called the "political theatrics of terror" has been extended in the 1990s from inner-city U.S. neighborhoods, where it still continues, to the border region with Mexico. Operation Last Call, a vigorous roundup of "Mexican-looking" people occurred in Texas in 1998, was a statewide assault by Immigration and Naturalization Service (INS) and police agents, descending upon hundreds of homes, catching up 116 immigrants in El Paso alone, over six hundred more throughout the state. The captured included a few "hardened criminals" but, reportedly, just as many "model non-citizens."[72]

The practice is repeated throughout the country. The key is surprise and drama, especially sudden unexpected violence. In 1996, border agents and local police used a massive mobile force to sweep through Jackson Hole, Wyoming, yanking Hispanic workers from restaurants and homes, even off their bicycles. They rounded up 153 of them, confining them in a holding pen and giving them identification numbers, scrawled on their forearms with large black markers. Over fifty were eventually released after this trauma when distraught family and friends could produce papers proving legal residency. Those who could not show such papers were, according to local papers, transported to INS detention in a manure-strewn cattle truck. (INS detention centers, by the way, are a supplement to the prison archipelago in the U.S.A. today, holding twenty thousand people who are suffering conditions often criticized by Amnesty International for human rights violations.[73]) Parenti again expresses concern here: "The jumble of tropes at work in this real life allegory [in the Jackson Hole spectacle] are as obvious as they are grotesque: mass arrests, numbered forearms, cattle cars."[74]

We may not like to hear observers like Parenti suggesting comparisons between U.S. security forces in Wyoming and the cattle cars of past genocidal horror. Nor will many citizens welcome my comparisons of police theatrics in U.S. neighborhoods to the similar dynamics of abduction and torture worked by an Argentine junta in its war against its own citizens in the early 1980s.

Even if we conclude that the evidence is not there to place the United States on a list of countries enacting genocidal repression in the early twenty-first century, a sufficient number of similar dynamics exist to warrant concern and vigilance. Just the two elements of police-military cooperation and the commitment to high-tech public spectacles of intimidation are important warning signals. Will we heed the warning signs and act to correct the situation in time?

Recall that the newly equipped and empowered U.S. police forces have grown up at the same time as the spectacular rise of the U.S. prison industry. Indeed, the buildup of the U.S. prison archipelago, with its unprecedented rate of construction, is itself a kind of spectacle, a grand SWAT operation worked upon our social landscape. Both the rise of prisons and the rising up of paramilitary policing make a show of spectacular force in the nation today.

Poor and immigrant communities feel most directly the spectacle and its terror. Other groups of U.S. residents, especially our threatened middle-class and white communities who (often wrongly) think they are safe from such official terror, are induced by the spectacle of paramilitary sweeps and SWAT actions to support and rationalize the powerful displays of state power.

Many kinds of spectacle are available. As Parenti points out, the SWAT operations are not the only ones dominating public space. There are many other ritualized displays, ranging from the courts to prison and jail visiting rooms, cell blocks, and the ongoing distribution of television shows like *Cops.* Spectacle creates its own kind of space. The theorists of contemporary spectacle have called it hyperspace. Among other qualities, hyperspace has a power to enthrall, to numb a citizenry by fascinating it with dramatic display while the direct victims of spectacular actions receive distributed terror.

Chapter 2 will consider the possible motivation for such spectacles of terror, and Chapter 4 will indicate what can be done to counter this kind of rule by spectacle. First, though, we need to consider an additional dimension of public terror, state-sanctioned executions.

Executions as State-Sanctioned Ritual Killing

The death penalty in the United States can be seen as the paradigmatic action of a political theatrics of terror that is disseminated throughout U.S. life at the turn of the century. As the very word *execute* suggests, there occurs the actual carrying out of a state's executive power: here, a power to take life, to transport one of its people from the realm of the earth's living to the other side.

The power to execute is a near absolute power invested with the state, and as Robert Meeropol has suggested, the granting of such absolute power most surely tends to corrupt. (Meeropol's own parents, Julius and Ethel Rosenberg, were executed in 1953 when he was six years old.) He reminds his readers of British Lord Acton's famous warning: "Power tends to corrupt and absolute power corrupts absolutely."[75] When the state is given the power to execute, it is given absolute power, the power to take life. According to Meeropol, giving away that power, as people do, is to sacrifice popular sovereignty to a government tending to corrupt absolutely. I conclude this chapter with commentary on how state-sanctioned ritual killings are, in fact, corrupting our social system. They function not to serve the people but as another mode of today's theatrics of terror.

The state's action does not just work a change upon the victim of an execution. It also is a highly ritualized action, with a drama that has a certain effect upon others among the living. As a ritualized action, with elaborate protocol, it not only executes one condemned man or woman, it also acts as a kind of executive order impacting the whole populace. In short, it is theatrical, done for a wider audience. Today, an increasing number of these state-sanctioned, ritual killings take place, and these give us an opportunity to examine capital punishment's theatrical effect.

The Practice of the Death Penalty in the U.S.A. In 1999, the United States was executing its people at a rate of two per week, falling just below that rate because of the holidays at year's end. The final total was ninety-eight, the highest figure registered for any year in the last forty years. There are now over thirty-six hundred people on U.S. death rows. With new laws expediting application of the death penalty and limiting inmate appeals (launched by the Anti-Terrorism and Effective Death Penalty Act of 1996, passed in response to the 1995 bombing of the Federal Building in Oklahoma City, which killed 169 people, including 15 children), we could be seeing, within several years, execution totals in the hundreds for a single year. We have already had executions of two or three on a single day; this could become much more common in the future.

It is not simply the sheer number of executions or of the death row population that is troubling. More troubling is the fact that while the ready use of the death penalty is more frequently made, studies continue to confirm its unconstitutional and unfair application. It is still a penalty that catches up the innocent and can catapult them into a state of death, for which no recompense can be given them. Since 1976, for every eight people executed, one on death row has been found innocent.[76] Moreover, those released owe their good fortune not to the system that is working to correct itself but to other citizens' actions and pressures coming from outside the judicial process.

The death penalty is almost universally a punishment for the poor, for those without the money to get competent counsel. The adage remains true about the death penalty: "Those without the capital get the punishment."

Most disturbing is the way that racism, which I discussed above as a cumulative bias throughout the criminal justice system, is operative in application of the death penalty. The racial bias of the death penalty continues to be confirmed by study after study. In the state systems, although only 12 percent of the U.S. population is African American, 40 percent of the death row population is African American. In some states, like Pennsylvania, 60 percent of the death row population is African American. On the death row of the federal system, over 75 percent are minorities. On military's death row, 87.5 percent are minorities.[77]

In Chapter 2, I will clarify how the system of governance in the United States today actually serves elite groups, which benefit from the death penalty and other punitive measures that fall disproportionately and unjustly upon racially stigmatized groups and upon economically disadvantaged classes. Here, I want to highlight that the death penalty is not just a matter of growing numbers and unfair application. It is also meant to have a certain theatrical effect, to register terror in the wider public to reinforce the power of the state over all of our lives. This theatrical effect persists, even while many debate the various theories of deterrence, retribution, or today's most popular "just desserts." Major intellectual inconsistencies and failures attach to all of these theories. This is not my primary concern here. In whatever ways the death penalty is justified (and the justifications can change from time to time), the theatrical effect of implementing the penalty endures. The death penalty's ability to register its theatrical effect, an effect that terrorizes, is what is at issue here.

Excursus on the Ethics of the Death Penalty. My own commitment to abolishing the death penalty, therefore, is not rooted primarily in philosophical and ethical discussions of theories of punishment (Does it deter? Is it a just dessert?). If I were to enter that discussion, however, I would be among those opponents of the death penalty who nevertheless admit there is a logic to dessert, that is, to the idea that if you commit heinous, intentional murder, you deserve death yourself.[78] Moreover, if someone were to kill one of my daughters or someone from my circle of friends, I admit that I might very well feel a rage that desires the execution of the murderer. (I am not sure of this, though; I might, like some murder victims' families I know, become so sick of killing that another death would seem pointless and undesirable.)

I can admit and endorse this logic of deserved execution while also intellectually and morally opposing any duty to execute those who may deserve to die for their crime.[79] This opposition is rooted in arguments that there are just too many negatives that are afflicted upon us all when a state government takes to itself, or is given by its citizens, the power to execute even those who are thought to deserve to die. Not only is there evidence that the practice of executions brutalizes the general population and may actually be involved in increasing homicides,[80] it also causes the growth of an expanding "bureaucracy of death" (the sharing of information across state lines about how to execute and with which technologies),[81] risks killing the innocent,[82] exacerbates racism and classism, and more.[83]

Most of all, I argue in this book that any seeming duty to execute is contravened by the fact that the practice of execution is a terrorizing tactic that over time creates illegitimate state power. This is the crucial negative factor that should lead us to abolish the death penalty. It is a factor rooted not just in love for the criminal, in forgiveness, or in some assumptions about how we are a civilized people today. No, the argument is rooted in a concern for a just political order, free from the kind of state repression that works first against communities of color and the poor but ultimately against all of us.

Let us remember that we have the death penalty in our legal codes today, and as the frequent practice we observe today, not because some wise ethicists once gathered together and decided, "Hmm, murder is a serious crime, and so we need the ultimate penalty of death to express society's outrage over murder and help victims find closure." No, those are only rationalizations for a habit of using the death penalty that long had been etched into U.S. history. We have the death penalty today because we are still living out a historical legacy that resorted to official killing to expropriate the lands of commoners and indigenous peoples, to enforce slavery and lynching practices, to terrorize members of labor unions in struggle.[84] This is the source of the actual practice and energy of the United States' stubbornly persistent death penalty. That history is why we must abolish it, whatever might be our ethical and usually abstract rationalizations for its use.

Realizing this historical legacy leads us to examine the death penalty today as it functions as part of a theater of terror that in turn perpetuates an unjust political and economic order. We can begin to track these by exposing the different circles upon which executions make their impact.

Ritual Experiences of Execution Spectacles. The tremors of terror radiating outward from the ritual of execution are felt first of all by those people who are in the prison house itself, where the death penalty is carried out. The case of Ziyon Yisrayah (Tommy Smith) offers one example. He became the second black man executed in Indiana in 1996 for a single detective's death, even after a prosecutor admitted he did not know for sure how the detective died. During his execution by lethal injection, prisoners throughout the penitentiary cell block kept up a drumming on prison bars and walls to indicate that they knew what was going on in the execution chamber. The scene is reminiscent of some fiction: during the execution of Archie Koerner in Brand Whitlock's novel, *The Turn of the Balance,* the other convicts in the prison house were awake and their own "demoniacal roar shook the cell-house."[85]

During executions in Missouri, the chaplain and psychologist are dispatched among the other prisoners to help lower "inmate stress levels."[86] Prison wardens have to prepare various controls on prisoner outrage when the death penalty is carried out, and these controls are applied not just to keep a lid on the rage but also to extend and reinforce the prisoners' overall sense of being under control by state power.

The tremors of executions are also felt and evident among many others who are involved in preparing for and carrying out an execution. These persons make up a complex network of people, including governors, their staffs and secretaries; directors and commissioners of corrections offices; wardens,[87] guards, prison staff; doctors, nurses, clergy; manufacturers of lethal serums and other instruments of execution; executioners themselves; cleanup crews; families of the victim, the executed, and the executioners. What do families of executing personnel talk about at the supper tables in Texas and Virginia before or after an execution? Maybe they don't talk about the day's work of execution at all. Perhaps they just head for the mall or settle back to catch the next sitcom or sports spectacle.

However different may be the perspective of these parties on the crime committed and the execution being meted out, these are all joined together in one complex social function, in what Stephen Trombley has termed an "execution protocol." A protocol is a form of ceremony and etiquette established for official state functions. State power in the United States today has and maintains an elaborate protocol for guiding the many who participate, including doctors and the clergy, in the ritualized killing.[88]

The tremors from an execution are also felt among those who are outside the formal protocol, among the wider public. Here, too, is a certain predictability of response, a kind of choreographed dance, especially between public citizens and the media. Radio disc jockeys and other talk-show commentators orchestrate lively on-air debates about the death penalty. Then, often both death penalty advocates and abolitionists gather outside prison walls during an execution. Whatever we may think about a particular execution or about the death penalty in general, we all suffer the spectacle. We all are often part of the ritualized killing that has event status.

The spectacle of any one execution or the spectacle of the thirty-six hundred people on death row, who are marked by both class and race, is of a different sort from that of the paramilitary sweep. If our executions were public hangings and torture, as marked many of the past, there would be a certain similarity. The spectacle of the paramilitary sweep is designed to be public, to terrorize through seeing, through display of force, through beholding bright light and marked uniforms of authorities.

In the case of state-sanctioned ritual killing, though, lies a more subtle orchestration of revelation and hiddenness. Revealed to us are the numbers of the executed and those marked for later execution. We hear some reporting of what the executed persons did or ate before they died, about how they died, and who witnessed their death. There are some things disclosed about executions. The state with the most executions, Texas, seems to bask in disclosing and recording details about the last words and last meals of executed persons, as a look at the Texas Department of Corrections Web site shows. (See "Select Bibliography: Essential Web Sites.")

Just as much about executions, if not more, is hidden. In the first place, most executions are carried out deep within the guarded penitentiary. It is not easy to get clearance for entering, even if you are a designated witness. And even if you are a witness, you don't see much. When Ziyon Yisrayah was executed, his friend and advocate Julie Carson was seated in front of a curtained window that opened out upon the chamber where he was to receive the lethal injection. What she saw was an already sedated and prostate Yisrayah, lying on a table, not awake. The lethal needle was applied. Then the blinds were quickly drawn. End of execution.

The curtained window is a good metaphor for the general theatrical way that the knowledge of the death penalty distributes terror. The curtained window both shows and conceals: it allows us to see the deed but then shrouds the victim from our sight. The opening and closing curtain also dramatizes the sense of theater that I have been suggesting is crucial to an understanding of how punishment is applied and how its messages are disseminated in society today. The opening and closing of the stage curtain in any theatrical event has not only the function of showing and concealing but also of building a sense of drama. The dramatic sense derives from the tension built up between what is not yet seen and what is about to be seen.

Executions, by being both widely applied and present, yet also shrouded, take on a certain dramatic tension that is disseminated among the public. While executions today do not involve the direct dramatic spectacle of the paramilitary sweep, they nonetheless are a very powerful mode of spectacle. The revelation-hiddenness dynamic builds up a kind of awe, a spectral mystery that is especially appropriate to most people's sense that the ultimate and always numinous boundary of life is being dealt with here. The state, with its dramatic and awe-inspiring spectacles of execution, with its carefully orchestrated ritualized killings, takes on a kind of religious function. This is not just because it exercises an ultimate power over life and death, but because it uses and constructs rituals out of this process of killing and dying. The practice and protocol of execution, we might say, is a kind of human sacrifice, like that maintained in religio-imperial systems of the past. In those cases also, human sacrifice often functioned as a way for political elites to try to reinforce their position and privilege over and against perceived threats to their power.[89]

It may be true that the death penalty, and the protocol for its ritualized killing of selected victims from among the thirty-six hundred in waiting, is a theatrical process. Is it, however, a theatrics designed to have a terrorizing effect to shore up someone's power? That was Molly's suggestion when explaining why we have terror at places like Rikers Island. To show the death penalty as a human sacrifice that in fact does have such an end in mind, we need to examine the entire apparatus of Gulag America within the landscape of U.S. wealth and its accumulation. That will be the concern of Chapter 2.

Conclusion: Lockdown America as Threat to All

> The carceral network does not cast the unassimilable into a confused hell; there is no outside.
>
> —Michel Foucault, *Discipline and Punish*[90]

Why should any of us care about the terrors of lockdown America? That's a question I have had posed by more than one friend or colleague. Those of us who pose such a question often assume that the terrors are for others, for someone else. In fact, one such questioner said up front not only "Why should I care?" but also "The police appear to be protecting me in my neighborhood quite well, and the prisons seem to be ridding my world of 'bad actors' and criminal elements. Why should I care at all, when it serves many of us so well?" Those formulating such questions also often acknowledge that they live in an affluent, professional, and predominantly white community. Why not just enjoy this protected life?

Such a query dramatizes the importance of discussing lockdown America as a threat to us all. To my mind, the two million people in U.S. prisons, the epidemic of police brutality, and the burgeoning of death rows are a massive scar on any public compassion, any fellow feeling we might share with all of our contemporaries. From this standpoint, lockdown America is a threat because it destroys that whole fabric of fellow feeling. It disrupts and divides the unity we want to feel and build, with our neighbors and with all humanity.

In my opinion, the terrors meted out by lockdown America are a violation of my dignity, even though I am a relatively affluent Anglo-Norwegian benefiting from the entitlements of being a white male in the United States. To have my position and bodily safety dependent upon a system of domination, which is more and more the reality for affluent white America (as the next chapter will confirm), is an affront to human dignity. I prefer that my place and position, whatever it is, be a function of a mutual give-and-take between myself and all others, where love and justice are both given and received among us, where opportunities and resources are shared. To live protected within any version of a gated community diminishes me, is an affront to my dignity, as well as an unjust action to others. I cannot really breathe freely, if my life and security are a function of a boot planted on the throat of someone else.

I know that many others do not share this feeling and find it unrealistic or idealistic. In fact, many have a counter-feeling, and sometimes counterarguments that drive in another direction, holding that any functioning social unity and well-being requires a division of bad folk from the good or better, a submission of some to the disciplines of prison, police force, and death penalties. I cannot here engage in a full-scale moral critique of each of those dimensions of lockdown America. I can say, by way of concluding this first chapter, why the terrors of lockdown America are threats to all of us (and not just to my dignity or fellow feeling), why they do not serve the best interests of even those who are outside prison.

Everything I write in this concluding section is based on an argument that it is an illusion, a self-defeating one, to regard the victims of lockdown America as other than us. This was expressed and analyzed well by Michel Foucault, whose words lead off this section. His sentence is difficult to understand even when read in the context of his entire book, *Discipline and Punish: The Birth of the Prison.* Wrestling with his meaning, though, is well worth the effort.

Foucault's basic idea is that our prisons and punishments are really only a part of society's numerous other ways of disciplining bodies.[91] Society exercises this discipline not only in its punitive institutions (say, prisons), but also in preschools and other educational institutions, in the workplace, on sidewalks and highways, through social mores about sexuality and marriage, in medical institutions, insurance provisioning, through repeated exposure to mass media images, in organizations for the mentally ill, and so on. All these make up an elaborate network that shapes and disciplines bodies and their everyday performance. Foucault refers to these, in their totality, as a "carceral network," a "carceral archipelago"—employing the term *carceral* to signify the disciplining, or the "in-carcer-ating (from Latin, *carcer,* prison) of the flesh (*caro*).[92]

Within this carceral network, the prisons should be seen as punitive institutions that occupy one extreme place along a whole continuum of society's disciplining of bodies. Prisons are not places radically other to where the rest of us live, even though some media images prompt us to think that way about prisons and the imprisoned. Foucault reminds us that we are all part of a carceral network that includes the prison. We are all on a continuum of an always-functioning and all-pervasive disciplinary regime. None of us is outside of this network. In contrast to the prison institution, which we often take to be the confused hell where society places unassimilable people, the carceral network is omnipresent.[93] There is no avoiding it. "There is no outside," as Foucault says, out of which to cast somebody into some other place.

Given this reality of the carceral network, we are all more closely related to the prison than we are taught to think. In fact, if you look at prison life and culture (by reading, say, *Prison Life* magazine) you will find prison life to be quite reminiscent, for all its differences, of experiences in the wider society. Even the punishments, the regimentation, and the excessive brutalities operative in the prison are often only more intense versions of the regimens and practices that characterize the general population. As Christopher Taylor observed about even the genocidal terror in Rwanda in 1994, "The culture of terror does not depart radically from the culture of ordinary sociality. It is the same, only more so."[94] My earlier portrayal of how males making punks of each other in prison mirrors sexual role relations between men and women outside prison is just one example of this.[95]

In this context, the famous epigram often attributed to Fyodor Dostoevsky becomes all the more important: "A society can be gauged by how it treats its prisoners." This quotation is often interpreted as meaning only that you can discern how compassionate or cruel a society is by looking at how compassionate or cruel its practices are within prisons. Clearly, however, we must extend and deepen the usual interpretation of Dostoevsky's words. As his many great works signal, whether *Crime and Punishment, Brothers Karamazov,* or others, the lives we know almost everywhere—in family, workplace, maybe even in our dreams—have their regimens, forms, and constraints, and these are mirrored in all their flaws and virtues in the brutal regimes of the prison and prisoners' lives.

From this perspective, we are all struggling, as are the imprisoned, to comply with, manage, or avoid what regimens (some good, some not so good) do to us. The patterns played out upon or dished out to the people in our prisons are the patterns that are played out upon or dished out to us. Our claims that the imprisoned are just bad and in a different world from ours are often trumpeted only to protect ourselves from the sometimes frightening truth that we, like them, are wrestling with the same issues, with regimens that may or may not be for our own good.

Because we all are on a continuum with the imprisoned, living with them in one carceral network, it is not unusual for those who are in the outer prison to find that certain life crises, certain traumas, can easily and unexpectedly catapult them into the real prison of razor wire, Plexiglas, steel, and guards. Sometimes it is poor health, a divorce and family conflict, a lost job, or a series of lost paychecks that lead many a person to straddle the line between the legal and the illegal, and then slip into the netherworld of prison. Although many previously had thought themselves to be quite other to the world of the imprisoned, they learn that the journey is not quite so discontinuous as they thought from the world of one regimen to another.

Why, then, is lockdown America a threat to all? As a first response, I remind us that it is a place to which all of us can go, a place that we should know well because it is but an intensification of the places where we all already are.

Moreover, the sheer numbers of the imprisoned, with the new high rates of imprisonment, should also lead us to see the problem as one affecting all of us. When we imprison our fellow residents at the rate we now do in the United States—565 persons per 100,000, a per capita rate six to ten times higher than most other countries (including European ones but also China and Russia)[96]—we are exposing greater numbers of us to an intensification of the carceral regime we all endure. As the social order bureaucratizes to deal with the increasing numbers of the actually imprisoned, the regimens we all inhabit become influenced by those expanding bureaucracies of control. We all can begin to experience more regimentation in our lives, for example, in the domains of taxation, financial transactions, at school, in neighborhood policing, and elsewhere.

In other words, what is at stake with the rise of lockdown America is the freedom of the entire population. All societies, democratic ones included, need a regimen, perhaps, in the sense of social forms that shape culture and make possible a certain order across the generations and among social groups. It is a crucial struggle, however, to control these necessary regimens so that human freedom is not sacrificed and domination does not become the pervasive structuring principle of the society. The rise of today's prisons, where more and more prisoners are subordinated to the point of spirit death, is a threat to the life of freedom in the society at large. It is no wonder, then, that activist lawyer Gerry Spence relates the rise of prisons to a pervasive threat to the freedom of the entire American populace.[97]

Spence, in fact, writes of the U.S. population as "new American slaves,"[98] arguing that social forms today are replaying the legacy of slavery. This latter point has often been made by a number of African American thinkers, especially by law professor Derrick Bell, in his book *Faces at the Bottom of the Well: The Permanence of Slavery.*[99] It should be of additional concern to us all if the building of prisons not only threatens the entire social fabric of freedom but also returns U.S. culture to a form that is structured by slavery.

The replaying of the legacy of slavery is being suffered, above all, by the populations that have always been most vulnerable to slavery, those exposed to the white racism operative in the Americas. The 70 percent in prison who are from communities of color and the 50 percent of prisoners who are African American bear tragic witness to the continuous structuring power of the racist heritage of slavery in America.

Today, language about the return of slavery is not uncommon. It is in use, for example, in many a hip-hop song, where black youth rap about the big prisons on northern landscapes of Pennsylvania or New York as looming like new "slave ships."[100] Such lyrics are not rooted in mere poetic license or hyperbole but in the real historical connections between prisons and the institution of slavery. The U.S. prison system has always had an apartheid character, writes philosopher C. George Caffentzis.[101] Especially after the Civil War and the announced abolition of slavery, the prisons became the major locus for the continual enforcement of slave conditions for black Americans. In short, today's prisons are enmeshed in the legacy of slavery just as today's capital punishment is in the legacy of lynching.[102] We cannot commit ourselves to executing and prison building, especially at the current rates, without resurrecting in America the ugly structural injustices associated with lynching and slavery.

When that past is resurrected, it will spread the sinister effects of unjust racial killing and confinement throughout what Foucault termed the entire carceral network. The entire disciplinary regime, which is inscribed in the structures of civil life, will increasingly present us with a cruel choice: either becoming a part of an overseer's culture (an option open only to an ever smaller elite group), or living in the culture of the slave. To trust as heavily as we now do in prisons and executions brings that cruelly bifurcated world closer to the places where we all live. It is to allow our entire civil order to lurch toward the worst side of the United States' historical experiment in nation building. In this way, too, lockdown America can be seen as a threat to us all.

There is a final sense in which our commitment to and tolerance of prisons and death penalties is a threat to the general good of us all: it entails a loss of a democratic society's most precious quality, that is, its popular sovereignty.

This argument, I believe, has been made most convincingly by Robert Meeropol, executive director of the Rosenberg Fund for Children. I have already cited some of his words. He and his brother are the only children to have lost both their parents to execution by the U.S. government. His statement about how the death penalty is not just his own pain but is also a threat to general popular sovereignty is worth quoting in full.

> There is also a more subtle, but still powerful, anti-capital punishment argument: [The death penalty] is anti-democratic and inevitably corrupting. One of the promises of the Constitution is that the people are sovereign. In other words, the only rights we the people cede to the government are those that are specifically enumerated in the Constitution. Americans' suspicion of concentrated governmental power is probably best summed up by the nineteenth-century British Lord Acton, who said: "Power tends to corrupt. Absolute power tends to corrupt absolutely."
>
> The imposition of the death penalty, the power of life and death, is a form of absolute power. *Give people in government that power and they will abuse it.*[103]

Meeropol goes on to comment on how corrupt the government became in its executing of his parents, and today's studies of the death penalty document how governmental applications of executions continually compound error, incompetence, and corruption.[104] The crucial link in Meeropol's argument is that when the government executes, it has to demonstrate perfection. That can rarely be done. Execution, the terminating of a life, demands a perfection, Meeropol argues, that can only be intended and therefore rests more and more on pretense. Such pretense easily breeds a governmental culture of cover-up and corruption.

The death penalty, which has always been "the paradigm act"[105] of a criminal justice system that manifests and reinforces racist practices, is a threat to all of us, Meeropol is arguing, because we all experience the risk posed by the death penalty to our popular sovereignty. The more we trust ourselves to the execution protocols at the heart of lockdown America's terror, the more we put our entire democratic system at risk. No wonder that even some of the founding fathers, particularly the Quakers, believed the death penalty to be inappropriate for the democratic governance they dreamed and fought for. Marcus Rediker, an American historian at the University of Pittsburgh recalls

Benjamin Rush's lament, for example, that "an execution in a republic is like a human sacrifice in religion," and Rediker refers to other cases in which some early fighters for democracy saw the death penalty as anathema to real democratic freedom.[106]

Any of us who cherish democratic ideals, who value our own freedom, have every reason to resist the bureaucracy of unfreedom, lockdown America, that rises in our midst today. To facilitate that resistance, however, we will need to understand it better, to see through its correctional pretensions and into the ways it actually serves to protect an imperial order. The next chapter takes aim at that understanding.

2. theatrics and sacrifice in the U.S.-Led Imperium

> The suffering of the conquered and colonized people appears as a necessary sacrifice and the inevitable process of modernization. This logic has been applied from the conquest of America until the Gulf War, and its victims are as diverse as indigenous Americans and Iraqi citizens.
>
> —Enrique Dussel, *The Invention of the Americas*

The argument of this chapter is that the terrors of Gulag America function theatrically, providing spectacles that have a negative impact, first of all upon those marked as poor and racially other. Such spectacles, involving the sacrifice of these especially marked ones, are carried out, however, in a way that also constitutes an intimidating display for exercising control throughout the wider society. These spectacles function on the domestic U.S. scene and also reinforce a global empire that is not identical to the nation of the United States but is anchored by the U.S. hegemony over military power.

This takes us more deeply into the notion of theatrics. In its most general sense, *theatrics* is simply the art of theater. In a more specific sense, it is a collection of dramatic mannerisms that are calculated for effect. Sometimes we use the word in a way that suggests theatrics are not important, as when we say, "Let's spare the theatrics and address the issue squarely." Here, the dramatic mannerisms are seen as a distraction from something else held to be more important.

This overlooks, however, the real power in theater and drama. We all know that the dramatic mannerisms, the theatrics, the acting out have effects. Issues analyzed and points made without theatrical display, without flourish, often go unnoticed. It is the essence of theatrics to be noticed. It is their role to have an effect, and theatrics are a visible and visceral way to have effect. Sometimes, theatrics are short-lived and powerless, and their effects quickly dissipate. For systems that use theatrics and are heavily institutionalized with long histories, however, theatrical display is a very effective tool of power. Gulag America, as analyzed in the previous chapter and with its six dimensions of terror, is a theatrical force of this sort. It is characterized by exaggerated self-display and drama. We must now ask why: as theatrical, what is its calculated effect?

I argue that the spectacle and spectacles of lockdown America involve the sacrifice of certain so-called surplus populations. These are groups both disenfranchised and often portrayed as "other" (by race, gender, class, culture) whom a society's policy-makers often see as expendable. A sacrifice of such groups is effected through isolation of them, rejection, exclusion, paramilitary-police intimidation and crackdowns, imprisonment, and execution. Such a multiform sacrifice helps maintain a public order that today is increasingly dominated by an elite class in the United States. Not all members of a surplus population need be sacrificed. Enough are, however, to keep others complacent and under control.

The practice of domination by an elite within the United States is coordinated with an imperial practice globally, where U.S. military force (or the threat of it) is increasingly necessary to support emerging transnational globalization. The terrors of lockdown America are the sacrifices demanded of many people who dwell at the heart of the U.S.-led imperium. Indeed, the spectacle of their sacrifice may be necessary to the well-being of a U.S.-led global empire, the *Pax Americana.* By this chapter's conclusion, I will have argued that the sacrifices extracted from many U.S. residents can be seen as a way to build up a dominant domestic elite that in turn is necessary for enabling the global reach exercised by the United States.

Gulag America's Calculated Effect

We may be put off by the notion of calculated effect. It suggests one or a few persons who intentionally create processes that terrorize. Is it not simplistic to talk of a criminal justice system, with its many judges, police, court, and corrections personnel, and complex laws, as having an effect that is calculated? Is the multidimensional terror of Chapter 1, and all the human suffering borne by direct victims, and indirectly by society at large, really an effect that is calculated?

Certainly no one person can do the calculating and work the effect. Nor can any one group or cabal of conspirators be identified as the workers of the multidimensional terror at work in Gulag America. At a systemic level, however, looking at how patterns unfold historically and are reinforced in many small ways in the present, we can describe sectors of our social life that benefit from the present configuration of Gulag America and other sectors that seem to be its targets. This is not as abstract a point as the reference to systems and sectors might suggest. Molly, the Rikers Island prison educator, explained the logic when she suggested that people who want a nice life and neighborhood in some sections of New York City "need" a ghetto and "need a prison," especially with all its "short-term terror and revulsion." It is time now to trace the dynamics of that need and to show more clearly how the theatrics of terror in Gulag America serve what Molly called the "attractive lives" of some sectors.[1]

Production, Punishment, and the Sacrificial Myth

The key to understanding why Gulag America rises today is to consider our present system of punishment within the context of the production of economic wealth in the recent history of the United States. Not every punishment can be explained in this way, but in order to understand today's organized and startling theatrics of terror, we best begin our understanding by viewing the punishment system in relation to the system that produces wealth.

We live in a capitalist economy whose defenders claim to champion the importance of free trade internationally and a market economy domestically in which all residents can compete. U.S. residents may have different ideological stances toward capitalist modes of production. Some may believe that the milieu of the United States allows every person with diligence and creativity to thrive and meet his or her basic needs. Others of a more liberal persuasion know this milieu doesn't exist and so advocate for special assistance to be given those who cannot survive.

Except for the more radical critics of capitalism, many in capitalist societies do not question that our way of creating wealth involves giving some people a right to hold more than many others may have. Greater accumulations of money and property by some in contrast to others is not held to be problematic. There are rules and laws about how one accumulates one's wealth, laws that are often poorly and unfairly enforced, but simply to hold wealth that exceeds that of another in your social group is no fault in itself, according to the system of production in U.S. social life.

The founding fathers agreed. What James Madison called the "various and unequal distribution of property" in his *Federalist Paper X,* is simply a fact to be lived with. He recognized it as the most durable and common cause of "faction," but he helped to design a government that did not remove or mitigate this difference in economic wealth. He only sought to control *faction,* the conflict and effects arising from the disparity.[2]

Many, from almost any side of the spectrum of ideologies about capitalism, note that capitalist societies that feature a marked or rapid growth of disparity between those who have much and others who have little will risk instability. There will be faction and a threat of rebellions from socially corrosive groups. A system of economic production, while accepting some degree of what Madison called "various and unequal distribution of property" is always walking a fine line between maintaining a smoothly running society with economic differences and becoming chaotically dysfunctional because those who are on the downside of economic difference are rebellious and unhappy. A capitalism that chooses to live with economic inequality has built into it, then, the need to control the potentially harmful effects of that inequality.

In this need to control faction and rebellion lies the seed of the connection between a system of capitalist production and the system of punishment. Today's elaborate system of punishment, with its theatrics of terror, has grown from this seed and exerts control over potentially rebellious factions. Today's factions, I will argue, are one result of the startling emergence of a new economic disparity in the U.S. population. We have a system of terrorizing punishment, meted out directly to more than two million people in prison (a disproportionate number of whom are people of color), because unequal distribution of property and general economic disparity have reached greater, nearly unmanageable levels. To control resulting faction, wealthier sectors have had to intensify means to control the lives of the less fortunate.

Even though the punishment system has reared its head in today's special terror of Gulag America, this use of force and terror to guard a system for creating wealth is not a new dynamic in the United States. It has long precedent, and it is a nearly habitual mode of existence bequeathed to the present by American legacies of Indian wars and institutionalized slavery. The building of the country and forging of its economic life were achieved, first, through the largely violent wresting of land from indigenous peoples here and by their forced removal and confinement to designated lands and then to reservations. The U.S. nation-state was born in acts of violence. Its very possession of land as a base was derived from and is maintained by acts of force.[3] Richard Hardt and Antonio Negri have also suggested that the root of contemporary U.S. imperial abuses "should be traced back to the very origins of the country, to black slavery and the genocidal wars against the Native Americans."[4]

Moreover, the industrial revolution in the United States, as in most of Europe, depended significantly upon a slave trade that involved elaborate mechanisms for regimenting the bodies and lives of those taken from Africa and maintained in the institution of slavery. The legacy of slavery here has hardly died out with the nineteenth-century emancipation of the slaves or even the turn of the twenty-first century.[5] Some of us are enraged by this truth; others rationalize it out of some kind of historical realism or through talk about the ambiguities of history. Although we may mask the horrors of the past, it remains true that we live today in an economic order that is dependent upon a history of subjecting other bodies and groups to confinement, forced labor, and worse. "The slave production in the Americas and the African slave trade" were a "pedestal of superexploitation on which European capitalism stood."[6]

Philosopher and ethicist Enrique Dussel has described this process, this dependency on slavery, as but one example of how the ethos of modernity is structured in the West. The expanding and dominating ways of Western colonialization dawned in 1492 and depended upon a "myth of a special kind of sacrificial violence which eventually eclipsed whatever was non-European."[7] The basic myth was that others, usually marked as Amerindian or African, but also as Arab and Asian ("Orientals"[8]), were viewed as material to be legitimately sacrificed for building up and maintaining a European-based modernity. The search for gold and silver in the Americas, pursued by the nascent capitalism of Europe,[9] entailed, for example, the death and desolation of enslaved indigenous workers.[10]

The silver mine of Potosí, in present-day Bolivia, served as a vivid example of how the search for valued commodities entailed the sacrificing of populations. "Four years before depleting the land, a mouth of hell was discovered into which a great quantity of people descended each year. These victims, sacrificed by Spanish greed to its god, work in the silver mine called Potosí."[11] Potosí, the "most bountiful of silver mines of all modern times,"[12] is described by Dussel as a metaphorical representation of "the mouth of Moloch, requiring human sacrifice . . . to the invisible god Capital, the new deity of occidental, Christian civilization."[13]

Nascent capitalism of modernity is a sacrificial economy worshiping money as its fetish, and sacrificing the "subjective corporeality of the Indian and African slave." So necessary is the sacrifice that it is rationalized as legitimate. Part of this process of legitimization involved racial disparagement of some others, who came to be seen as so much fuel for the palace. If those who are marked for sacrifice become unruly, they then are treated as victims meriting even greater control. It is then a short step to what Dussel calls the "gigantic inversion" worked by the European modern mind: "the innocent victim becomes culpable, and the culpable victimizer becomes innocent."[14] Dussel argues that the viewing of conquered and colonized people as "necessary sacrifice" is touted as the "inevitable price of modernization." It is accepted as such, especially by those who benefit from the sacrifice, and sometimes is made to seem so logical and necessary that even some of the victims acquiesce to the logic. "This logic has been applied from the conquest of America until the Gulf War, and its victims are as diverse as indigenous Americans and Iraqi citizens."[15] Dussel might also have noted as victims women, who often have been rendered as exploitable and as potential victims to be sacrificed for modernity.[16]

A present-day capitalism, touting free trade globally and celebrating the U.S. economic boom in the decade of 1991–2001, still lives out this sacrificial myth. The plight of Third World nations, whose poor sink deeper into an impoverished sprawl above which a small world of elites move, is general testimony to the persistence of sacrificed populations. The dying of Iraqi citizens, especially their children expiring at the rate of three thousand a month, is a specific and dramatic witness to the way sacrifice of some is rationalized for the health of the already wealthy countries.[17]

An example from my own cultural scene in New Jersey may be illuminating. When oil prices became uncomfortably high in the United States, as they did in early 2000, it was a common theme for callers and talk-show hosts of mainstream radio to say, "Let's just go back and bomb those Middle East places, do it right this time, and leave 'em just a 7-11 food store."[18] The fact that this could be stated so quickly, so unquestioningly, so blissfully unmindful of the human loss entailed suggests just how much we are steeped in a culture that accepts and assumes the right to sacrifice Third World populations to secure our way of life.

Such sacrifices are seen as necessary to the efficiency of Western culture and economy. Economist Franz J. Hinkelammert argues that this relation between "sacrifice" (even of genocidal proportions) and "efficiency" has been enthusiastically embraced by the West from the eighteenth century to the present.[19] Hardt and Negri have pointed out that this is so much the case that these sacrificed and subordinated others become necessary for dominant European and Euroamerican groups to maintain their very identity, their identity as "cultured," as "civilized," as "free."[20] In short, for supplying both natural resources (oil) essential for economic life, and also for nurturing North Atlantic selves' senses of cultural identity, the deaths of the poor are necessary. They are sacrifices that power the U.S.-led imperium. When in 1994 anthropologist Christopher Taylor was forced to flee the genocidal terror of Rwanda, where over a million lives were lost to a preventable slaughter that the West did little or nothing to stop, he returned to the peaceful world of the United States and mused, "How often our peace seems predicated on someone else's misery."[21]

When my colleagues and I were distributing leaflets to passers-by along the streets of Princeton, New Jersey, calling for an end to the siege of sanctions and bombs so devastating to Iraqi children after the Gulf War, it was not unusual to receive a response from a well-dressed shopper, "Bomb 'em all!" "Even the children?" asked one activist friend. "Every last one of 'em," was the reply. Such retorts indicate that amid all the progress Americans claim for our modern or postmodern culture, we still have not made any great advance beyond the sacrificial myth. We still live in an ethos of that ugly modernity that rationalizes the sacrifice of racially stigmatized surplus populations. Surplus populations, recall, are those disenfranchised and displaced groups, usually also racially stigmatized, whom policy-makers either neglect or assume to be expendable in the social order.

Cultural commentators today, especially those supported by major media corporations, rarely explore this history and the sacrifices upon which U.S.

and European governments depend. They also seem unwilling to discuss today's economic disparity, which has called forth its necessary complement, a terrorizing system of military application of force (as in Iraq) and the punitive regime of Gulag America.

In the next section, we must look more closely at the disparity between rich and poor that exists in the United States and that becomes a key motivating factor for putting in place the new punitive regime. The rise of an elite U.S. sector, which has accelerated over the past three decades, is not an unavailable story, but it is often untold. If we are to understand the U.S. prison industrial complex—the rise of Big House Nation—we must start telling that story.

A Strengthened Elite Class in America: An Untold Story

Celebrations of the millennium in the U.S.A. were replete with accolades for the nation's booming economy, the dream economy, as its beneficiaries have called it. This was especially true among those who measure economic health largely in terms of growth of the economy and the upward surges of the stock market. This decade's economic surge constitutes the most dramatic period of economic expansion in U.S. history.[22] The economic vitality of America's majorities, however, are not best measured by statistics concerning growth. Bullish days on Wall Street are not necessarily marks of economic justice.

Accompanying the dream economy is an economic disparity that has been documented again and again. In 1999, during the heyday of economic boom, Harvard sociologist William Julius Wilson introduced some sobering perspective. Wilson documented that along with the dream economy, a gap between rich and poor has been widening.[23] This gap has widened across the better part of three decades, most intensively in the last two. The rate of the widening had slowed by 1999 but was still widening nevertheless. It was yielding new cultures of the social elite.

At the end of the 1980s, this widening gap had already been documented by Kevin Phillips, a national columnist who had worked as a Republican campaign aide for Richard Nixon in 1968. In 1990, Phillips documented how the Reagan administration accelerated dynamics already under way since the 1970s and thereby unleashed new forces of economic instability and inequality. These new forces were marked by an increasing concentration of wealth in the upper 1 percent of the U.S. population. Between 1977 and 1987, the average annual family income for the lowest 10 percent of U.S. wage earners dropped by 10.5 percent, while at the same time the upper 1 percent of the population (already making an average of $174,498) actually increased their wealth by a whopping 74.2 percent.[24]

The 1999 studies by sociologist Wilson, looking at the same period and tracking the distribution of wealth, confirmed these statistics.[25] While education, inflation, and growth were "positive signs," statistics on the real lives of people could hardly be called positive. Household debt during these decades of growth, for example, had increased for U.S. families from 59 percent of disposable income in 1973 to "an astonishing 94.8 percent in 1997."[26]

Other indicators of economic life of U.S. residents were equally troubling. Over the century's last two decades, the U.S. had the most rapid growth of wage inequality in the Western world.[27] The number of those without health care was on the increase, and the numbers of those living in poverty who were not getting food stamps was on the rise.[28] By the middle of the 1990s, the United States had the smallest and fastest-shrinking middle class among the seventeen industrialized nations.[29] While more wealth circulates in the United States than in any country in the world, a higher percentage of our residents still live in poverty than in the other industrialized countries.[30] The Children's Defense Fund documented in 1999 that over four hundred thousand additional children slipped into "extreme poverty" after the Republican Party's provisions for cutting social services in its Contract with America began to take effect under Democratic President Clinton's signature.[31]

It is important to ponder this rising inequality and its troubling effects on increasing numbers of middle-class and poorer populations. All the more must we ponder it when celebrants of the present economic order proclaim that the economic growth benefiting an elite is a "rising tide that raises all boats." The rising tide doesn't always automatically raise all boats, at least not enough to lift people above their economic and political miseries. Sometimes, it can, as in the several decades immediately after World War II.[32] Today's markers of economic disparity are so pronounced, however, that this cannot be said of the economic growth spurt of 1991–1999. With the economy still booming into the new millennium, Richard W. Stevenson wrote in the *New York Times* that studies of this new growth "suggest that those at the bottom of the economic ladder are not benefiting much from the boom and, by some measures, are falling even farther behind."[33] When this growth slows, as it most surely will, the disparity, according to Wilson, could become a source of greater political and economic trauma and conflict.

Some of the most sober of economic and political analysts have been forced to draw conclusions about the American democratic system and its economic order that run quite counter to today's rhetoric of economic celebration. Anthropologist John Bodley, for example, studying wealth and economic power in "the American industrialist state," had to conclude from his findings that holders of economic wealth in the United States, with their ready and continual access to a growing network of transnational corporate powers, now make up one of the smallest ruling elites in the history of world cultures.[34] In such a setting, small businesses are increasingly taken over by large conglomerates that have access to transnational corporate wealth. Poor populations in the United States in the 1970s and 1980s, especially in the large inner cities, were used up and then abandoned, as manufacturers competed in a "race to the bottom," seeking ever lower wage labor, first in the Southern states and then wherever they could find it in Third World regions where tariffs and wages were low and workers were without effective unions.[35] Working communities are laid waste, and the disparity between their earnings and those of the average corporate CEO atop the economic order grows to outlandish proportions.

The rise of this economically powerful sector marks the twentieth century's final decades. A widening gap between rich and poor was powered by runaway spending, largely in the areas of military funding and military support structures. This was the great secret of Presidents Reagan and Bush who talked much of the need to cut federal spending as warrant for cutting social services, while spending vigorously on military costs that actually fueled indebtedness. It marked an effort that Phillips discusses as an economy shifted into "conservative overdrive," where there flourished a "conservative commitment to expansive debt."[36] With a few rhetorical changes, this supposedly conservative tradition was carried on by the Democratic president, Bill Clinton. Across the last two decades of the twentieth century and through three presidencies (Republican and Democratic), military spending has dwarfed funding for education and social services. In spite of that fact, the first U.S. president of the twenty-first century began his administration in January 2001 with a lament that the military had been neglected and required further reform and financial support.[37] U.S. leaders thus continue to ignore and therefore fail to redress the divide between classes that exists in their nation.

With this kind of bifurcation of the class terrain in the United States, systems that seek to maintain social order also go into a kind of overdrive. Economic production, which in capitalism always needs mechanisms to manage the faction provoked by unequal distributions of wealth and property, easily becomes dependent upon systems of punishment (with all the policing, sentencing, and institutions of confinement). Along with economic overdrive, then, comes a kind of punitive and disciplinary overdrive, one that functions to control the surplus populations left behind or who might be threatening to the mechanisms of economic boom.

The Punishment System and Controlling Surplus Populations

The kind of bifurcation of wealth and class sketched above creates social wreckage, we might say, debris that has to be managed, cleaned up, or dispensed with. This wreckage makes up the surplus populations that our economic system of production has to manage and that the United States controls today to a growing extent by systems of punishment and confinement.

Terms like *debris* and *wreckage* may be deplorable in their application to human beings, but they name how the system and elite power holders in the system often view groups of the population that do not find a comfortable place in the economic and political order. Christian Parenti, drawing from the work of criminologist Steven Spitzer, divided this wreckage into two categories: "social junk" and "social dynamite."[38]

According to Spitzer, *social junk* refers to people whose lives are worn down and nearly destroyed, barely holding together. These include the mentally ill, drug addicts, lonely and frayed drifters, alcoholics, and cast-off, impoverished elders. When an economic order no longer structures itself to care for such as these, then its officials must find mechanisms to get them out of the way. "They must be driven away from the beaches, malls, and tony shopping areas of resort towns and financial districts, and the pleasure zones of theme park cities."[39]

People who can enjoy shopping and theater in the big downtowns do not want to see the homeless and the hungry. Indeed, the renovated New York City of the 1990s, under the administration of Mayor Rudolph Giuliani, has announced itself as a place inhospitable to the poor. New controls were devised, therefore, for housing the homeless and for preventing unemployed persons from earning coins by washing the car windows of autos stopped in traffic.

Those who make up Spitzer's category of social junk rarely unite to orchestrate a potent resistance to the social forces that grind them down or to the legalized vigilante men that chase them around. They rarely pose a threat to the system, though they are a kind of blemish on the system. They are, as Parenti notes, a kind of "ontological threat" to the system.[40] They are only feared, if at all, because their very being discloses that something is wrong with the functioning of the economic order.

It is quite otherwise with the group identified by Spitzer as the "social dynamite." Here, there is fear and a sustained and organized wariness among the elite. *Social dynamite* names that sector of the population left behind by economic production who do pose the threat of social explosion. These often play roles in creating nongovernable spaces. Included here are the impoverished low-wage, working-class, and unemployed youth who often do not appear in statistical summaries of the economy. These youthful spirits are often not bowed and crushed by their disadvantage, and so they fight to be included in the social order.[41] They are called social dynamite because they are, or can be perceived as, a major threat to the functioning of the economic order.

These groups have always characterized the U.S. economic and political order. U.S. officials have often had to wage a veritable civil war against low-wage workers, farmers, and others—so much so, in fact, that historian Howard Zinn has referred to the big business war on labor as "The Other Civil War."[42] Children walking out on strike from textile mills in New Jersey in the 1840s, shoemakers doing the same in New England, and the Black Panthers of the 1960s—for all their differences, these share a historical role of being deemed social dynamite. As such, they provoke unease and repression from established agents of control.

Such groups are often forced to live on the edge of social legality and even when engaged in fully legal behavior, they are presented and hunted as criminals. Such has been the fate of groups like the Young Lords and the Black Panthers, as well as "gang-groups" like the Bloods and Crips in Los Angeles, whose "thug life" was often mixed with programs of social renewal and liberation.[43] Participants in the unemployed councils organized by the Communist Party in the 1930s may also be termed social dynamite, given the ways they acted to force the stoppage of evictions in New York's Lower East Side.[44]

From the perspective of officials who live atop a political order marked by disparity, such groups are threats to order and power. Especially in a system that is made up of both class hierarchy and racial hierarchies, social dynamite will be viewed as a major threat. Groups of young people—especially those who organize in the Black Panthers, Young Lords, the American Indian Movement (AIM)—will be marked by class and race (as Indian, black, Hispanic), and subject to repression. At one point in the 1970s, every member of AIM was targeted by the FBI for surveillance and almost all of its leadership was tied up with time in court and prison.[45]

An economic order rooted in a system of production that tolerates a hierarchy of economic opportunity marked by race and class will have to devise systems of control and punishment to deal with social dynamite. This need to control yields the kind of policing, imprisoning, and executing we see today in the political theatrics of terror. Parenti's words are again effective.

> Controlling [social dynamite] requires both a defensive policy of containment and an aggressive policy of direct attack and active destabilization. They are contained and crushed, confined to the ghetto, demoralized and pilloried in warehouse public schools, demonized by a lurid media, sent to prison, and at times dispatched by lethal injection or police bullets. This is the class—or more accurately the caste, because they are increasingly people of color—which must be constantly undermined, divided, intimidated, attacked, discredited and ultimately kept in check with what [Frantz] Fanon called the "language of naked force."[46]

We see a political theatrics of terror, therefore, pervading our punishment system today. It is functioning in overdrive to exercise control during these decades marked by severe economic disparity in the U.S. social order. In fact, nearly all of the recent legislation designed to create and support the new building of prisons, the longer sentencing, the ethos of a newly equipped, paramilitary police force, and the expedited execution process has come hand in glove with the processes that have also augmented economic disparity. This process began with the refurbishing of U.S. police forces through grants beginning in the 1960s through Lyndon Johnson's Law Enforcement Assistance Administration. There quickly followed the Omnibus Crime Control and Safe Streets Act of 1968, the Comprehensive Drug Abuse Prevention and Control Act of 1970, the Racketeering Influence and Corrupt Organizations Act of 1970, the Comprehensive Crime Control Act of 1984, the Anti-Drug Abuse Acts of 1986 and 1988, the Violent Crime Control and Law Enforcement Act of 1994, the Illegal Immigration Reform and Immigrant Responsibility Act of 1996, and the Anti-Terrorism and Effective Death Penalty Act of 1996.[47]

These acts of legislation across the last several decades, all with virtuous sounding titles, came into being during the rising economic disparity created by the conservative overdrive detailed by Kevin Phillips, William Julius Wilson, and others. The political theatrics of terror was a necessary complement to a political economy that put rich and poor into greater conflict with one another.

How Terrorizing Punishment Serves the Economically Powerful

Many are conditioned to offer up justifications for this rise of organized punitive force in our times. First, some will argue that it is precisely these more stringent measures that have cleaned up our cities and neighborhoods and have reduced crime. This overlooks the fact that the burgeoning prisons and pervasive paramilitary policing are completely out of proportion to any reduction of crime.[48] Moreover, as I noted in Chapter 1, the majority of the controlled and confined are not there for reasons of violent destruction of persons or the social order. They are subjected to prison terror and spirit death for violations for which restitution and correction could easily be made by other means.

More prisons and more authoritarian policing are not only cruel and terrorizing, but increasingly they are being seen as only a temporary stopgap against intransigent social problems that require more imaginative means and a challenge to the economic order of things. Even in New York City, where strongman Mayor Giuliani persuaded many (for a time) that his strong policing was reducing crime, public confidence in using punitive force is evaporating in many places.[49]

Second, a justifying response claims that we have to do something about those individuals who fail to act responsibly, who drop out, who can't get it together, who are disruptive and violent. Yes, we do need to do something about them. There will always be some who are violent, usually because they themselves suffered severe violence as children from either abusive parents or disadvantaged neighborhoods or contexts.[50] For some, a more controlled environment will perhaps be necessary, at least temporarily. Confinement and isolation, however, do not heal one for responsible participation in public life.[51] No, our public addiction to the construction of prisons and confinement and to a whole system of punishment for controlling surplus populations only absolves us of the need to think about and invest creatively in new modes of social community that might nurture people left out and behind and might prevent crime-inducing conditions.[52]

Before the recent and dramatic rise of the prison population, our surplus populations were absorbed by a social order that had an admittedly imperfect welfare system. It was a system that dealt with some of the needs of the economically disenfranchised. Moreover, before the conservative overdrive beginning in the 1980s, certain controls and limitations on employers existed, such that they were encouraged to make concessions to their workers. With the last decades' removal of that welfare system and the deregulating of employer obligations, combined with a failure to think about creative improvements to welfare and labor rights, a well-funded punishment system has been built up to absorb the poor.

So, yes, we need to do something about the troubled and disruptive souls in our social order. What we have chosen to do, however, is to close down the creative social action and revisioning that might mitigate the problems. Instead, we have built up an unimaginative network of warehouses for the poor. If there is creativity and imagination exercised relative to troubled and disruptive people, it seems more often applied to devising ever new modes of profiting from the systems of confinement.[53] We have really yet to try doing that something, which would entail well-organized and well-imagined social justice and empowerment for the historically most vulnerable in our population.

A third justifying response, however, might say that the rise of the punishment system just happens to correspond temporally with the rise of economic disparity. There is no causal connection, insists this response, between today's economic disparity and the system of prison, police, and death penalty. To the contrary, there is a causal logic, and even Molly (the educator at Rikers Island) could make the connection quite bluntly between terrorizing punishment and the protection of wealth amid an era of economic disparity. Punishment systems do function to serve those who already have economic power. So valuable is this function that we can say that stark economic disparity helps cause, and also creates (indeed, needs) institutions of punitive control and also theatrically intimidating spectacles of control.

As Parenti has pointed out, the theatrics of terror expressed through massively built-up prison practices and support systems make two major contributions to the security of elites atop a disparate economic order. These help us see the processes that link economic disparity with the punitive buildup, enabling us to see how they are causally connected, not just temporally coincidental.

First, quite obviously, massive punitive force serves an economic elite by moving aside the social junk from the places the elite likes to inhabit and by controlling and seeking to eliminate social dynamite. Both of these surplus populations are put out of the way, dispensed with, neutralized. The debris, it is thought, is thrown out.

The use of force to protect those atop a disparity of economic wealth is so well known that elite voices themselves acknowledge it. Regarding international politics, George F. Kennan, who was ambassador to the Soviet Union and a major Cold War theorist, argued that military force is a part of a "pattern of relationships" necessary to ensure that a country like the United States, with only 6 percent of the world's population, can continue to use the 50 percent of the world's resources upon which its prosperity is based.[54] Although Kennan was developing his realpolitik in an international frame of reference, the same principle applies for managing disparities of wealth and power on the domestic scene. Systems of force will always be justified as being for everyone's protection, and there are examples of that, but their basic role is to protect the present disbursement of wealth. The more that disbursement is unequal, the more force will be necessary. In trying to explain the mass of new legislation and runaway prison construction of the 1980s and 1990s, it is most logical to look to the need to protect the disproportionate wealth of a new elite. It is certainly much more logical to look to that explanation than simply to assume that citizens were less responsible during those decades and hence more in need of policing and imprisonment.

Second, the system of punitive terror creates through its prison culture a predator population that, when it returns to the street, has negative effects on neighborhoods and societies. The production of predators further reinforces economic disparity. Predators frighten and disorganize poor neighborhoods, driving many of the members of these communities right into the arms of powerful security forces and law enforcement officials for protection. Prisons, amid disparities of economic power, therefore, become halfway houses lining the vicious circle that reinforces the power of economic elites. Surplus populations are criminalized and moved into prisons, where significant numbers are trained more intensively into a predator class. When predators return to the streets, to live again among the poorer communities on the outside, they then become additional reasons to justify the further criminalization and imprisonment of the poor's own neighborhoods. The term *predator* may seem dehumanizing and extreme, but prisons transform some people into animal-like, destructive forces that later wreak havoc on neighborhoods outside.

As this circle continually gets played out, more and more people—both outside and inside the prisons—begin to see Big House Nation as the normal abode of our life and spirit. The big stick seems necessary to life itself. Many of us seem to want to accept vigilance and control. We become acculturated to an ethos of domination. Indeed, we have been pressured to respect and functionally to worship a whole culture of vigilance and control. Officials seeking election make easy entrance to office by riding residents' fear of real or imagined criminals. They preach a law and order gospel that finds a ready acceptance among a citizenry taught to confuse spectacular enforcement and rigorous vigilance with just governance. Political leaders thus serve up spectacles of fighting crime, not only through news shows but in law enforcement sitcoms like *Cops.* As sociologist Zygmunt Bauman notes, "Fighting crime, like crime itself, and particularly the crime targeted on bodies and private property, makes an excellent, exciting, eminently watchable show."[55]

In sum, it is not only self-serving and naive but also illogical to claim that the rise of prisons and the new punitive regime simply accompany by coincidence today's emergence of a new economic elite. To the contrary, the regime of theatrical terror is necessary to and services a political economy in which a U.S. economic elite must steady itself atop a startling economic imbalance.[56]

From Gulag America to *Pax Americana*

What I have argued so far is that the forces of lockdown America serve an elite minority who govern a markedly disproportionate share of economic power within the United States. A similar relation between organized force and a powerful elite thrives in the international theater of U.S. dealings. The internally thriving gulag has grown up along with the rise of the United States to its oft-noted status as the unrivaled superpower.

With the demise of the Soviet Union in 1989 and 1990, U.S. leaders had a unique opportunity to redirect Cold War military funds toward meeting the social and economic needs of surplus populations on the U.S. home front. Instead of doing that, the administrations of George Bush Sr. and Bill Clinton pushed through legislation and policies that consolidated the building up of Gulag America and fueled the need to build up and to exercise U.S. military power. Military assaults in Panama (1989) and Iraq (1991) conveniently justified the need for continual reinforcing of the U.S. post-Cold War military establishment.

Ronald Reagan, as the Soviet Union was crumbling from within, had already established the U.S. role as military policeman for an era of globalization, with bombing missions sent out to deliver international spanking-raids or to consolidate U.S. power, as in Grenada (1986) and in Tripoli, Libya (1988).

It was George Bush who put the military into its post-Cold War overdrive with the invasion of Panama and the Persian Gulf War—both requiring the demonizing of leaders whom the United States had previously supported and groomed: Manuel Noriega in Panama and Saddam Hussein in Iraq.[57] Bush's policies were continued by President Clinton's own approval of bombing missions against Iraq. These occurred in 1993, in 1998 and 1999, and then continued on a sporadic basis in tandem with a devastating sanctions policy that still keeps Iraq under a veritable siege condition.[58] Clinton also bombed a pharmaceutical plant in the Sudan in 1998 and on behalf of NATO powers led the bombing expeditions against Serbia in 1999.

The bombing raid against the Sudan, justified as necessary to punish terrorist attacks against the United States, was named Operation Infinite Reach. The title for this military operation is a revealing bit of hyperbole. It bespeaks U.S. leaders' understanding of their right to claim unilateral action across the globe to protect perceived or real self-interests. The U.S.-led NATO bombing missions of Serbia in 1999 were carried out without even seeking United Nations approval. Not only the globe but the entire twenty-first century has been staked out as American. Clinton's administrative officials used imperial speech continually, as when departing Secretary of State Warren Christopher proudly announced in 1998 that the next century would be "the American century." Mickey Kantor, U.S. trade representative, referred to the twenty-first century as the "New American Century."[59]

Academic and media pundits in the decade of the 1990s have become accustomed to talk about U.S. power as grounding a *Pax Americana*. This is a kind of global peace that is enforced and ordered by U.S. power and domination, carried out with a kind of imperial confidence that is not unlike that shown during the times of *Pax Romana*.[60] At the end of the Gulf War, President Bush glowed as he delivered his State of the Union address before Congress in 1992: "A world once divided into two armed camps now recognizes one sole and pre-eminent power, the United States of America. And they regard this with no dread. For the world trusts us with power, and the world is right."[61]

In a Pentagon document released to the public in the same year, officials made quite clear their imperialist intentions—thought to be benign and good for the world, of course. It read, "Our first objective is to prevent the re-emergence of a new rival," especially, the document continued, from among "the advanced industrial nations."[62] To clarify the intention, a few more lines from the document stress the point: "The U.S. should be postured to act independently when collective action cannot be orchestrated. . . . The world order is ultimately backed by the U.S. . . . We must maintain the mechanisms for deterring potential competitors from even aspiring to a larger regional or global role."[63] Such an intention to dominate the globe and a unilateral right to intervene anywhere has never been questioned by the Clinton administration, however true it may be that the United States is also unwilling or unable to intervene to settle all global conflicts (as in Russia's harrowing attacks in its war in Chechnya of 1999 and 2000).

Powerful media outlets in the United States and the world dwell quite comfortably, it seems, with the mantle of imperial power resting upon the nation. As the bombing of Serbia began in 1999, for example, the *New York Times Magazine* featured on its cover an essay by one of its chief columnists, Thomas Friedman. In the essay, after celebrating the global era and the Internet where "we are all connected and nobody is in charge," Friedman acknowledged that the U.S. military is the "hidden fist" keeping the global order in place. "McDonald's cannot flourish without McDonnell Douglas, the builder of the F-15."[64]

If being an *empire* is a matter of being a state that exercises a "governing relationship of political control through imposition over the effective sovereignty of other political societies," as political scientist Michael Doyle would have it, then the United States qualifies as an empire. Indeed, Doyle suggests as much. Moreover, if *imperialism* is defined as "the process of establishing and maintaining an empire,"[65] the United States also possesses policies that clearly qualify as imperial in nature. To be sure, the U.S. nation-state is not today "the empire," as Hardt and Negri point out, but the United States is the privileged, imperial player in creating and supporting the global network or transnational entity that is rightly called empire.[66]

My discussion here of U.S. imperial power is not meant to turn this book into a project on international relations. The imperial role of U.S. foreign policy and positioning is certainly relevant, however, to our understanding of lockdown America. As Doyle points out in his study of some six different imperialist formations in the past centuries, empires attain their global reach through effective consolidation of a "dominant domestic coalition."[67] Granted, the United States as superpower is enmeshed in and protects an entire network of transnational connections and agents, and gains power from doing so. It is also indispensable to U.S. participation in global empire, however, to create an administrative structure of domination at home, with a centered state apparatus. Securing the dominant domestic coalition is crucial to the centering of power necessary for imperial pretension and global power play.

The groups that ride atop the current economic disparity in the United States today and that have successfully forged the theatrics exercised in Gulag America constitute such a dominant domestic coalition. This coalition is built from both political parties and includes key participants who hold no elective office but who shape governing power over the state of things for most Americans from within corporate worlds.[68] They constitute in the United States what John MacArthur has called a "bipartisan political oligarchy" that serves big business and global trade.[69]

Conclusion: Surplus and Sacrifice in the U.S.-Led Imperium

With the rise of Big House Nation, we are not just seeing another experiment by well-intentioned leaders in how best to deal with our criminal element. We are not simply witnessing fed-up people suffering so-called compassion fatigue, who now have agreed to hand over two million of their neighbors for warehousing and nearly four thousand for death. Nor are we witnessing some institutionalized tough love that is part of some new moral vision insisting that citizens take responsibility for their own lives or face the punitive consequences.

No, Big House Nation serves up a theatrics of terror for the function of maintaining the power of a newly strengthened elite, a dominant domestic coalition that has risen to new power in the last three decades. It has built its power internally by creating economic disparity with new enforcement strategies and by being able to flex imperial muscle globally, especially since the fall of the Soviet Union.

Lockdown America, as a way to deal with surplus populations amid growing economic disparity, can be seen as a system of sacrifice within a U.S.-led imperium that practices domination on both internal and global fronts. Because the United States still cycles and recycles white supremacist proclivities and practices, this is not just a sacrifice of the poor. It is also a sacrifice of people of color, and of the racially stigmatized poor. The disproportionate suffering borne by people of color, under the aegis of an American imperial power, is not marked only by the preponderance of blacks, Hispanics, and Asians in U.S. prisons. It is dramatized also by the state of Africa, a whole continent rich in natural resources, which is kept in bondage to U.S.-led elite nations that enforce bonds of fiscal debt upon them. Africa's people thereby are maintained in a state of risk to ever new ways of dying daily and dying-out. At this writing, the dominant domestic coalition in the United States is working to sign with African leaders a trade bill that introduces Africa to the global market but on terms that do not threaten U.S.-led economic and political control over Africa's political economy.

The populations being sacrificed for and in the U.S.-led imperium, who are deemed as surplus, may be above all the children of Iraq. According to the World Health Organization and other human rights and advocacy groups, in the year 2000, Iraqi children are dying at a rate of more than three thousand per month.[70] This phenomenal rate of deaths began in 1991 with the U.S. bombing of Iraq, termed by former U.S. Attorney General Ramsey Clark as the largest aerial bombardment in world history. The bombings have continued over nearly a whole decade so that the aerial domination of the country amounts to "the longest sustained U.S. air operation since the Vietnam War."[71]

After her own visit to Iraq in 1996, Leslie Stahl of the CBS news show *60 Minutes* asked U.S. Secretary of State Madeleine Albright whether the total loss of half a million Iraqi children was troubling to her. Albright responded on air: "I think this is a very hard choice, but the price, we think the price is worth it."[72]

The deaths of these children, not to mention the host of others (totaling a million and a half when adults are added), have increased each year throughout the decade of the 1990s and into the new millennium. It is a decade-long march of horror that roughly parallels the unprecedented expansion of the U.S.'s so-called dream economy and the rise of that dominant coalition that has forged both lockdown America and *Pax Americana.*

Given the dependency of the U.S. economy on the political terms it enforces in the Middle East's oil-rich countries,[73] the children dying in Iraq since the 1991 bombing and sanctions policy constitute a continually extracted sacrifice for the maintenance of U.S.-led global empire. The terrible deaths of these children has become the lifeblood of the dominant domestic coalition now enshrined in the U.S.A., whose military is the hidden fist of globalization. There is every reason to recall anew the observation by Martin Luther King Jr., that the United States is "the greatest purveyor of violence in the world today."[74]

Our study of lockdown America, then, exposes an ugly practice: the sacrifice of surplus populations here at the heart of empire's superpower. Because of deep-running currents of white supremacy in Europe and the United States, the sacrifices will most usually be of people of color. Especially wherever U.S.-based corporate power wants energy from oil and gas, there will occur the exertion of imperial force. As I write, U.S.-backed armies are demanding sacrifice (in the form of loss of land and forced removal of their communities) from the indigenous Maya of Chiapas, Mexico, and from the indigenous U'wa of Colombia, both of whom inhabit lands rich in oil, gas, and other natural resources.

The way of the cross in lockdown America, then, is a way across a terrain that is a locus of empire. It is a terrain where people—deemed surplus, junk, or dynamite—are sacrificed to maintain a public order in the United States and increasingly to sustain the U.S.-led global imperium. The sacrifice of some in the United States is through the spirit death of long-term imprisonment. For others it comes through the direct loss of life via the state-sanctioned killing called capital punishment, which also pulls the power over life out of the hands of citizens and puts it in the hands of the state. For still others the sacrifice comes in the form of de facto extrajudicial executions, as in the killings of youth of color through excessive police force. For many others of us in the encroaching outer prison, there is a certain sacrifice, a loss of self and public dignity that occurs when we live by fear—of police, of their sweeps and nighttime raids, of enforcing agents standing ready with their surveillance and ever more calibrated modes of draconian penalties.

If the way of the cross takes us into this kind of place, onto this kind of killing field, what might be a way through it? How is the way of the cross not just another march to slaughter, swelling the number of innocents sacrificed? How can it be a wielding of the cross that resists the rites of sacrificial death demanded by the powerful?

When we raise these questions, we begin to glimpse the way of the executed God. Along that way, we will find release from our captivity to a political theatrics of terror and from the indignities of forced sacrifice in the U.S. imperium. We will find our way toward a theatrics of counterterror.

part two

A Theatrics of Counterterror

The basic fact is that Christianity as it was born in the mind of this Jewish teacher and thinker appears as a technique for the oppressed. . . . It was upon the anvil of the Jewish community's relations with Rome that Jesus hammered out the vital content of his concept of love for one's enemy.

—Howard Thurman, *Jesus and the Disinherited*

3. Way of the Cross as Adversarial Politics

> Mark's story of Jesus' last days . . . is an intensely political drama, filled with conspiratorial backroom deals and covert action, judicial manipulation and prisoner exchange, torture and summary execution. . . . And we do well not to forget that this very narrative of arrest, trial and torture is still lived out by countless political prisoners around the world today.
>
> —Ched Myers, *Binding the Strong Man*

What kind of practice is required to redress the agony of our times, in this era when new economic disparities in the United States are reinforced by a strengthened punishment regime? What way ahead is there for survival and flourishing?

Christian groups and communities of faith have often sponsored programs that address issues of economic inequality, the poor, and the imprisoned. But we need a more forceful and dramatic response if we are to take on today's political theatrics of terror.

Christians today, I argue, must participate in a theatrics of counterterror. From this chapter on to the end of the book, I present the main lines of this needed theatrics, an organized forceful way of acting out our faith. The way of the cross begins with what I present here, in Chapter 3, as an adversarial politics. The way of the cross is especially distinguished, though, by what I will discuss in Chapter 4 as dramatic action and then culminates in the unceasing organizing of peoples' movements that I present in Chapter 5.

Manifesting such a theatrics of counterterror derives from the very heart of the religion of Jesus. I endorse emphatically Myers' position, as rendered in the quote given above, that it is the nature of the story of Jesus to be one of contestation and resistance vis-à-vis the punitive ways of empire. I say this with full knowledge that Christendom, established Christianity, has often abdicated its powers to challenge politically enshrined terror. Christianity has long tolerated or made common cause with the terrorizers who build imperial regimes of oppression. This, however, is Christendom's betrayal of its Jewish teacher, Jesus, one who offered a daily spiritual life—of survival, resistance, and flourishing—to those who suffered indignity and disinheritance in an ethos of empire. As Howard Thurman stressed so well in his book *Jesus and the Disinherited,* Jesus' teachings on love, extended even to the enemy, were "hammered out" and forged on "the anvil of the Jewish community's relations with Rome."[1] Everything we know to be distinctive about Jesus' teachings is diminished and cheapened if we forget that Jesus was a Jew, a man from the beaten-down but fiercely independent region of the Galilee. It was from that locale that Jesus forged the way of the cross upon the anvil of imperial might.

The reinterpretation of Christian faith that I am offering in this book for responding to the crises posed by lockdown America is not to suggest that I believe Christianity to be the only or best faith tradition to fuse with activism today. Quite to the contrary, the spiritual practice most demanded by today's political crises must be an interfaith one. In fact, I believe that this interfaith dimension of political resistance today is already at work. People of struggle, informed by a wide array of faith traditions (Muslim, Jewish, engaged Buddhist, Yoruba, and several spiritual traditions of Caribbean cultures, as well as Christian traditions) are all enlivening the current struggle in the United States.

If this book gives nearly exclusive attention to reinterpreting Jesus, his way of the cross, and resources of Christianity, it is because I am seeking to move my own tradition into a closer and more effective solidarity with those forces of an interreligious spirituality that are working for justice today. Given that Christianity remains such an important religious influence in the United States, revisioning its heritage is an essential contribution to ecumenical, interreligious, and broader public movements for justice.

The Galilean Jesus

Christian faith as adversarial politics and as a vigorous movement-oriented force is grasped more easily if we take with new seriousness a Galilean perspective on Jesus of Nazareth. If Christians are to contribute to a theatrics to counter the terror of the day, we will need to reappropriate consciously the Galilean identity of Jesus.

Galilee, the major site of Jesus' ministries, was not just a quiet pastoral scene where some gentle savior-shepherd taught his noble truths. It was rugged terrain, a site of contestation, of independent communities in struggle with what empires do to common folk while seeking to maintain control of a vast domain. This Galilee, if fully understood, bequeaths to Jesus and his way of the cross a crucial and distinctive quality.

Without their Galilean frame, Jesus' teachings and life are abstracted from the site of imperial contestation that was Jesus' unique setting. Without thinking Galilee when thinking Jesus, we derive a Jesus easily accommodated to imperial power rather than the Jesus who resisted it. The meaning of Jesus' Galilean identity influences the way the rest of this book unfolds. It accounts for this chapter's focus on adversarial politics as well as the emphasis in Chapter 4 on dramatic action and the stress in Chapter 5 on the building of peoples' movements.

First of all, the way of the Galilean Jesus is marked by resistance to empire. Galilee was a district that, throughout its history, had regularly been subordinated to "outside rulers, usually from the great empires."[2] Galilee itself was rarely the main target of imperial powers, since it featured rugged terrain and was at a remove from the major navigable waterways. Richard A. Horsley has explored the social, economic, and political meanings of Galilee across the pages of two important works, *Galilee: History, Politics, People* (1995) and *Archaeology, History, and Society in Galilee* (1996). From his work, it has become clear that Galilee was not the primary target of imperial control, especially in the intentions of the Roman powers of Jesus' day. More important to Rome would be the fertile Great Plain or the temple-state in Jerusalem, or other regions that provided a buffer with rival empires. Nonetheless, Galilee was an important frontier region, and control of it was crucial to empire. It was a "crossroad of empire."[3]

The empires, therefore, treated the district of Galilee with a distinctive style of control, one that bred a fierce and independent ethos of resistance, persisting from the time of the earliest Israelite tribes into the resistance efforts in the fourth century.

> . . . Rulers generally "administered" an area to the extent necessary to extract the desired economic revenues but otherwise did not interfere much in the relatively autonomous social-religious life of the villages and towns. . . . In the case of an area such as Galilee, those two factors likely provided mutual reinforcement of the desire to be left alone. The sense of being remote from the ruling center and the experience of relatively greater independence among frontier people during times of imperial weakness would have served to sharpen the experience of subjection when an imperial regime tightened control in the area.[4]

The Galilean struggle with empire, together with the conditions that nurtured a tradition of independence, meant that resistance to empire was a mark of the Galilean ethos. Whatever one says about Jesus' life and teaching, they cannot be thought apart from such an ethos—an ethos that bred opposition and resistance. Therefore, this work will begin with an explanation of Jesus' way of the cross as entailing an adversarial politics. Such a politics will appear foreign only to a mind that forgets the Galilean-ness of Jesus. Rome did not forget Jesus' Galilean origins. In fact, we do well to remember Luke's rendition of the Roman charge against Jesus: "perverting our nation . . . *from Galilee* to this place [Jerusalem]."[5]

Being adversarial and being political can be seen as very natural to a teacher from Galilee, in spite of long-standing Western teachings that have separated a spiritual Jesus from a vigorous politics. The main question will become not was Jesus adversarial and political, but how and in what ways did he work out his adversarial politics. How did he appeal to, express, maybe revise the Galilean ethos of independence and resistance? As we shall see in this chapter, not only Jesus but also the apostle Paul and the early Christian movement display an anti-imperial, adversarial stance that must be recovered.

Let us take careful note that what I term a Galilean anti-imperial posture and the Galilean ethos of resistance is not to endorse the easy oppositionalism I criticized in the Introduction.[6] Galileans did not have the luxury of standing in some pure nonimperial space, so as to fight the empire. As is the case with many subordinated people, Galileans also had to adapt to the imperial ethos even while resisting it. Marianne Sawicki's recent study of first-century Galilee has shown persuasively how Galilean resistance often included accommodation "to the incursions of empire while offering real and symbolic resistance."[7] This should not lead us to place accommodation on equal footing with resistance. No, resistance is what encompasses accommodation in the Galilean ethos. Accommodation is but a necessary feature of resistance. Some modes of accommodation are cowardly capitulations to oppression; often, however, they are strategies that have resistance as their aim.

The necessity of accommodating even while resisting is one of the main reasons that the community of Jesus' followers, after his death, often had to resort to stealth and to the casting of their refusals of empire in a myriad of symbolic and creative daily acts. After establishing in this chapter the adversarial politics of resistance in the faith of the Jesus movement, it will be necessary to discuss creativity and dramatic action (Chapter 4) as ways to practice adversarial resistance. But let us return now to the other traits of the Galilean Jesus.

A second trait is the way that the Galilean Jesus is marked by exposure to economic deprivation and political subordination. Galilee's situation featured not only distant rule by alien powers but also daily experiences of economic deprivation and political subordination.

Economically, Galilean villagers' produce and revenue were heavily taxed, and often by three bodies regnant in the first century, when the Jesus movement(s) were emerging. Herod was one of these, demanding revenues from Galileans for his various building projects.[8] Herod, though, was a client-king who also had responsibility for making sure that additional revenues were collected for Rome. Then, in addition to Herod and Rome, the third source demanding revenues was the priestly aristocracy to the south of Galilee in Jerusalem.[9] Both Herod and Rome used that religious hierarchy to reinforce their political and economic domination of Galilee.

Not surprisingly, then, the addressees of Jesus' ministry were people whose socioeconomic plight was visible and tragic. The crowds were not well-secured inhabitants with time to explore an internal mysticism and piety. What we might call mysticism and a spiritual syncretism were assumed in Galilean religion and ritual.[10] What was more salient for Jesus, spiritually, was the desperate plight of the people who came to him. They were most certainly, in the main, the people (*ho ochlos,* the crowd, the masses), those suffering the poverty, hunger, and despair associated with a disintegrating village structure burdened by heavy taxation and drain on their resources.[11] In Sawicki's terms, Galilee was a "severely stressed system struggling to persist in the face of massive and deliberate imperial incursions."[12]

A political subordination was necessary to keep the economically deprived under control. There were administrative centers, fortresses, soldiers, an elaborate array of informers (connected religiously as well as politically), all necessary to keep Galilee subdued, its diverse bandits and rebel groups under control.[13] The mix of this subjugation with a village ethos that valued pride and memories of past struggle spawned a resistance that never died. Long after the times of Jesus, Galilee would be referred to by dominant imperial elites and religious leaders seeking respectability as a rebellious and impious place. When fourth-century Christians, for example, distinguished themselves by a care of the sick and poor that surpassed any such practice by Hellenistic and Roman communities, they were referred to as "those impious Galileans."[14]

In short, Galilee was predominantly a rural village community where large groups of the poor suffered poverty and indebtedness. Galileans offered up their desperate forced labor, their foodstuffs and animals, to service the religious and political system of the privileged who lived in the urban centers—whether it was the city of Sepphoris, Tiberias as built by Herod Antipas, or Jerusalem to the south. Galileans had their lives extracted from them on a daily basis. They were living sacrifices to a system where local elites (political and religious) joined with the imperial system of Rome and its brutal tyranny.

This political subordination of Galilean village society does not mean that Galileans knew only the agrarian life and should be thought of as isolated in rustic peasant cultures. Quite to the contrary, they had to know and adapt to the cultural impositions of Mediterranean and Hellenistic structures upon their environment. They knew, therefore, the industries growing up around the Sea of Galilee, the modernizing ways of empire in cities like Sepphoris and Tiberius. Even Jesus, who admittedly had a primary sense of belonging with peasant populations,[15] also showed knowledge and familiarity with some of the finer ways of privileged and Romanized Herodian classes.[16]

Finally, Jesus' Galilean-ness meant a consciousness and concern about his people's struggle for their lands. Again, this too is implicated in the foregoing discussion of Galilee, but it deserves distinctive commentary. Village life, understood as a peasant economy and culture, was a landed life. Village leaders and populace were dependent upon the land, lived in close proximity to its changes and fragilities. According to Horsley, even under the severe stresses of taxation, tribute, and political domination, which tended to destroy the villagers' connection to the land, peasant households during Jesus' day had not been driven off their lands. They did function with a severe level of indebtedness that maximized despair and tended to work disintegration of family traditions and their village pattern of "land tenure" based on family inheritance.[17] These patterns, in turn, were under constant pressure from "landed estates" owned by royal officers and priests resident in the urban centers surrounding village rural settings.[18] The lines of contention and resultant debates about land ownership and indebtedness were legion.

Jesus' concerns about land, processes of nature that are present in a land-conscious culture, are registered in the gospel accounts. Just to take Mark, for example, the parables are exemplary, focusing on seeds, sowers and planters, vineyards and laborers, harvests, soil, fig trees, birds and animals.

Jesus' parables should not be seen, as Ched Myers rightly observes as "earthly stories" in rural Palestine to be mined for some "heavenly meanings." No, they are in Jesus' teachings more like an "agrarian eschatology," a vision of the future in which land and cosmos are respected as somehow working together to subvert imperial rule over the land.[19] A Galilean Jesus, a way of the cross insurgent and flourishing from Galilee, cannot omit this importance of the land.

Most recently, Sawicki has stressed this relatedness to land (including the way water crosses the land) as a key way to understand the "Galilean idiom" in which the gospel was first articulated."[20] For Sawicki, this is an idiom not so much of how Galileans were situated upon the land, so much as one about how they moved across it: how they circulated themselves, their kin, their resources, and their cultural values amid and against the traumatizing currents of empire. Jesus, then, is presented by Sawicki not just as located villager but as one moving amid villagers and elites, even while "refusing" those urban interior spaces that introduced Roman disruption and occupied the land unjustly.[21]

All three of these traits of a Galilean Jesus give a concreteness and specificity to understanding Jesus' way of the cross and by implication to understanding authentic Christian faith and practice today. A Galilean faith, holding the meanings discussed above, will enable us to move our understandings of Christian practice closer to the struggle with lockdown America and *Pax Americana* today.

In light of the cultural and political meanings of Galilee, it is not surprising that theologian Virgilio Elizondo would see Jesus' Galilean-ness as crucial for understanding the struggles of Mexicans and Mexican Americans with the U.S. imperial state that bounds the Mexican nation. Elizondo sees Jesus' Galilean locus as full of theological import for people wrestling with both empire and the multiple identities taken by people who are "multiply rejected" when living near and within empires.[22] The result is a cultural practice of resistance marked by *mestizaje*—cultural mixing as a mode of resistance to empire.

Sawicki, too, finds this *mestizaje* in the way a Galilean Jesus crossed lands, waters, kinship lines, and other categories. Perhaps her words render Jesus too much as a versatile hero, but she does point to the kind of mercurial transformation that resisters to empire must often manifest. Concerning the inscribed customary practices of gender, society, and political life, Sawicki writes:

> In Jesus' day those practices were not engaged in placid maintenance of a traditional society; they were disrupted by and creatively adapting to the incursions of empire. Jesus himself fits into no one simple category. He passes as a Judean gentleman at Hellenistic symposia meals, but he also passes as a Galilean waterman on the docks at the Magdala fish-works. The frontiers of his land project into his soul: indigenous Galilean, transplanted Judean, dining with Herodians and Romans. He is *mestizo,* culturally mixed, out-caste, transgressive of borders.[23]

In sum, Jesus' struggle in a Galilee repressed by client-king Herod, by imperial Rome, and by a religious elite centered in Jerusalem who reinforced both was a struggle that anticipated and can inform our own today. This struggle is the way of one who was executed by state power. Those who follow his way now may also suffer the way of some execution, but because it is the way of the executed God, we may expect some flourishing. That flourishing this book explores as a theatrics of counterterror.

The rest of this chapter looks just at the adversarial politics necessary to the theatrics of counterterror. How can such an adversarial quality be seen at work in the basic sources of Christian faith and practice?

Jesus and the Soldiers of Empire

The adversarial nature of Christian practice is displayed above all in the narratives about the executed Jesus of Nazareth. Narratives about the moment of Jesus' process of execution and the moment of his death make this point clear. Consider that of the Gospel of Mark.

In this text, after Jesus' cry of dereliction, after the rending of the temple curtain, after a report of Jesus' breathing his last, then, in that moment of Jesus' death, a voice says, "this man was [note the past tense] God's son" (Mark 15:39). In the moment of the executed one's death, there is this opposition between Jesus who draws his last breath, on the one side, and another who shapes breath and tone to announce the end of Jesus. The voice was that of a Roman soldier, a centurion. He later reappears in Mark's text to confirm the fact of Jesus' death to Rome's Pontius Pilate.

Notice how in this biblical text, the profound difference between the dead and the living, between the one without breath and the one with voice, is marked by this opposition of Jesus and a soldier, of Jesus and a centurion in Rome's empire. Whether you follow a tradition that sees the centurion as making here a confession of faith in that moment or as quietly, with authority (maybe even with a bit of imperial gloating) marking the triumph of Rome over yet another challenger, the point is that Mark presents an opposition: Jesus and Rome's soldier.

If, as many Christians believe and confess in diverse ways, it is God who is here disclosed in and with Jesus, with a Jesus who dies this way, then it is God revealed on a cross over and against the representatives of empire, in opposition to a state power whose brutality is marked by the tool of torture upon which Jesus of Nazareth was executed. The narrative of the cross is draped with an adversarial symbolism.

When working with the notion of the executed God,[24] it is important to allow these adversarial symbolics to take deep root in our consciousness, to flower in our thinking and practice. We face an opposition: between Jesus and the soldier, between Jesus and his God on the one side and Roman state and officials on the other. The fact of this opposition is more important than just the simple fact that he was dying, or even that he was dying a horrible death. Our own existential angst about death, loss, and decay, and about the psychophysical trauma of dying can lead us to read-in all kinds of other meanings into this death of Jesus. He did not just die and suffer horrible psychic and physical pain, he did so in the way of those who are held to be in opposition to the established, imperial powers of the land.

As we shall see, the kind of opposition he had mounted to imperial power was complex. The eventual crucifixion of Jesus by Rome's Pilate was not only due to Rome. Certain religious elites wanted Jesus dead also, leaders who themselves, at least sometimes, spoke of their own opposition to Rome. Moreover, traditions portray one of Jesus' own disciples, along with other figures in the crowds of Passover, playing a role in Jesus' eventual betrayal to the Romans for crucifixion. Even with all these complexities, it is the opposition to Rome that is inescapably built into the Markan narrative, especially into accounts of Jesus' death.

Soldiers took him to the courtyard and mocked him, whipped him, scarred the forehead with thorns, pressed a poor countryman into service to carry Jesus' instrument of torture. It was the decision of Rome's Pilate that determined the final outcome: the King of the Jews was put to death alongside criminals deemed to be seditious to the ways of empire. In light of this military presence at Calvary, we must speak not so much of "the death of Jesus" in general, as of his "execution," an "imperial crucifixion of Jesus."[25]

Much, if not most, of Mark's narrative about Jesus' execution cannot be taken as historically accurate. The narrative features are, in Crossan's terms, more a "historicization" of prophecy than they are a "remembering of history."[26] Nevertheless, the feature of opposition to Roman empire, which is evident in the narrative, lifts up an important trait of Christian historical practice. It is expressive of Mark's own experience, within communities following Jesus, of a "lethal persecution" by Rome in the 60s and 70s,[27] and also of an opposition that, as we have seen, also characterized Jesus' Galilean setting of the 20s and 30s C.E. This opposition between empire and Jesus' followers dogged them immediately after Calvary,[28] and, as I will show, into the efforts of Paul in the 50s.

In sum, what emerges from the Markan soldier scene is an opposition that characterized almost all of the kingdom movements catalyzed by Jesus. It is an adversarial politics that throws a sense of opposition onto the tapestry of our understanding of God and of practices of Christian faith. To follow in the way of the cross is to practice a politics that is adversarial to empire.

How Adversarial Was Jesus' Politics?

To what degree was the politics of opposition signaled in Jesus' execution really adversarial? Many might retort, "Not very." As the way of the cross suggests, his posture was ultimately nonviolent: his message and work have been characterized as a quietist alternative to the revolutionary zealots of his age, and there are precious few suggestions that Jesus was an organizer of the disenfranchised, as we would identify that role today.

Moreover, there is the whole weight of Christendom invoking Jesus' name, while either supporting status quo politics or seeking to live apart from politics of any sort. There are important instances of engaged Christians and church folk supporting political movements that are critical of standing political systems, but they are a rarity.[29] Even when vigorously engaged, they often present themselves with such strong discourses of peace that *adversarial* is not a word one would readily use to describe their style and ethos. Many Christians might even view the word as out of place in a gospel of love and reconciliation. With Jesus' apparent distance from adversarial politics and the witness of the most visible churches, it is understandable if we mutter, "Not very" to any suggestion that Jesus had a politics adversarial to empire.

Both champions and critics of Christendom, however, have overlooked the fact that an adversarial politics is lodged in the ways of the Galilean Jesus. I have already summarized the Galilean ethos as one of resistance, with distinctive ways of being resistant that could include both stealth and open revolt. The rest of this chapter will seek to characterize two interpreters of the Jesus movement as further developing a view of Christian practice as adversarial: Paul the apostle and Mark the writer of the earliest Gospel.

Pauline and Markan resources do not give us historical descriptions of Jesus and his life, such that we can derive a detailed and heroic biography of a politically adversarial Jesus. I am not seeking to construct Christian thought around some left-wing Jesus model, as if we could ask the pious question, "What would Jesus do?" and now answer simply, "Fight the empire!" I do believe, however, that emerging studies and historical reconstructions of Jesus in his context, and of the larger Jesus movement of women and men, tend to confirm my claim that a strong sense of opposition and resistance to empire characterized the key events and movements giving birth to movements that led to Christianity. That fact should not make it strange at all for Christians today to interpret their faith and practice as entailing resistance to imperial formations.

I will refer to historians who confirm this viewpoint regarding Paul and Jesus, continuing to cite texts like those of Richard A. Horsley, John Dominic Crossan, Marianne Sawicki, and Elisabeth Schüssler Fiorenza. These may wince at my failure here to accent all the very real differences existing between them. This group taken together, however, reinforces the case for viewing Christian faith and practice as that of an adversarial politics.

Many biblical scholars and investigators into early Jesus and Christian movements might also find my claim about the adversarial nature of Christian practice to be somewhat banal. Is it not obvious that Jesus' followers grew amid a necessary opposition to empire? Yes it is. It is worth risking our belaboring the point, however, if for no other reason than that Christendom in the West (and elsewhere) so often still cozies up to empire, either by outright sacralization of empire or by locating its spiritual concerns in some sphere of practice that entails no contestation with state imperial systems. I risk belaboring the point, then, in order to remind us all just how integral resistance to empire is to Christian faith.[30]

Both Paul and Mark are writing well after Jesus' death: Paul, some twenty years later; Mark, some thirty or more. Yet they both give us a reading of Jesus that, when put in the context of the Roman world that Jesus, Paul, and Mark all shared, begins to offer a portrait of what I am calling the adversarial politics of Jesus. Paul and Mark together give us clues as to how adversarial Jesus' politics were and clues also about what it means to be adversarial to empire.

The Anti-Imperial Paul: Imprisoned and Executed by Rome

The term *anti-imperial*[31] does not sum up everything Paul did or taught, but it is perhaps a designation most ignored about his work. Ignoring it is to miss the *orientatio*[32] of his life, his fundamental way of situating himself in his work and world. His supposed end as a prisoner executed in Rome was fully consistent with the anti-imperial posture of his work and teachings. Paul's anti-imperial life, his "anti-imperial message of the cross," has become the subject of scrutiny for a growing scholarship.[33] Here, I want only to highlight some basic features of his anti-imperial gospel, in order to establish this formative apostle, Paul of Tarsus, as one source of a Christian adversarial politics of Jesus.

To study Paul is to study an early theologian whose writings predate the crafting of the gospel narratives of Jesus. By the time of Paul's writings, the Jesus movement had already spread throughout Judea, Galilee, and Asia Minor. The movement continued simultaneous to Paul, and at times independent from him, with some members reaching Rome before Paul did, as suggested by the fact that Paul had written ahead to the church there before his own arrival.[34]

The Jesus movement(s) already had a basic "preached message," or kerygma: "The man Jesus' teaching, and all the acts of his life (such as his healing miracles), had been given definitive approval by God himself, who has raised this Jesus from the dead. Jesus is, therefore, not only the promised Messiah of the Jews but has shown forth in the works and deeds of his life what God expects of each human being. He is the model whom we all must imitate."[35] Paul's own work strengthened the connection between Jesus and the expected Jewish Messiah, but went on to make a distinctive contribution, holding that this messianic one was also the cosmic Christ, the awaited one and savior (*sōtēr*) for all the nations. As with much of the Jesus movement, Paul's cosmic Christ is forged out of the heritage of Jewish messianic traditions and Paul's own impressive rabbinical training.

Paul's writings in the 50s C.E. presuppose not only this kerygma but also the activities or what Sawicki has called "the paleochurch,"[36] the diverse network of followers of Jesus who continued after Calvary in the 30s and 40s. I do not discuss this paleochurch, the traits of the groups that continued with Jesus' movement immediately after Calvary. I anticipate this period to be clarified by the ongoing research (and debates between) works like Crossan's *The Birth of Christianity* and Sawicki's *Crossing Galilee*.

What does seem clear is that the slightly later works of Paul (50s C.E.) must be seen in relation to the ethos of this paleochurch (30s and 40s). What I will here present as Paul's anti-imperial and adversarial politics amid Roman empire is an expression of a diverse and broad paleochurch resistance to empire. The paleochurch deployed a resistance as a kind of "stealth operation" to empire, using its own "indigenous idiom" to subvert and resist empire through daily, "small-scale refusals" of its hegemonic tentacles.[37] This was a genuine adversarial resistance to empire, even if it did not destroy imperial control and even though the paleochurch deployed no obvious and facile "liberation" rhetoric.[38] Paul's own anti-imperial rhetoric was, in part, his construction, but it didn't come only from him. The resistance in early Jesus movements laid some of the groundwork for Paul in this regard.

Paul's anti-imperial stance has often been obscured. Especially his apocalyptic vision and sensibility have been seized upon to give the apostle's theology a distinctively otherworldly spin. Biblical critics and worlds of the faithful in Christendom have therefore often collapsed his apocalyptic vision into a depoliticized and spiritistic Christian faith. This is to miss both Paul's particular anti-imperial posture and the strong political dimension belonging to apocalyptic vision generally.[39]

The anvil upon which his apocalyptic sensibility and cosmic Christ were forged was the plane of empire that Paul moved across and upon when he encountered young Christian communities in tumultuous struggle with the way their allegiance to Jesus came into conflict with the imperial cult of emperor worship and political hegemony. Not surprisingly, Paul's formal declarations of Jesus as Christ and "son of God in power" (Rom. 1:4) occur in his last letter, to the community of Rome struggling at the heart of imperial power.

Paul has been interpreted by many Christians, especially in the United States, as being the chief Christian orchestrator of a Christendom that only obediently submits to standing powers and never resists them. Paul's writing in chapter 13 of Romans has become the standard citation here: "Every person must submit to the supreme authorities. There is no authority but by act of God, and the existing authorities are instituted by him; consequently anyone who rebels against authority is resisting a divine institution, and those who so resist have themselves to thank for the punishment they will receive."[40] As I write, some Christian churches in Philadelphia, Pennsylvania, argue that they cannot oppose the death penalty because it is the law of the land, and Romans 13 supposedly mandates acceptance and obedience of this law.

This passage from Romans 13 is not as clearly compliant with imperial authority as it may seem. There are now numerous discussions of the context within which Paul is likely to have uttered these words, contexts that make this far from being a Christian maxim that should hold in all settings. Some scholars suggest that this was Paul offering special counsel to some Christians who, if they did not guard internal unity of purpose at a particular time of social conflict, would risk the very real threat of imperial intervention into the community by the emperor Claudius.[41] There are also numerous other interpretations of a similar nature. Moreover, the text in Romans 13, in any comprehensive, biblical, or Christian perspective, would surely have to be balanced with Revelation 13, where government becomes "the Beast" and out of which God's people are called to make their exodus. More importantly, proempire readings of Romans 13 are very out of keeping with both the life and pervasive teaching of Paul, which, as I will show, has a vigorously anti-imperial dimension.

With the letter to Rome and in his other writings, we can see the major contours of Paul's anti-imperial hermeneutic and practice. This has three foci: (1) an anti-imperialist grammar, (2) the building of solidarity around a revered one who was crucified as a seditious criminal, and (3) the forging of alternative communities amid the very world of empire. Although Paul shows this anti-imperial posture, this does not mean that he was the most radical or contentious of resisters to Roman empire. By no means. Others forged a more radical practice. Nonetheless, Paul's apocalyptic theology and vision of Christian faith must be acknowledged as politically significant in its first-century milieu.

Paul's Anti-Imperial Grammar

The first focus of his anti-imperial posture takes us to the very language of Paul's theology. His thought and practice display an anti-imperial grammar. Indeed, Paul takes some of the dearest terms of his discourse from the imperial world, then bends them back upon the claims of empire to champion the greater power of the way of Jesus. It is a kind of grammar that I will call dialectical in the sense of both embracing and subverting the language of empire. Paul's gospel is a discourse that steals empire's own terms and uses them against it. In this, Paul perhaps shared in the paleochurch's "stealth operations" of resistance to empire.[42]

The very notion of gospel, *euangelion,* is a case in point. It is a term that originates neither from the early Jesus movement(s), nor from the Septuagint (the Greek translation of the Hebrew testament dating from third-century B.C.E.).[43] *Gospel* was a term for the glad tidings that announced and eulogized military victories of Roman campaigns or the celebrations and sacrifices made on behalf of the emperor, who was uniquely proclaimed as *sōtēr* (savior), one who brings world peace, the enforced peace of Roman power, the *Pax Romana.*[44] Glorification of the emperor, indeed his deification, "gives *euangelion* its significance and power. . . . Because the emperor is more than a common man, his ordinances are glad messages and his commands are sacred writings. . . . He proclaims *euangelia* through his appearance. . . . The first *euangelion* is the news of his birth."[45]

When Paul forged a grammar dynamically structured around the terms *gospel* and *sōtēr,* he was, in effect, laying down a gauntlet to the standing political powers of Roman jurisdiction and to its own divine charter myths. Paul's couching the good news of Jesus as gospel and his talk of Jesus as savior (*sōtēr*) bringing salvation, *sōtēria* (see 1 Thess. 5:8-9, Phil. 1:28; 2:12; Rom. 1:16; 10:1; 11:11; and 13:11), would certainly be heard as an alternative claim not only about the cosmos but also about victory and power in very concrete domains of earth and politics. Paul's gospel set forth an alternative lord to the imperium's claims to possess saving power, a clear challenge to the imperial cult running from Caesar Augustus to his successors.[46] Our enforced distinctions between religion and politics, church and state, often render us tone deaf to both what Paul was saying and what the people were hearing: a theological-ethical-political challenge to the claims of the empire that structured their daily lives.

Paul used other terms from the imperial cult in order to forge his own anti-imperial grammar. Each term and its anti-imperial connotations warrant elaborate unfolding. Here, I only point to their major anti-imperial potential.

Paul's use of the Greek term, *pistis* (faithfulness or loyalty), also participates in the dialectical embrace and subversion of imperial language. It is an important term in Paul's repertoire, describing God's faithfulness or loyalty to all the peoples and the world. This could not help being seen by Paul's contemporaries as a challenge to the Caesars, who often proclaimed their loyalty to the peoples, their faithfulness to unite all the peoples. In the *Acts of Augustus,* as Dieter Georgi points out, "faithfulness" is an explicitly announced virtue of Caesar's religion. "Under the princeps of Augustus many previously unbefriended peoples 'discovered the *pistis* of the Roman people.'"[47] The Romans propagated and monopolized the entire framework of terms about faithfulness. *Fides,* the Latin synonym of *pistis,* appeared frequently on coins. The cult of *fides* grew stronger under Augustus, as "Caesar represented the *fides* of Rome in the sense of loyalty, faithfulness to treaty obligations, uprightness, truthfulness, honesty, confidence, and conviction."[48] When Paul appropriates, especially in Galatians and Romans, the language of *pistis,* he is again stealing from the imperial vocabulary and pointing to a new lord.

The very term *lord* (*kyrios*) qualifies as another example. When Paul applied the term to Jesus in his work in Thessalonica, a vigorous center of Roman administration, Paul and his supporters were attacked for "acting against the decrees of Caesar." Karl Donfried has identified the various kinds of oaths of allegiance to Caesar that the community at Thessalonica could have violated, but he notes that the simple use of the term *kyrios* for Jesus, when the term had been used for Caesar throughout Eastern Mediterranean regions, "could easily be understood as violating the 'decrees of Caesar' in the most blatant manner."[49]

Consider the notion of peace (*eirēnē*). Especially with Augustus, the Caesars had laid claim to the rhetoric of peace. It was intrinsic to Caesar's status as *sōtēr* to be the one renowned for bringing and enforcing the peace for all the known world. Scholars of empire still speak of the "Augustan threshold,"[50] a phrase denoting imperial administration so vast and efficient, so definitive of assumptions of the way things are, that the exercise of state violence is either accepted or unnecessary. It is an efficient, well-ordered peace—the *Pax Romana.* This peace was recognized throughout the empire, not only by elites but by many other sectors of social life, including lower classes.[51] The emperor demanded and expected reverence for the Roman peace, the force designed to hold the world together.

Paul's frequent use of *eirēnē,* especially in the letter to Rome, suggests again his forging of a grammar of contestation with imperial power and pretension. When writing to the Christians in the Roman center of Thessalonica, Paul includes use of a phrase with deep political roots, "peace and security" (Greek: *eirēnē kai asphaleia;* Latin: *pax et securitas*). He set this politically charged phrase (similar to today's politicians' rhetoric about "law and order") in the context of his discussion of the coming "day of the Lord," an event to "shatter the false peace and security of the Roman establishment."[52] As this indicates, his famous apocalyptic orientation is not an otherworldly discourse but a theopolitical challenge.

Note that I am not simply extracting a few inconsequential terms from Paul's writings. Gospel, faithfulness, Lord, peace—these are all central structuring notions of his reflections on Jesus, and they carry, in the context of Roman imperial control, a definite politics of Jesus. A similar dialectic of embracing and subverting imperial terminology can be seen at work with other key Pauline terms: "*parousia* (the coming of Jesus)," which is often used for the coming of a king or emperor; "*apantēsis*" (festive greeting of the Lord), which is taken from the rhetoric of greeting kings and dignitaries entering political centers;[53] "*archontes* (the powers) referring to cosmically charged political forces that "hold creation in thrall through the instruments of earthly oppression."[54]

Yes, Paul has a cosmic Christ, and the powers of evil he addresses have a kind of cosmic and even metaphysical beyondness, if you will, vis-à-vis the politics of Rome. Yet, and this is crucial, we neither understand the apocalyptic Paul nor his cosmic Christ except through the adversarial stance he assumes and sharpens by critically engaging the political claims of the imperial cult. Recall that the imperial cult, for all its political ideology and practice, also made cosmic, religious claims. Rome's gospel and Paul's gospel do not represent an opposition between a political force and a religious force. No, this is a struggle between two visions and two communal ways of inhabiting the earth, both of which are inextricably political and religious. Both are freighted with this-worldly concern for flesh-and-blood human beings; both are full of cosmic and religious meanings and aspirations.

Solidarity around a Revered One, a Seditious Criminal

Paul's anti-imperial posture is more than this grammar that dialectically embraces and subverts the vocabulary of empire. Paul also centers himself and gives to his adversarial practice its distinctive marking by yoking his gospel to an executed criminal, the Christ crucified in Jerusalem. There is perhaps no statement more emphatic than the one Paul sent to the Roman city of Corinth, colonized and then repopulated by rabble sent by Rome. To the Christians there, Paul wrote: "When I came to you, brothers and sisters, . . . I decided to know nothing among you except Jesus Christ, and him crucified" (1 Cor. 2:1-2). To the Galatians, Paul wrote: "It was before your eyes that Jesus Christ was publicly exhibited as crucified!" (Gal. 3:1).

Paul's central message about a crucified Jesus, as the last quote suggests, has a strong dramaturgical quality. It is a dramatic act for public performance. Crosses were set up all over the empire, and the early followers of Jesus lived near the torture, had to come to terms with its threatening display at every turn.[55] One might say that when Paul held up the crucified Christ as central to a salvific message, he was stealing the show, spiriting away the cross, as it were, from the theater of terror maintained by Rome for subordinating peoples and putting that executioner's device to use as a tool for the gospel's subverting of imperial power. It becomes a centerpiece on display in the Jesus' movement's theater of counterterror.

Paul's Lord, the *sōtēr* of his contestational glad tidings, was held up from among those consigned to the death penalty by imperial powers. This was not a respectable lord. Paul's gospel was seen as folly, shame, and madness. The younger Pliny called the sect built around the executed one a form of *amentia* (insanity).[56] Officials in the Roman system found it especially offensive that reverence should be paid to one who had been nailed to the cross by Roman authorities as a state criminal.

To be defined by a message about a crucified Jesus was to be defined as an adversary to Roman empire and all that it held to be good. It was to be marked as adversarial in four senses. These senses all overlap with one another and tend to align those faithful to Jesus with populations and sectors viewed as dangerous, shockingly ugly, and contentious.

First, the Jesus communities are marked as politically seditious. To see transformative power and peace as somehow bound up with this crucified one is to put the community on the side of sedition. The community would be seen as out of step with imperial power and approval, disloyal, and probably practicing political resistance. In the cultural logic of Rome, if you were among the crucified, all the more if you worshiped one in its number, you were probably seditious.

Second, the communities of the crucified Jesus, even if they had wealthy patrons, would find their lot cast, almost by definition, with the lower classes. Crucifixion was a punishment almost always reserved for the lower classes in the Roman empire, as is also the case with the death penalty's application in the twenty-first century United States.[57] American death rows ring with the popular maxim, Those who lack the capital get the punishment. Similarly, Roman philosopher and satirist Apuleius wrote, "*Crimen opes redimunt, reus est crucis omnis egenus*" ("Riches buy off judgment, and the poor are condemned to the cross.")[58]

Rome clearly saw application of the crucifixion as not just a deterrent but a terrorizing mode of control, especially wherever poorer populations and large slave populations threatened the system of imperial privilege.[59] Any who found peace alternative to Rome, or worse, who saw sovereign power wrapped up with the executed criminal Jesus, would surely be consigned to the lower classes in the public view. Educated elites would clearly have been scandalized, preferring the cleaner, undefiled, uncriminalized, unexecuted, and immortal gods of Greece and Rome.

Third, the Jesus community would be identified with the shamed. To be crucified or aligned somehow with the crucified was to be vulgar, located at the other end from any virtue, respect, or nobility. It was to have one's body marked and desecrated in a way that left no doubt about the worthlessness of the one so treated. To be a community of the executed Jesus under the crucifying power of Rome meant to be ignominious, and Celsus, a second-century Greek writer who criticized Christians as a threat to social stability, hung that label on followers of Jesus whenever he could.[60] The cross is referred to in the Letter to the Hebrews as a sign of "shame" (*aiskenei,* 12:2).

Finally, pervading all the above, is the sense of living among the terrorized. To be a follower of the executed Jesus, of the crucified one, meant not just suffering in general, not just solidarity with working or lower-class folk, not just to be shamed, but more fearsomely perhaps, to be among the terrorized. The crucified were to be made a display of. Hengel describes crucifixion as "a 'barbaric' form of execution of the utmost cruelty."[61] According to the testimony of Roman writer and politician Seneca and historian Josephus, who wrote about its practice in Judea, crucifixion was the mode of execution that gave full reign to executioners' caprice and sadistic whim.

Perhaps the multidimensional, adversarial stigma of a gospel linked to the crucified one is especially dramatized if we recall what the end was that often awaited the victims of crucifixion: being eaten by dogs. This only compounded the horror, was a terror to mind and body, especially in the many Mediterranean traditions that place a premium on burial and the body.[62] "Crucifixion was aggravated further by the fact that quite often its victims were never buried. It was a stereotyped picture that the crucified victim served as food for wild beast and birds of prey."[63] John Dominic Crossan has suggested that if we want to see into the heart of the cross's terror, "follow the dogs."[64]

"To know nothing among you except Jesus Christ, and him crucified"—for Paul to state this, to preach it and teach it, was to be adversarial in the utmost degree.

Forging Alternative Communities amid the Empire

Let me finish presenting the anti-imperial Paul with a discussion of the kinds of alternative communities he sought to create. These, too, manifest his adversarial politics of Jesus. Paul settled for no mere preaching of his gospel. Anti-imperial grammar was matched by tireless work to build alternative communal forms.

Those whom I know to read Paul free from ecclesiocentric piety usually come away from his writings with the impression that he seems a bit crazy, at least eccentric. Thomas Cahill's generalist survey of Christian texts captures the spirit found in Paul's writings better than many a traditional commentator. He calls Paul an overachiever, "an either/or kind of guy, an absolutist for whom the matter under discussion would always be All or Nothing."[65] Add to all this the statements about women being silent in church and submissive to husbands, attributed to him in 1 Corinthians 14:34-35 and in the pseudo-Pauline texts, and then those of us hungry for liberation and earthly justice are prone to toss aside this Paul of Tarsus.

Nevertheless, even a feminist like Elisabeth Schüssler Fiorenza has pointed out that Paul is not the chauvinist he has often been made out to be, even if he is not the liberationist many seek. Indeed, he did leave the door open for a consolidation of a vicious imperial patriarchy that would come to mark and mar much of Christendom's history. Yet at the same time, he affirmed equality and freedom in community in a way that even loosed some of the fetters that restrained women in the Greek and Roman worlds.[66] Caesar Augustus had created special legislation to reinforce marriage as the expected norm. Later emperors ratified this with special taxes and sanctions on the unmarried and with laws promoting remarriage. Schüssler Fiorenza's summary is crucial.

> At the end of the first century, the emperor Domitian reinforced the Augustan marriage legislation particularly in order to strengthen the leading families of the empire. It is therefore important to note that Paul's advice to remain free from the marriage bond was a frontal assault on the intentions of existing law and the general cultural ethos, especially since it was given to people who lived in the urban centers of the Roman empire *It stood over and against the dominant cultural values of Greco-Roman society.*[67]

The frontal assault that Paul forged in the domain of marriage practice is a signal of his overall adversarial practice amid traditions and privileges of empire. The fact that Paul worked to build communal alternatives to empire around a politics of the crucified Jesus does much to explain why religio-political elites went after him. In Macedonian Philippi, Alexander the Great's old capital, Paul was stripped and publicly flogged. In an Athens marketplace, he was ridiculed and shouted down. In Corinth, he was charged with offenses before the Roman proconsul. He was imprisoned in Ephesus where his work also started a riot, from which Paul had to flee. He was imprisoned for two years, apparently in Caesarea Maritima because of his refusal to bribe the procurator. Going up against empire and building communities that know nothing but the executed, crucified Jesus had their costs, as he explained to his hearers in the Roman colony of Corinth.[68]

This life of adversity was born of an understanding of an adversarial practice seeking new community in the context of empire. It was the living out of the value of *eleutheria* (freedom). So fiercely held was the value that when slaves were initiated through baptism into Christian community, they expected their emancipation.[69] Schüssler Fiorenza, following Wayne Meeks, is right to identify Paul's famous baptismal formula as a veritable "performative utterance" heavy with political and social import: "As many of you as were baptized into Christ have clothed yourselves with Christ. There is no longer Jew or Greek, there is no longer slave or fee, there is no longer male and female; for all of you are one in Christ Jesus" (Gal. 3:27-28).[70] This is a sign of what Daniel Boyarin has called Paul's "passionate drive for human unification, for the erasure of difference and hierarchies between human beings."[71]

What Schüssler Fiorenza calls the Christian communities' "praxis of coequal discipleship" has been elaborated by Richard A. Horsley in his study of the assembly at Corinth and Paul's attempt to build there "an alternative society." It is in this Roman colony that Paul preached the madness of the crucified *sōtēr* (savior), and it would have been received as madness. The gospel of the crucified subverted the position of the elite supported by a Roman terrorization of subordinated peoples. Paul built and nurtured alternative communities among the terrorized, the "lowborn, and despised,"[72] and if he worked also with elites, with the "higher born," they were called to make common cause with the despised.[73] Adversaries to Paul's work and gospel could discern immediately that this gospel was not a reverence of the empire's glad tidings.

Not surprisingly, then, the Corinthian community, as "alternative and adversarial to empire," had to avoid the public marketplaces, grow slowly and sporadically as a "network of cells."[74] Paul cultivates these communities' sense of autonomy from the world, not simply because the world, culture, or bodies are generally fallen, but because they are the domains of empire, hierarchy, and devastation for crucified peoples. He especially urged the Corinthian community to settle its disputes away from dominant society and especially outside of its courts.[75] Similarly, the citywide festivals in Asia Minor should be avoided, again not out of some mere sense of the contagion of paganism, but because they were religio-political celebrations of empire, of the imperial cult of ritual domination and control.

Paul's admonition to avoid these social relations is less like a fundamentalist minister warning of the pagan, secular world and more like novelist Walter Mosley's recent admonition that Americans at the millennium swear off TV-filtered news and media entertainment, together with sports spectacles and overconsumption of alcohol, so that they can free themselves from their chains.[76] Paul's adversarial politics of Jesus seeks to nurture new fundamental forms of social relation against the streams of imperial control that shape body, mind, and spirit.

Even in the realm of structuring economic life, Paul's work featured an alternative practice. We cannot idealize Paul here, for he himself had his power plays, and he developed his own patronage system as he moved from city to city. He was a Roman citizen, and though he might "count it as nothing" in the ultimate scheme of things, he could count on it, at times, for aiding his work.[77] Nevertheless, Paul's writings show that he worked tirelessly to create a Corinthian assembly whose economic relations were dramatically counter to those structured by the imperial milieu. In a milieu in which monetary resources often followed a vertical path of tribute extracted from poor laboring classes, Paul sought to organize a "horizontal movement of resources from one subject people to another for the support of 'the poor among the saints at Jerusalem' (Rom. 15:26)."[78] Even though this alternative horizontal movement was fledgling, it was nevertheless a significant alternative. It was to nurture a "network of assemblies" shifting moneys between despised communities, exemplifying a way toward a different mode of political economy, different from the tributary one of the Roman order.

This anti-imperial Paul is, again, not all there is to Paul and his work. It is, however, essential to understanding him, and it grows out of the center of his self-understanding, "to know nothing" (1 Cor. 2:2) among his peoples but the executed, crucified *sōtēr.* This points toward an adversarial stance, a kind of "social radicalism" that Stephen Patterson argues Paul shared with Jesus traditions.[79]

This theologian and church builder probably died at the hands of empire for his social radicalism. Paul's end is often described as simply being one of the many deaths that Christians suffered under the persecution of Emperor Nero. But evidence exists that Paul and Peter were probably charged and convicted independent of that persecution and probably before it.[80] Dieter Georgi suggests that Paul's crime was one of treason: not the more passive crime of refusing to sacrifice to the emperor but the more active offenses of "political aggression."[81] As a Roman citizen Paul "enjoyed" the privilege of not being crucified, as was Peter. His was a death by beheading. Although there is a bit of privilege in this, it is still an act of imperial removal, a death come as execution at the hands of the same powers that planted crosses to terrorize potential resisters, a death in conformity with Paul's life and his anti-imperialist work. It was a death that has always been an embarrassment to the later Christendoms that compromised with empire, built empires, and became crucifiers and executioners themselves. Those Christendoms forget the Paul who lived and died amid an adversarial practice that helped birth communities flourishing amid and against imperial ways.

In doing so, Paul lived out the Galilean identity of Jesus, a trait that pitches Christians in resistance to empire. In this, despite all the discussions that pit Paul against Jesus, there is a remarkable kinship in the basic *orientatio* of their lives and work. Without referring to the Galilean theme as such, Paul's fundamental idea of the election of the world's nobodies expresses a core concept similar to the message Mark developed for Galilee.[82]

Let us now return to the Galilean Jesus, this time as presented by the gospel writer Mark, who positions the narrative about Jesus on the dramatic stage of Galilean culture and politics.

Mark's Gospel: A Drama of Anti-Imperial Resistance

About a decade after Paul's death, Mark wrote his gospel, an interpretation of Jesus' life and message, the origin of which has been located everywhere from Rome (see William Lane's commentary on that gospel), to rural Syria, and also in Galilee itself (see Howard Kee's work).[83] The Gospel of Mark surges forth from amid some of those subordinate and restless peoples whom the empire's crucifying ways struggled to keep in check. Just after or at the time of Mark's writing, Judea and Jerusalem were under siege by imperial forces. Execution by crucifixion marked the fall, five hundred per day at one point, according to Josephus, with totals reaching to the thousands. Whether Mark is written from Galilee or from some other locale, it is clear that it is written about what I have described as the Galilean Jesus. Moreover, like Paul, Mark is written out of a sense of the resistance and struggle of the paleochurch to Roman occupiers of the land. In fact, Mark displays a very intense spirit of seething Galilee, as a land under both Roman terror and rebel recruiting. Wherever Mark's community was, it knew, as Crossan reminds us, a "lethal persecution" by forces of empire, as well as social discrimination and political opposition.[84]

The time and context of Mark's writing is not that of Jesus, and so the Jesus of Mark's gospel is not the historical Jesus. Galilee (which is the locale of this gospel's narrated story) in the time of the author of Mark's gospel may in fact have been more turbulent and rife with Roman repression than in Jesus' time. Herod Antipas had the seething rural area of Galilee of Jesus' day well pacified by administrative control, by the enervating drudgery of poverty for the rural poor (the breadbasket for supplying the urban centers), and by swift preemptive strikes against leaders who even hinted at insubordination, as evidenced by his arrest and the execution of John the Baptist.[85]

The increasing and omnipresent cruelties of empire in the days of Mark's narrative motivate him to present Jesus and his way in a stark and dramatic juxtaposition to imperial terror. The result is that Mark's gospel functions as a terse witness to Jesus, who lived, taught, and died within the *locus imperium.* Let us admit that Mark as a writer projects his world onto that of Jesus. It is a legitimate and understandable projection. Rome's power dominated the world of Mark as much as that of Jesus, especially after Roman imperial administration had crossed the "Augustan threshold" in the early years of the first century,[86] becoming a generation-transcending, brutal machine. Mark's Gospel, the earliest one, offers no piety of easy triumph. There is barely even a resurrection of Jesus in this Gospel, a fact that gives some believability to the cautious and astute reader who senses all that Jesus was up against in Roman-dominated Palestine and that would so challenge Jesus' followers in years to come. Nick Cave, the punk-rock singer, crashes into biblical discourse his own refreshing summary: "Mark's Gospel is a clatter of bones, so raw, nervy, and lean on information that the narrative aches with the melancholy of absence."[87]

Such a spare Gospel throws into stark relief the opposition of Jesus to imperial power. It is no accident, therefore, that I began this chapter on the way of the cross as adversarial practice with the oppositional scene of crucifixion, where Jesus and the world of Roman soldiers are in dramatic juxtaposition. This death in opposition to imperial authority was consistent with the nature of Jesus' life, and Mark's Gospel also brings that out. Because the idea that Christians are to be adversaries to empire is still an alien notion for many U.S. Christians, I must note just a few more features of Mark's Gospel to cement the point.

To begin with, Mark's grammar is, like that of Paul, an anti-imperial grammar. From the first line announcing "the beginning of the good news of Jesus Christ" (1:1), Mark steals the term *gospel* (*euangelion*) from the proclaimers of military and imperial victory and plants Jesus at the center of the story's announced glad tidings. Such a planting amounts to a supplanting. The revered one is not Caesar, but a soon-to-be-executed Jesus, "from Nazareth of Galilee" (1:9). This is not unlike the way Luke would apply the term *sōtēr* to the birth of Jesus in Bethlehem and so supplant Caesar Augustus' well-known role as savior and maintainer of peace.[88]

Confronting the Temple-State

Jesus' own journey to execution as a potentially seditious teacher who needed to be put to the cross is most starkly presented in Mark's Gospel by Jesus' contestation with the temple-state system in Palestine. The temple-state was the centralizing point in Palestine where lines of power—religious, political, economic—all intertwined and produced a common result: the subjugation of poorer populations throughout the region.

> From the tithes and other dues to the priesthood and temple, through repayment and interest on loans, and even through the contributions

> that Diaspora Jews from around the world sent to the temple, surplus wealth flowed into and piled up in Jerusalem. There were no mechanisms, however, by which these resources could be channeled to the people most in need. . . . Rather, some of the surplus wealth was used on luxury goods or simply stored in the temple treasury, in the form of valuable metals or objects.[89]

The temple was the central site symbolizing and anchoring the power of religious elites, as well as of the economically and politically powerful. Rome accommodated itself to much of Jewish religion, and in spite of Jewish contestation with Rome, the temple also became a site of daily sacrifices made to Rome.[90] We know of these sacrifices because their cessation reportedly marked the fall of Jerusalem after the revolt of 66 to 70 C.E.[91]

The Jesus of Mark's Gospel takes direct aim at the exploitative religio-politics of the temple-state. Writing out of his interest in the Galilean Jesus and from his own sense of Galilee as occupied territory, Mark had to veil his specific references to Roman usurpation and colonization. Nevertheless, as my discussion of Jesus' crucifixion has already suggested, Mark registered clearly the opposition to Rome and its supporters.

Dramatic Encounters with Empire

Mark's contestation and resistance to the religio-political centralization of power in the temple-state is registered in a narrative rich in dramatic presentation. In fact, Mark has such a keen sense of dramatic encounter that we might speak of him as a playwright, maybe even a choreographer of acts resistant to empire. Each act could receive lengthy commentary. Here, I simply call a few of them to readers' attention, in order to establish the potential for understanding the gospel as adversarial practice.

After stealing the notion of gospel from the realm of announced Roman military victories and applying it to the executed teacher from Nazareth, Mark has Jesus announced and baptized by a loved, wilderness eccentric, John the Baptist. No sooner is that connection made than we learn that John is hustled off under arrest (1:14) and later executed (6:27). This gospel is clearly a drama in which its leading proclaimers are caught up in matters of life and death in a land where potentially ruthless leaders guarded their power.[92]

Jesus' ministry in Mark begins with a number of healings and exorcisms that create great amazement in Galilee. The amazement is not the "Wow!" called forth before a demonstration of supernatural power, which our more secular minds today might stumble over. No, the people's amazement, time and again in Mark, is presented as due to Jesus' claiming authority by these actions. His enemies are not shown contesting the reality of the transformations worked by Jesus, whatever they were. These acts were not startling because they miraculously suspended natural process. His enemies are seething, instead, because he supplants their authority over the people, which they possess by reason of their place in the temple-state system of the imperial ethos.

The scribes are an especially noteworthy group who often felt their authority to be subverted. Many of them constituted an academic, political, and religious elite who often become Jesus' archenemies across Mark's narrative. Mark presents them as being sometimes supplanted by Jesus as teachers in the synagogues (Mark 1:21-22). At other times, Jesus seems to usurp their power to decree "forgiveness of debt," which they exercised by overseeing proscribed sacrifices in the temple cultus.[93] The scribes slide easily from their religio-academic status to outright political agents. As Ched Myers has noted, the scribes' and Pharisees' frequent visits to Jesus (for example, Mark 3:22 and 7:1) allow them to appear as "government investigators from Jerusalem."[94]

Jesus violated the authority of the purity laws when he touched lepers. When he declared people forgiven, he was blaspheming the cultural debt code, which mandated sacrificial acts for forgiveness. He assumed his presence to be that of the Jewish apocalyptic "Human One" ("Son of Man/Son of God") who restored people to wholeness, without insisting that they define themselves according to the sacrifices and role statuses mandated by elite religio-political officials and the temple system.[95]

On one occasion, Jesus is portrayed as provoked to rage, when certain officials were watching to see if he would break Sabbath law and perform an act of healing. Jesus is moved from his rage to an intentional crossing of the line and an open, flagrant violation, claiming nevertheless a justifying mandate: "Is it lawful on the Sabbath to do good or to do harm, to save life or to kill?" (Mark 3:4). After Jesus is portrayed as restoring a withered hand and looking at religious authorities with anger and grief, the Pharisees are described as going off to plan his execution in the chambers of the Herodians (3:6). Myers well describes Mark's narrative here, by noting that Jesus' actions appear as a kind of "civil disobedience as theater."[96]

Jesus' critical actions against religious officials were not an "anti-Jewish" practice; nor should our interpretations of Jesus' resistance to religio-political authority be seen as an anti-Jewish posture. Jesus the Jew was not anti-Jewish. He was, though, in resistance to and under suspicion from many who held or who revered established powers, and these could be the political elites of Rome or the religious elites of Jerusalem, or both together. We miss the essential point of Jesus' adversarial politics if we take an anti-Semitic route and suppose Jesus to have adopted a pervasive "anti-Jewish" perspective.[97] Just as much do we misunderstand Jesus, however, if we fail to admit how he was positioned against leaders of the Jerusalem elite whose religious practice could serve imperial power.

Jesus' dramatic disobedience was a challenge not only to the temple and to religious elitism, but by reason of the temple-state's inscription within the imperial ethos (remember the sacrifices offered on behalf of Rome on temple grounds), this religious disobedience was also a contestation of the imperial power of Rome. Jesus' disobeying a temple law about forgiveness is merely religious only in the minds of those who would see religion and politics as of different orders. In Jesus and Mark's day, that kind of bifurcation did not operate. Especially these types of religious actions of disobedience would have put Jesus at odds with the powers and privileges of a religio-political, imperial order.

The confrontation with Rome is most dramatically presented, perhaps, in the healing-exorcism story of the Gerasenean demoniac (Mark 5:1-21). Mark presents this story with more elaborate detail and dramatic flair than any other in his Gospel, save the narrative of Jesus' trial.[98] The demon exorcised is none other than one who is given the name Legion. In the Palestine of Jesus or Mark, that name would most likely mean a division of Roman soldiers. In fact, the whole story resounds with military imagery, with Jesus presented as summoning out the fierce military demon, jousting with it, and finally sending it away from the land, banishing it, as it were, into a running herd of swine that is drowned in nearby waters.

The designation *herd* (*agelē*, 5:11) applied here to the swine, was more frequently applied to bands of military recruits.[99] New Testament scholar J. Duncan M. Derrett also points out that the word used for Jesus' dismissing of the demon into the swine (*epetrepsen*) connotes a military command, and that the rush of the pigs into the sea to drown was like a military charge (*ōrmēsen*) into battle.[100] Myers appropriately draws the parallel here to the enemy soldiers "swallowed up by hostile waters" in accounts of Pharaoh's chariots and army being cast into the Red Sea during Israel's liberation from Egypt (Exod. 15:4).

In short, the demon named Legion who occupies and is exorcised from the body of the Gerasene man is a drama in which Roman military power is represented as occupying and then being banished from the body politic of Palestine. Moreover, as Myers also notes, the possessed man shows many signs of the traumatized and colonized person explored so well by Frantz Fanon, and the Gerasene's liberation is told in a way that appears as the "cathartic response of the subjugated."[101]

With this story, Mark's Gospel leaves no doubt that the way of Jesus is an adversarial politics challenging the imperial colonizers of Rome as well as the religio-academic elite. They are two rooms in the suite of power in Palestine, which Myers calls the "colonial condominium."[102]

Dramatic Entry into Jerusalem

From this point in Mark's narrative, the gospel writer takes up many issues, but the story drives on to the execution encounter and the opposition to Rome at the cross that I have already described. It may be important to recall, however, that when Jesus is described by Mark as entering into Jerusalem for the final drama of trial and execution, he does so with still more theatrics of contestation vis-à-vis the temple-state. Mark presents Jesus' last campaign of action as a dramatic repudiation of the temple. Even his disciples were prone to marvel, indeed revere, the wonder of the temple on which Josephus and almost all commentators could not help but remark. Jesus proclaims that it would be destroyed (although, if he was writing before the actual burning of the temple in 70 C.E., Mark gets the mode of destruction wrong; it was not destruction by demolishing its stone work). When Mark has Jesus predict this destruction, we have Jesus again repudiating the ultimacy of the temple and what it stood for. Jesus thus gives his last sermon in this part of Mark, sitting "opposite the temple" (13:3).

Such a position, a facing in opposition, captures well the opposition Jesus played out in his theatrical entrance to Jerusalem. In what Myers insightfully calls "carefully choreographed street theater,"[103] Jesus is depicted as entering on the foal of an ass, mimicking the triumphant entry of military victors with their glad tidings of conquest. His destination? The temple. He comes neither as Roman military commander nor as Jewish rebel fighting to restore the temple and Davidic kingdom. He does come, however, with an adversarial politics that contests the amalgamation of religious and political power in the temple-state.

Once on temple grounds, Mark makes it clear that Jesus is about an "unrelenting critique of the political economy of the temple."[104] As Paula Fredriksen points out, we do not know what actually went on in the visit by Jesus to the temple. Moreover, the temple grounds were so vast that his actions may not have rippled widely with much dramatic effect.[105] Yet, in Mark's narrative, we see the fruit of Jesus' life and actions as remembered and creatively shaped by Mark, who wrote under conditions of an imperialist ethos similar to those of Jesus' period. Mark's words here need full presentation.

> And [Jesus] entered the temple and began to drive out those who sold and those who bought in the temple, and he overturned the tables of the money-changers and the seats of those who sold pigeons; and he would not allow any one to carry anything through the temple. And he taught, and said to them, "Is it not written, 'My house shall be called a house of prayer for all the nations'? But you have made it a den of robbers." And the chief priests and the scribes heard it and sought a way to destroy him; for they feared him, because all the multitude was astonished at

this teaching. And when evening came they went out of the city. (Mark 11:15-19 RSV)

Jesus' words here are presented as the words of critique uttered by the great Hebrew prophets, particularly Isaiah and Jeremiah. Mark's Jesus points his criticism at the officials who are privileged by the temple-state hierarchy and by a system expropriating wealth and life from the poor, its religio-political sanctioning of theft. Crossan describes Jesus' actions in the temple as being a "symbolic destruction, in deed and word, against the Temple," and that it is this, in fact, which "led immediately to Jesus' arrest and execution in Jerusalem at Passover."[106] Sawicki suggests that this destruction may have been more than "symbolic," since the dramatic action also threatened to "interrupt the commercialized flow of sacrificial animals through the Jerusalem temple."[107]

After the destruction and on the way out of the city, the disciples question, maybe from a lack of faith manifest as timidity, how it is that temple power can be so questioned. They were questioning how such impressive power could be countered. Is there a way to rival both temple-state and Rome? Responding to the difficulty of believing that Jesus' adversarial practice could ever bear fruit against powers like these, Mark's story has Peter notice a withered fig tree that Jesus earlier had cursed. How is this a response to those with a timid faith, one that wavers before the forces of temple and empire?

Jesus' curse of the fig tree is a puzzling part of Mark's story, until we recall that the withered fig tree is a literary symbol of illegitimate, unfruitful state power. There are few, if any, nonsymbolic trees in Hebrew literature.[108] Jesus' curse of the fig tree would clearly be understood by Mark's readers as a repudiation of the temple's claims to be bringing peace and security (*pax et securitas*) in the land, and a demonstration of the power of Jesus' way over the state power that the temple mediated and reinforced. The story of Jesus' curse of the fig tree is Mark's way of saying, "Don't trust the exploitative temple-state powers. They are unreliable. Do not revere that religio-political enshrinement of imperial power." Jesus prompts Peter, who sees the withered fig tree, to have the kind of faith that can rival imperial power when all the odds say, all the pundits proclaim, that empire cannot be defeated. Jesus' adversarial faith believed otherwise.

This adversarial faith, with a similar logic of disrespect toward empires thrives in the hearts of many people today, those (in fact and metaphorically) who are locked down in the *Pax Americana.* Journalist Mumia Abu-Jamal wrote these words from a death row cell in Pennsylvania:

> Conventional wisdom would have one believe that it is insane to resist this, the mightiest of empires. . . . But what history really shows is that today's empire is tomorrow's ashes, that nothing lasts forever, that to not resist is to acquiesce in your own oppression. The greatest form of

> sanity that anyone can exercise is to resist that force that is trying to repress, oppress, and fight down the human spirit.[109]

Conclusion: Being Adversarial: Christians at the Crossroads

Once we free our contemporary minds from the fetters of Christendom, which historically has seized, reinforced, or compromised with imperial dominations, we are then free to see Christian faith as adversarial practice to empire. Paul and Mark, two founding visionaries who present Jesus of Nazareth and his gospel to us, bring us face-to-face with the Galilean way of Jesus, as a way that suffers and resists empire. Such adversarial practice has characterized many groups and traditions in resistance to class hierarchy, racist supremacy, or militarist nationalism. Thankfully, followers of Jesus who contest imperial ways have never been completely absent from history, even if the ways of Christendom have held a stronger sway over the centuries.

There are followers of Jesus in almost every movement of resistance to imperial domination, even if they are only sometimes scattered like seeds hidden on the broad and rugged landscape of resistance. It is important to acknowledge and nurture this Christian presence, however, because it has a distinctive contribution to make as we build interfaith coalitions against the enforced ordered peace proposed by a Rome, by a U.S. militarized global power, or by any other imperial force. Christian adversarial practice makes a distinctive contribution. As Chapter 4 makes clearer, such a practice moves to the heart of the political theatrics of terror as constructed by imperial powers and steals the show through a theatrics of counterterror, which is both cathartic and liberatory for those treated like surplus populations, held down and ground under by imperial control.

I am well aware that the anti-imperial reading proposed in this chapter on adversarial politics will be hard for many Christians to embrace, and this not simply because it requires a new way of seeing Christian faith and biblical narratives. There is also required a willingness to make a decision to be adversarial. The way of the cross, when it is not simply a matter of passive acceptance of one's own relative lack of power or a willingness to sacrifice others to vicarious slaughter (both distortions of the way of the cross often offered up by Christianity), demands decision.

The way of the cross as adversarial, and as requiring a decision, is reminiscent of the Congo cosmogram of West Africa, which has shaped some African Christian understandings of the cross. A cosmogram is a diagram of the cosmos, which crosses a vertical north/south axis with an east/west axis and then affixes meanings to the cosmic directions and to the movement of the sun from east to west. Meanings for everyday life are often read off of this image.[110] In contemporary Haiti, much influenced by West African traditions of the cosmogram, the cross image is often interpreted as a kind of crossroads, a place where two beams (vertical and horizontal axes) cross, yes, but also a place where believers are thought to be at a crossroads, challenged to make a decision, to deliberate about alternatives.

The cross as crossroads might prompt, here, a closing meditation on the executed one who hangs on that Roman gibbet, who did not just die but did so in opposition to a regime of execution. Along the horizontal axis of the cross, we might trace the two hands and wrists fastened in opposite directions and see them as portraying the stubborn, hard truth that there are oppositions. In a world of postmodernist championing of complexity, ambiguity, play, of the kind of difference that often leads to indifference, we must meditate on the fact that there are adversarial agents and structures; "there are victims and there are executioners."[111] There is the killing power of Caesar and his state-sanctioned ritual killers, and there is the work for love and justice by those who often become the slain ones. There is state power and those who suffer and resist it.

Along the vertical axis, we might find occasion to contemplate the way we are challenged to make a decision regarding our own relationship to imperial systems. Will we stand up to imperial power, or bend down to, submit to, or tolerate, its victimizing ways? The cross of the one executed by empire is our crossroads.

How we make our decision to accept the terms of empire or to resist them may depend on how we envision the resistance to empire. Being an adversary to empire in the way of Jesus may depend on whether we can see that way as an effective mode of contestation. It is crucial, therefore, to understand the way of the cross as a theatrics of counterterror that steals the show, that wrests away power from the imperial usurpers of it. The next chapter points a way toward that kind of dramatic action.

4. stealing the show:
Way of the Cross as Dramatic Action

> This really means making the movement powerful enough, *dramatic* enough, morally appealing enough, so that people of goodwill, the churches, labor, liberals, intellectuals, students, poor people themselves begin to put pressure on congressmen to the point that they can no longer elude our demands. Our idea is *to dramatize* the whole economic problem of the poor.
>
> —Martin Luther King, Jr.

> Defense lawyers called the [bail] sum unprecedented and punitive, while a prosecutor portrayed [activist John Sellers] as the real puppet master in a protest replete with puppets and other theatrical agitprop objects.
>
> —Monica Yant Kinney and Angela Couloumbis, "Catalyst for Chaos, or Singled Out Unfairly," *Philadelphia Inquirer* (August 4, 2000), about the holding of Sellers on $1 million bail for misdemeanor protest charges, sustained at the 2000 Republican National Convention

The way of the cross is adversarial, yes, but the primary embodied expression of that way, under conditions of empire, is neither violent tactical maneuvering nor passive endurance. Both of these responses may be necessary in certain situations. Neither should be seen as by definition always inconsistent with the way of the cross. Nonetheless, the defining characteristic of Jesus' way of the cross is its prominence as adversarial, dramatic action. It taps the powers of creative, theatrical action. As is borne out in street movements today, and as reported in the *Philadelphia Inquirer* above, the theatrical has a power that can be seen as a threat even by repressive power.

Jesus embraced performative and dramatic modes of engagement and speech on the way to the cross. The cross itself was also a dramatic act within Rome's theater of terror. After Jesus' execution, narrators of the stories about him so crafted the memory of Jesus and wove in testimonies about resurrection and the power of God that a new and more expansive drama developed. It was a breathtaking drama that dwarfed the Roman theater, subordinated Rome's imperial pretensions to God's unfolding drama, a pageant of empowerment for the poor. The way of the cross thus steals the show from imperial power.

This defining characteristic of the way of the cross, dramatic action, is also the crucial center of a theatric of counterterror we need today. Dramatic action wielded against imperial forces is today more prevalent among activists not related to the church than among those from Christian churches. Yet the way of the cross, as highlighted by Jesus and the Jesus movement, foregrounds dramatic action, and thus followers of that way should become ever stronger participants in theatrics that rival imperial systems.

The theatrics of counterterror I am unfolding in this book will not be complete with our move here from adversarial politics (Chapter 3) to dramatic action (Chapter 4). We still will need to consider the building of organized movements (Chapter 5), which constitutes the culmination of a theatrics of counterterror in collective actions that resist and build alternatives to today's police brutality, the prison-industrial complex, and the death penalty. There is no way through lockdown America, no real resistance to it, without such movements.

In this chapter, our task is to show how the dramatic action along the way of the cross can be a force driving toward movements rivaling lockdown America and *Pax Americana.* After noting Jesus' own mode of dramatic contestation in the tumult of imperially dominated Galilee and Palestine, I will turn to the way sacrifice and spectacle intertwine today and how dramatic actions steal the force of that terror. We will be positioned, then, to set forth the major features of dramatic action as bodily contestation and as a creative enactment of new worlds. With such dramatic action as this, we begin to glimpse a new view of a triumph of God as a pageant of empowerment for dominated peoples.

My overall aim in this chapter is not to call readers into the streets to take up dramatic action against today's repressive forces. That needed call has already been issued and is being heeded. I am more interested, here, in developing a carrying frame for understanding why dramatic action is important for resisting and transforming lockdown America, and in discussing how such dramatic action can be viewed as intrinsic to Christian faith and practice.

Before going any further, I want to note that this embrace of drama and theater as a way to resist the political theatrics of terror today also honors what might be called the theatrical impulse already at work in oppressed communities. Those who live long under systemic domination experience both rage and a need to focus and control that rage. One of the means of this control, as James C. Scott has pointed out in his studies of the arts of resistance to domination, is fantasy, and in particular, the artful rendering of fantasies about how to "reverse and negate a particular domination." Sometimes these fantasies live only in the "hidden transcripts" of subordinated populations.[1] Yet they are the seeds of struggle to make an alternative, freer public world. The artful rendering of fantasy is itself part of that struggle. The fantasies can sometimes be fanned into the flames of open revolt. At the very least, the fantasies are part of the agency of dominated peoples. Through their arts, they survive, resist daily, and lay the conditions for more effective revolt when the time is right.

With this chapter and my highlighting of dramatic action, especially as it breaks out in bodily confrontation and creative enactment of new worlds, I seek to honor the way that a theatrics of resistance, or what Angela Davis has called an "aesthetic of resistance,"[2] is already under way, has long been under way, in the very subordinated populations being sacrificed today in lockdown America and *Pax Americana.* W. E. B. Du Bois pointed out how black communities had a whole history of "sorrow songs," an art form that suggested not subservience and escape, but resistance and critique.[3]

It is crucial to harness that theatricality of resistance, to stay close to it, as it were, while we forge resistance today. In that artfulness is also to be found the rage of oppressed peoples but chiseled and honed into a force for change. Rage and resistance without art, which some cadres of radical elites have served up to oppressed peoples, often just drives oppressed groups further down, producing rage that works either inner destruction of self by the self, or external destruction by dominating forces that bate their rage.[4] Rage forged into an aesthetic of resistance is an always operative, usually peaceful but militant, mode of adversarial contestation. We do well to allow it to blossom, especially now, into the theatrics of counterterror we so need. This chapter, which places dramatic action at the heart of resistance, is a way to acknowledge what Scott has called the "theatrical imperatives"[5] that issue from oppressed communities' own agency. We must now turn to the kind of theatrics played out along the way of the cross.

How the Executed Jesus Stole the Show

The execution that Jesus underwent may seem a strange way to play out an adversarial politics. How is his execution an act of resistance, theatrical or otherwise? I suggest it is consistent with the fact that his adversarial politics was not expressed in a simple practice of frontal assault. Frontal assault is usually a luxury afforded to the already powerful. There is a prudence in Jesus' politics of resistance, a practical wisdom that can embrace strategic caution and radical sacrifice without diminishing the effective power of resistance.

Other resisters of Jesus' day, at times, had to exhibit this caution. André Trocmé noted in his book *Jesus and the Nonviolent Revolution,* for example, that on one occasion, during the first decade of Jesus' life, an army of over ten thousand Jews gathered in the mountains to fight Roman forces. Legions numbering more than twenty thousand Roman soldiers were soon brought in, and Jewish leaders, though ready to fight as on other occasions, this time decided that prudence meant backing off.[6] Jesus drew some of his disciples from the ranks of militant Jews (Zealots) and never delivered unambiguous denunciations of militant organizing against Rome. Yet his rejection of the easy revolutionary rhetoric of frontal assault is clear, as Trocmé notes, in the lines that Luke recalled from Jesus: ". . . What king, going to encounter another king in war, will not sit down first and take counsel whether he is able with ten thousand to meet him who comes against him with twenty thousand?" (Luke 14:31 RSV).[7]

This act of taking counsel, expressed in Luke, is part of a general prudence and strategic caution that tellers' of Jesus' story often display. I suggest that it is in relation to this strategic caution that we consider the apparent defeat of Jesus' execution. The gospel writers portray this caution, and even the seemingly definitive setback of Jesus' execution as intrinsic to an adversarial resistance to empire. Moreover, the seemingly passive and ineffectual experiences take on adversarial force, become effective resistance, when rendered as creative and dramatic action.

The executed Jesus was a performer of drama in the context of the Roman imperium. The gospel narratives, by which we understand Jesus, are themselves continuations of a dramatic or theatrical contestation with empire manifested by Jesus along the way of his life. The creative drama of Jesus' life and the dramatic portrayals in the gospels steal the show.

To understand this notion of stealing the show, I stress again that crucifixion in the Roman context was a kind of show itself, one designed to have an important impact. Its repeated usage was meant to be a spectacle, a display, to mark the legitimacy of Roman power over subordinated classes and slave populations. "Crucifixion was," as Fredriksen puts it, "a Roman form of public service announcement: do not engage in sedition as this person has, or your fate will be similar."[8] Regarding Palestine and other territories under Roman control, Josephus made the point that crucifixions were often used as "spectacles" to induce Jewish surrender or to create fear for reducing future Jewish resistance.[9] In the aforementioned example of ten thousand Jewish fighters deciding to not risk total oblivion by taking on the Roman legions, Varus, the Roman legate of Syria, nevertheless rounded up two thousand Jews and crucified them, just in case they or others might contemplate rebellion again.[10]

The life that Jesus lived and the adversarial practice he displayed finally entailed walking into the heart of Rome's theatrics of terror, the citadel of its imposed rule, to risk what in fact befell him, being lifted up on a gibbet of torture designed to mark and consolidate Rome's power. Nevertheless, the life he lived and the way he was remembered made his death a show-stealing act.

In what sense does Jesus steal the show? In the gospel narratives of Jesus' execution, especially in their combining of that account with the stories of

Jesus' resurrection, there is a denial that the empire's capacity to execute Jesus can enact an ultimate power over life and death. Even in Mark, where we have very little talk of a resurrected Jesus, there is the affirmation that this executed one has returned to Galilee, that he has gone back to that agrarian land of suffering and resistance and somehow still thrives there, in spite of the empire's executing power.

Back to Galilee. This is a most significant locale for the drama-conscious evangelist, Mark, to assign as the site of the resurrected Jesus. It is the executed one returning to that place from which Jesus had come, among whose people he had forged a solidarity that brought him into increasing conflict with the politics of imperium and temple. The resistance was not quashed or quelled with the execution of the strangely seditious Jesus. So after his execution, puzzled disciples are told, "he is going ahead of you to Galilee" (Mark 16:7).

Let us not get hung up on whether the resurrection was a historical event or whether it happened in the way the gospel narratives say it did. Something happens in the dramatic narration of Jesus' return to Galilee, in his return to a renowned locus of resistance. We do not need exact historical information about that something in order to grasp the powerful witness, the powerful sense and conviction among his followers, that Jesus' life of dramatic practice and resistance was not quashed by his being submitted to the spectacular death of crucifixion. We do not need to have exact historical data about this, any more than we need it for deriving key perspectives for our everyday lives from, say, novels. Consider the way we learn great truths for our historical lives from works of fiction by Fyodor Dostoevsky, Richard Wright, Herman Melville, Robert Penn Warren, or Toni Morrison. We do not need to find exact historical matches for their characters: Raskolnikov, Bigger Thomas, Captain Ahab, Willie Stark, or Sethe, in order to encounter life-changing insights from their stories based on deft analogies to our lives now.

In a similar way, the gospel stories, as narrative renderings of a dramatic life, were intrinsic to the emerging new movements of resistance to Roman power. The narrated drama of Jesus' life and death came to mark a transition out of the power of imperial oppression. Jesus went to the cross, was made a show of by Roman power and by complicitous religious elites, but he also stole the show. Because the continuing force of Jesus' life seemed apparent even after the execution, a veritable force of saving power, a power of God, was identified with him. Caesar was neither *kyrios* (lord) nor *sōtēr* (savior), as so often trumpeted by the imperial cult. Now, especially through the narrated drama of Jesus' life, those titles are ascribed to an executed one and carried by a movement that lives out its remembrance of his way. Ultimate power is now associated with a whole way of life pointed to and acted out by this figure from Nazareth and Galilee, this one who catalyzed new common life and caring among the agrarian poor and entered into adversarial practice with the temple-state and Rome.

The spectacle of crucifixion, which long functioned for *Pax Romana* to beat down courage and resistance, now becomes the center of another narrative about power, a story that displaces Rome. In the gospel narratives, the cross is still a spectacular symbol, a great show, but now one that celebrates triumph over the crucifying empire and all that supports it. Rome is rendered by its own cross of torture into an interim power. The spectacle of the Roman cross is now wielded against terrorizing Rome. This is to steal the show.

As portrayed by Mark and other gospel writers, Jesus' execution could be a show-stealing act writ large, because his life already had been filled with dramatic, show-stealing actions. To claim, as he did, for example, that the ways of God were given with acts of simple caring and radically inclusive love, which included even a love of the enemy, was to startle, dramatically, the ordinary expectations of his hearers. Drama was everywhere in Jesus' life, teaching, and ministry, as narrated by the gospels.[11] He touched lepers and proclaimed forgiveness for commoners with stigmas and blemishes, without making them go through religiously prescribed rituals at official sites of religion and empire. This dramatized Jesus' conviction that full life could be had outside of repressive, official auspices. To teach all this in a way that challenged authority was to set up a drama; indeed, it was to steep his whole movement in dramatic confrontation.

Recall just the narratives about healing. Jesus is not depicted as healing all who were in need of it. As presented by gospel writers, the healings performed and narrated are those that are important for some kind of dramatic effect, a dramatic point to be made about where legitimate authority lies and does not lie. Yes, the healings are often portrayed as acts of compassion for the particular sufferers encountered, but the compassion is not limited to them. The concern for the particular sufferer (a centurion's daughter, a paralyzed person, a blind person, a Gerasene man with a demon) become occasions also to display a compassion for a whole people suffering under a complex, all-pervasive tyranny.

We have already noted how Jesus' entry into Jerusalem was depicted in the Gospel of Mark as a kind of street theater, one that played upon Jewish senses of messianic expectation and imperial traditions of military victors entering triumphantly into a city. Myers has suggested that Jesus is often shown as conducting actions with an eye to "carefully staged political theater."[12]

In sum, the show-stealing drama of Jesus' execution is the culmination of an overall penchant of Jesus to use drama as a primary tool for practicing resistance to empire. It radically contests exploitative power, yet it is not the kind of frontal assault that simply results in being quashed by imperial power. Violence is not repudiated at great length; it is more accurate to say that it is ignored, set aside as a somewhat contemptible, unimaginative resort to the same old ways. For effective resistance to empire, Jesus moves along the way of theatric contestation: the imaginative, artful, attention-getting, subverting power of dramatic action.

Amid today's political theatrics of terror in the United States—where prison construction, death penalties, and U.S.-led bombing missions are used to terrorize and control surplus populations who suffer economic exploitation—Christians must again find a way to steal the show, to forge their own drama, their own spectacle.

Sacrificing the Poor: Theatrical Spectacles of Fear and Fascination

The significance of an adversarial politics of Jesus, which embraces dramatic action as a mode of resistance, becomes clearer when we recall again just how much the forces of terror are today using theatrical spectacles as a mode of repression and control. In today's theatrics of terror, the spectacle is complexly related to a real sacrifice of the surplus populations we discussed in Chapter 2. We must understand this interaction of spectacle with the sacrifice of the poor, in order to view better how dramatic action, in a theatrics of counterterror, might be an effective resistance to the terror of the day, how it might steal the show.

My basic claim in this section is that today's spectacles of terror reinforce a continual sacrifice of poor and marginalized peoples by a tendency to keep viewers of spectacles in fear, or mesmerized and fascinated by state power.

Take, first, the fear. Fear plays a crucial role in subverting critique of unjust power, which otherwise might move from critique to outright resistance. The theatrics of terror we encounter today are not just the massive and brutal exercise of force, they are a way of exercising force that disseminates spectral awe and fear, causing many would-be critics to shut-down their resistance. Simone Weil's essay *The Iliad, or: The Poem of Force* eloquently explored this dynamic, showing how the "touch or sight" of something horrible, more than the direct pain of the horror, can paralyze and silence resistance—first among the direct victims, then among all who behold it.[13] Lee Bernstein, examining capital punishment and the rise of the prisons in the United States, uses Weil's arguments to show how today's law enforcement establishment can create a threat of violence that operates to "create an inability to react, to protest, or to critique."[14]

In a similar vein, scholars of contemporary spectacle frequently refer today to the power of the spectacle to create fear in citizen groups that might otherwise marshal resistance. Richard Hardt and Antonio Negri have summarized this well, arguing that "*the fundamental content* of the information that the enormous communication corporations present is fear." We do well to recall their words: "The society of the spectacle rules by wielding an age-old weapon. Hobbes recognized long ago that for effective domination 'the Passion to be reckoned upon, is Fear.' . . . It seems as if there is no place left to stand, no weight to any possible resistance, but only an implacable machine of power."[15] This fear is crucial to recognize as an effect of spectacle, but emphasizing only fear overlooks other effects of the spectacle that interact with the fear.

Consider, then, the important notion of fascination as another effect of spectacles in the theatrics of terror. The fascination I will discuss here is of two kinds. It is, first of all, a type of mesmerization that steeps citizens in distraction. Fascination is fueled, second, by a drama that exploits people's love and need for scapegoats, that is, their allowing certain select victims to stand in for them, somehow to exonerate them. Here, fascination is born of a self-interest that lets itself think that another's suffering is necessary for one's own or the general good.

Novelist Walter Mosley has discussed the first form of fascination, mesmerization, and distraction. His thoughts are important contributions to our understanding of spectacles as repression. Famous for his novels (*Devil with a Blue Dress, Always Outnumbered, Always Outgunned,* and *Blue Light*), he paused from his fiction writing to pen a millennial lament against the reigning optimism in the United States. In this work, *Workin' on the Chain Gang,* he suggests that U.S. citizens now seem to accept all the new chains being put on themselves and others, by giving themselves to spectacle and becoming, as he put it, a "chain of fools:"

> Of all the constraints placed upon us, two of the most powerful are those of spectacle and illusion. Chains are expensive, as are surveillance tools and armed guards. The best way to keep a worker working is to bedazzle her or him. . . .
>
> Organized sports are perfect for these ends. Ferdinand Marcos distracted a whole revolutionary movement in the Philippines by hosting the Thrilla in Manila, the battle royal between Joe Frazier and Muhammad Ali.
>
> Sports are good, sex is better. Movies, celebrations, mud-slinging elections, or a grisly string of murders . . . can also be perfect for the derailment and subsequent pacification of the masses.[16]

Mosley might also have mentioned the military junta in Argentina that employed powerful public relations firms to throw attention upon the World Cup soccer match in Buenos Aires at the same time that the junta was implementing a Dirty War that would take the lives of some thirty thousand innocent civilians.[17] He might also have mentioned the spectacle of the O. J.

Simpson trial that captivated the attention of a whole populace, while the nation's social services were gutted by Contract with America legislation in Washington, D.C.

While surplus populations are being sacrificed, then, we are mesmerized amid the terror by a continual spin of images. Some of this mesmerization comes from the spectacles of force directly applied to dominated groups, some from the spectacles that numb us in an ethos of distraction. Meanwhile, the already powerful benefit from this politics of mesmerization.

Now consider the fascination that exploits the scapegoat mechanism. This is especially relevant to our consideration of punishment spectacles: a whole industrial complex of prisons catching up two million people, the ritualized executions, the swashbuckling paramilitary police tactics of our day. In what ways does a scapegoating mechanism function in these spectacles?

There is a deep-running propensity in our culture, and also other cultures, to displace the faults and violence spread throughout the entire body politic onto a few bodies that are made to suffer the public shame and punishment for which the whole system bears responsibility.[18]

There are many examples of this scapegoating mechanism played out today. Violence may be almost everywhere, in our families and neighborhoods, as well as in our international policies, but instead of focusing on the pervasive violence, we in the United States often turn our focus upon a few violent offenders stigmatized by race: black males or other persons of color.[19] I believe that one of the reasons we have a disproportionate number of people of color on our death rows is not just the much studied cumulative racial bias in the criminal justice system, but also, more particularly, because a largely white populace is often prone to construct punishable evil as a black or dark problem.[20] Thus, that group projects its general concerns about violence upon a few scapegoated ones. . . .

In the 1980s, there was prevalent a general greed and a will to hoard among much of the U.S. populace, of which the conservative overdrive in that decade, as we have seen, took full advantage. Did citizens focus that generalized greed as the problem? No, instead, they followed in lockstep behind politicians' easy rhetoric about the irresponsible black mother, the welfare queen.

The white middle classes experienced a general economic insecurity in the 1980s and 1990s. Did they focus resistance on the elite sectors from where the policies came that put middle- and lower-income groups in jeopardy? No, instead, they often scapegoated immigrants, largely Mexican but also Asian Americans and others, for their sense of threat.

Because of the propensity to make scapegoats of others, usually of racially stigmatized poor others, the spectacles of terror fascinate. They fascinate not only because they offer a mesmerizing show, but because many experience a kind of absolution of their own fault and responsibility. When experiencing today's theater of terror and punishment, then, people are not only taught to fear state power, they are also attracted by theatrical transactions that promise, or seem to promise, security, as their own violence and faults are dramatically projected onto the punished few.

It is ironic that the numbers of the punished few in the United States are growing now to the ever greater numbers they are, the thirty-six hundred on death row and the two million incarcerated. These figures will probably continue to grow until we discern that our terrorizing punishment reflex is, in fact, a vicious act of self-destruction, an attack upon ourselves and the whole social system being projected out onto others. In a very real sense, when we execute and imprison in the ways we do today, we are killing and walling ourselves in. Until we see this, today's theatrics of terror will continue to exploit fascination with scapegoats to build up an ever more virulent and vicious lockdown America.

Christianity bears much responsibility, along with some other myths and ideologies,[21] for perpetuating the scapegoating mechanism. Many Christian sources—including the writings of the apostle Paul and the Gospel narratives, but especially later Christian theologians—used notions of sacrifice in the Hebrew scriptures to interpret Jesus' death as a necessary sacrifice for saving the many. Jesus was described as a kind of scapegoat, able to have all sin and evil put upon himself, thus to take away from us the wrongs attributed to or suffered by others. Such Christian readings, taught to countless generations of Christian people,[22] have disseminated the destructive idea that we can derive a better life now or in some future time of salvation by means of someone else's sacrifice. From this perspective, Christian scapegoating interpretations of Jesus' death bear a significant responsibility for today's theatrics of terror, as we suffer it in the form of prisons, endemic police brutality, and state-sanctioned executions. Christians who wish to counter this theatrics of terror with something really new, must lay aside the scapegoating myth of Jesus' death.

Jesus' execution was not a salvific event, and I have not presented it as such in this book. His execution was a part of a whole way of the cross, entailing his adversarial politics, his creative and dramatic contestation with religio-imperial power, and the organizing of movements in Jesus' name that continued after his death. All this is what is salvific, if you wish to use that word. In other terms, it is all this that reconciles (or yields a healing unity) and that liberates (or makes real integral freedom from oppressive structures).

In Chapter 3 of this book, I have already summarized the adversarial politics. Here, in Chapter 4, I am examining the way this adversarial politics involved dramatic and creative contestation. Jesus entered the Roman theater of terror at Passover and acted up differently there, so differently, in fact, that fledgling and crucial movements would spring up in the wake of his death. But again, Jesus did not go into the imperial theater to become a scapegoat. No, he was, in fact, contesting the whole lethal, religio-imperial, scapegoating regime (recall how Rome used crucifixions as examples, as public signs inscribed on the bodies of the tortured few in order to help anchor a general public order).

Along this kind of way of the cross, a way of adversarial contestation, dramatic action and continuing movements, we fight not only the fear of spectral state power but also the fascination that mesmerizes and feeds off any collective illusion that these sacrificed ones are suffering and dying for all of our good.

We must turn, then, to ask more concretely what dramatic and creative action might mean in our own time. What does a theatrics of counterterror look like anyway?

Dramatic Action: Bodies on the Line, Worlds Created

The way of the cross, through its theatrics, is a mode of dramatic action that challenges the terrorizing, spectacular theatrics of imperial power. The most effective dramatic action is, as in the case of Jesus, nonviolent action. Affirming this, however, must entail also careful qualification. Even though I have much respect for the history and the concept of nonviolent direct action, I hesitate to use *nonviolence* itself as the key term for characterizing Christian action. This is because nonviolence is neither the first nor the only trait of the action that is so necessary for countering imperial terror today.

The defining quality of this action is not nonviolence, first of all, but artful and adversarial performance. Nonviolence is necessary to such a theatrics, as I will show, and without it truly creative action usually destroys itself, but it is not the defining trait of Christian dramatic action. I embrace nonviolence not so much as an end in itself, therefore, but as a means toward artfully and most effectively confronting imperial power with genuine alternative ways of living.

It must also be acknowledged that, from the perspective of history, sometimes—and I stress sometimes and not as a rule—strategic and limited violence has been an effective tool against imperial oppression. Nevertheless, even when that seems the case, it is not so much because of the violence itself, so much as it is the dramatic and creative modes of its application, modes like those I discuss in this chapter around the themes of bodily contestation and creative enactment.

I will here present the two major traits of the notion of dramatic action as I envision them and then conclude by showing why especially the second of these traits entails nonviolence. The major traits are, first, bodily confrontation with institutionally applied physical force, and second, the creative enactment of new worlds. Bodies on the line, we might say, become occasions for creatively enacting new worlds so to counter the ways of empire.

Bodily Confrontation with Security Forces

Dramatic action has its first trait in people's willingness to put their bodies on the line, in confrontation with imperial forces of control and repression. These forces may be applied by security officers with billy clubs. These may be prison guards with their keys, their ammunition, weaponry, water cannon, airpower. They may impose bars, cells, razor wire, and prison walls to confine bodies. Oppressive forces may end lives with the injection needles, electric chairs, hanging nooses, and the firing squads of execution protocols, as well as with the military artillery, bombs, and planes used by the forces of *Pax Americana.* Also included among security forces' repressive modes are what they can do to activists by pressuring their employers, ensnaring them in financial debts and obligations, or fabricating charges of criminal conduct.[23]

These are all examples of ways that today's political theatrics of terror can function, and a theatrics of counterterror will be marked by adversaries to empire who dramatically confront, who demonstrate against, imperial power's use of this force against human flesh and its flourishing. This confrontation is usually occasioned by the intentional violation of standing laws in a way that risks, and usually invites, the application of physical force to the demonstrators. Demonstrators receive in their flesh (through arrest, imprisonment, being carried bodily, being physically threatened in a host of ways) the effects of physical force.

Exemplary of such intentional violations would be the so-called illegal marches carried out during the civil rights movement in Birmingham and Selma, Alabama, of the 1960s; the symbolic destruction of nuclear weapons by demonstrators in the United States during the 1970s, 1980s, and 1990s; the blocking by unarmed Maya women and children of U.S.-supplied Mexican army tanks in Chiapas, Mexico, of the 1990s; the mounting of the steps of the U.S. Supreme Court in 2000 or the closing down of the Liberty Bell shrine in Philadelphia in 1999 by opponents of the death penalty who also organized for a new trial for death row prisoner Mumia Abu-Jamal. In all these cases, those in an adversarial position to organized and institutionalized terror intentionally violated a law and suffered the application of force to their bodies: police clubs, handcuffs, body and strip searching, confinement in jail or prison, and so on.

In many cultures of protest, this bodily confrontation with institutional force is often called direct action.[24] It is a form of nonviolent protest that directly confronts violent forces. The meaning of direct is set by a contrast to indirect nonviolent action. This latter includes the whole set of life actions in which nonviolence is practiced: family, child care, self-care, eating habits, friendships, investing, and so on. These lifestyle domains are all spheres of nonviolent expression and action, but they are comparatively indirect applications of resistance to a violent world. When bodies are on the line, coming up against forces representing institutionalized violence, then the direct application of nonviolent action is evident.

I find this distinction between direct and indirect action helpful for distinguishing different ways to practice nonviolence. Christian action, however, is not distinguished by opting for one or the other, direct or indirect. Both may be options in need of consideration. Again, the crucial identifier of adversarial Christian politics, under conditions of empire, is creativity and drama. The best practitioners of what is often called nonviolent direct action often confirm this by rendering their actions as dramatic and creative ones (using mime, puppetry, dance, marches, surprise tactics, innovations that capture the imagination, and more). Direct is not the best way to describe this effective and unique action. Hence, I use the term *dramatic,* or *creative,* to highlight the contestational force of the action.

Nor does the word *direct* describe sufficiently the kind of action suggested by Christian narratives as attaching to Jesus' adversarial politics. Indeed, at times, he was direct (as when he overturned money-changer tables in the temple and brandished whips). At other times, though, he was hardly direct at all, advising silence, suggesting caution and prudence in the face of overwhelming force, even submitting to apparent defeat. All these kinds of action, even though not direct, should not be characterized as indirect. Again, it seems best to call them dramatic and creative. It is in these ways especially that they become adversarial to empire.

As bodily confrontation, Christian action becomes particularly dramatic, and using one's body to act up amid empire has some special effects that are crucial for taking on imperial terror today. This is rooted in the fact that forces of repression often have a special impact on our bodies. To be sure, imperial power also works upon its citizens' minds in ways as real as anything it does to their bodies. Powerful groups in our society thus invest heavily to create media and other cultural mechanisms of control, which often work so effectively that repressive measures against the body are unnecessary. Yet I would argue that analyses of the historical record of imperialism and of present imperialist structures reveal that application of force to the body is the heart of its terrorizing ways. Dominant powers take aim at our minds, yes, but also at our sphincter muscles. They seek to register state terror in our gut.

This is often hidden from our view, especially by those who wish to deny the reality of imperial force, or who wish to give it a friendly face. Sometimes, however, even those who celebrate *Pax Americana* and its glory will admit its roots in physical force. One of these is journalist Thomas L. Friedman, who often argues for the value of the current globalizing economy and for U.S. domination. We do well to recall, as I noted in chapter 2, that Friedman admits the necessity of physical force and of wielding it against unruly groups. Behind the maintenance of the present free trade system, he says, is "the hidden fist," that is, U.S. military force: "The hidden hand of the market will never work without a hidden fist—McDonald's cannot flourish without McDonnell Douglas, the builder of the F-15. And the hidden fist that keeps the world safe for Silicon Valley's technologies is called the United States Army, Air Force, Navy and Marine Corps." Extolling the virtuous power of militarily anchored, U.S. geopolitical power, Friedman concludes, "Without America on duty, there would be no America Online."[25]

All this suggests that the persuasiveness of political and economic values (disseminated and reinforced in the ethos of globalization[26]) are significantly dependent upon a capacity to dominate the body and to do so through military and other modes of physical force and intimidation.[27]

Because the body is such a crucial site for anchoring a political theatrics of terror, our theatrics of counterterror must mount a dramatic resistance of bodies confronting bodies, where adversarial practice is registered on the physical level, even though imperial powers have amassed and rendered themselves seemingly invincible by firepower, military hardware, and, domestically, with the prison-industrial complex.

How does this dramatic action by bodies really constitute effective resistance? The willingness of demonstrators employing dramatic action that pits bodies against established security forces makes two major contributions toward effectively eroding imperial domination.

First, it exposes the empire's willingness to use and perpetuate itself by physical force. The confrontation of demonstrators' bodies with security forces highlights the way imperial control, in spite of its sophisticated rhetoric claiming to rule by a freely given consent of the people, has to maintain itself by physical violence. Exposure of a dominating system's use of brute force is crucial to mobilizing resistance. It is crucial to eroding the compliance of citizens who are schooled and induced by media to think that reigning powers are virtuous and consensually endorsed. Especially when demonstrators act in a way that makes clear the system's faults and when they absorb in their bodies the blows or constraints put upon them, then they are forcing others to consider, maybe even to see through and challenge, imperialist claims to legitimacy.

Martin Luther King Jr. frequently pointed out that marching peoples' bodies dramatized evil, that this drama was crucial to "mobilize the forces of good will."[28] Dramatic action that confronts organized physical force, thus, has the benefit of exposing the empire's dependency upon coercion.

Second, demonstrators engaging in bodily confrontation offer to citizens who practice it a partial antidote to the fear generated by a dominating system's theatrics of terror. If it is true that imperial power maintains itself in great part by creating spectacles of force that evoke fear in the public, it is crucial that a theatrics of counterterror have some antidote for the way this fear takes up residence in the body, in one's physical being. Wisely crafted dramatic action, which involves your body going up against imperial force, actually helps rid the gut of the terror the state seeks to implant there. Protestors cannot do this all the time, and often one must know how to protect one's body from imperial security forces as well as to risk confrontation. Nevertheless, bodily contestation is one crucial ingredient when creatively enacted. It helps people break free from the somatic weight of psychic and social terror in which an imperial ethos often steeps us. By deliberate, well-planned, and intentional violation of some laws and customs, demonstrators take some control over the way physical force is applied to their bodies in an exploitative milieu. In so doing, they face terror, absorb it in their bodies, as it were, even while resisting it. One might say that any violence resulting from dramatic action (even just facing up to police phalanxes or being handcuffed) creates in members of resisting movements an anti-body, one that vaccinates them against susceptibility to imperially induced fear and terror.

In sum, dramatic action through bodily confrontation makes significant contributions to a theatrics of counterterror. First, by means of their very physical theatrics, dramatic actors (demonstrators) expose the brutal attempts of imperial domination to use physical force, and, second, dramatic actors increase their own freedom from the fear and terror that empires inscribe in our bodies.

Bodies that undertake such contestation, with such effects, were part of the secret of Mahatma Gandhi's rivaling of British empire. For him, bodily confrontation was part of the power of "truth-force" (*satyagraha*).

> Even today the more direct uses of satyagraha always include the body and the meeting of bodies: the facing of the opponent "eye to eye," the linking of arms in defensive and advancing phalanxes, the body "on the line"; all these confrontations symbolize the conviction that the solidarity of unarmed bodies remains a leverage and a measure even against the cold and mechanized gadgetry of the modern state.[29]

Creative Enactment of New Worlds

The bodily confrontation with established powers is usually, of course, a confrontation between bodies of unequal force. The dominating system has the firepower, the armies, the phalanxes of police, which are increasingly organized on military models, even on the U.S. domestic scene.[30]

With such an imbalance of forces, the mounting of effective dramatic action, which might really serve a theatrics of counterterror, is no easy matter. To face this difficulty, the confrontations worked by dramatic action must develop more intensively their character as a theatrics, as drama. Activists must plan and interpret these confrontations as performances, as art-full, if you will, as creative enactments. Such a cultivation of creativity makes three essential contributions to movements trying to counter today's theatrics of terror.

First of all, by cultivating creativity in their confrontational engagements, demonstrators compensate for the disparity of physical force by galvanizing wider public and moral support. A theatrics of counterterror that builds an aesthetic sense into resistance benefits from a creativity that displays actors' values and concerns for a broader public. This display is crucial for galvanizing wider support for movements of resistance against terrorizing domination. Creative and aesthetic expressions in confrontation, then, are not merely an ornament to struggles of resistance; they offer no simple entertainment while demonstrators undertake some more real action of resistance. No, aesthetic expressions are necessary to survival, essential to resistance. They strengthen resistance to empire so that it can present itself as a formidable challenge on a playing field that often seems uneven due to overwhelming imperial power.

When frontal assault is not available to subordinated peoples, as it often is not, creative and aesthetic expression of confrontation can encourage and invite support from others. This aesthetic dimension already exists in much civil disobedience, in the show created by the mere fact of confrontation when, say, unarmed demonstrators position themselves against armed forces. The aesthetic sense is augmented, however, when demonstrators add marching to their rallies, which may also involve singing, as was so powerfully enacted in the civil rights movements across the South. Or, there may also be the art of an orchestrated silence, so impressively used in the great Silent March through New York City in 1917, organized by the National Association for the Advancement of Colored People to protest the race riots and lynching against black Americans in East St. Louis.

The creative sign may be carried in a demonstrator's single lit candle or in any number of surprising acts of aesthetic resistance that capture the imaginations of others. There is a long history of such creative displays.

- When Pontius Pilate introduced the emblems of empire into Judea, Jews in 26 C.E. theatrically prostrated themselves en masse and exposed their necks to the swords of surrounding Roman soldiers. Pilate withdrew the Roman standards.
- Ida B. Wells organized a mass exodus from Memphis, Tennessee, in 1892 to protest lynchings and discrimination against blacks.

The ritual and public burning of draft cards from 1964 to 1975 dramatized resistance to U.S. military campaigns in Vietnam.

Mark Dubois chained himself to a riverbank and so stopped the filling of a reservoir, thus helping to preserve a wild and scenic river that had been threatened by development.[31]

Resistance against General Pinochet's military rule in Chile was broken open in 1983 by people "banging on pots and pans and blowing whistles."[32]

U.S. activists in 1986 provided round-the-clock, visible accompaniment and "escort service" to human rights activists in Guatemala who were under threat from death squads.

Demonstrators with disabilities fighting for civil rights legislation in 1990 did not just show up for a rally in Washington, D.C., they crawled "out of their wheelchairs and up the steps of the Capitol to underline their demands."[33]

On July 3, 1999, demonstrators for Mumia Abu-Jamal closed down the Liberty Bell in Philadelphia, ringing bells and chanting, "Let freedom ring for Mumia."

In 1998 and 1999, thousands of activists carrying white crosses featuring the names of those slain by Latin American military forces marched illegally into Fort Benning, Georgia, where many of these military officers had been trained by the United States.

Opponents to capital punishment in the United States were arrested while staging a die-in in front of the U.S. Supreme Court in February 2000. Other abolitionists showed up at the Republican National Convention in Philadelphia, in July of the same year with flyers depicting the convention as "The Executioners' Ball." The lead practitioners of the U.S. death penalty (Governors George W. Bush of Texas with 150 executions and Tom Ridge of Pennsylvania with over 200 signed death warrants) were represented on the flyer by the black-and-white sketches of José Posada, showing them as skeletons in gala costuming.

In November 1999 (Seattle, Washington) and in April 2000 (Washington, D.C.) demonstrators used new modes of costuming and dramatic street theater to interrupt the annual meetings of the World Trade Organization, the International Monetary Fund, and the World Bank, whose officials set terms for global market that usually privilege the corporate few at the expense of the majority populations.[34]

In each of these actions involving civil disobedience, some creative sign, some aesthetic display (the lying prostrate, the die-in, the lit candle, the song, the artistic flyer, street theater, the chaining of one's body) accompanies the act of bodily confrontation. When these acts bear fruit—say, in undermining military dictator Pinochet in 1983 or in galvanizing widespread protest to the Vietnam War—the creative moves are essential. They give the confrontation a quality of aesthetic display, the drama that drives the word *demonstration* into its full and original meaning, *monstrare,* to show, reveal.

This aspect of creative show has accompanied almost all the actions of civil disobedience that invite and receive broader public support. Courageous confrontation cannot do without the aesthetic dimension if it is to invite the broader public that can bring both numbers and moral force, helping to make up for what the resisters lack in comparable physical force. Rebellious confrontation that can be embraced by a wide public needs artful creativity.

It is, in fact, the art of rebellion, which, according to Albert Camus, is what generates collective force from resistance.[35] Rebellious art has the fruit of building collective force that can rival otherwise overwhelming oppressive force. This collective sense, bred by creative confrontation, is what is necessary to make up for the disparity of force in the confrontation with established forces of terror. Straight-out violence tends to be ineffective and alienates a broader public. Nonviolence also must be done with an aesthetic sense, but one of its advantages over violence, which now can be noted, is that even without much creative flair (as in a simple "sit-in"), there is a creative and dramatic impact issuing from a surprising and vulnerable encounter with overwhelming force. When, however, nonviolent action deploys fully dramatic theater and really develops the aesthetic sense consciously, it intensifies its public impact.

Creativity's second contribution may be harder to communicate, but I believe that artists and lovers of art will know what I mean and that demonstrators themselves often intuitively and unconsciously are aware of the point. Resistance that remembers and employs the arts, also fosters hope. It nurtures a felt sense of connection between present struggle and future realization. Through artistic creation, resisters to the present order are allowed to taste the future, we might say, to feel themselves already in the future for which they work. Art has a capacity to *re*-present, or make present, what it depicts. It is, again, not just an ornament, not a mere decoration that points to some more real, substantive political world of transformation still to come. Creative expressions anticipate future worlds often so effectively that these worlds are made present before their realization. Especially with music, maybe above all with popular dance music, bodies in resistance move into and within a world where the future is not only anticipated but somehow known now.

Acts of civil disobedience are frequently referred to as acting up. One group, ACT UP (AIDS Coalition To Unleash Power), is exemplary in its acting up, with an artistic flair. ACT UP aims to help people recognize how drug companies profit from people with AIDS and how government turns its back on people with AIDS.[36] When we act up artfully, something more than confrontation is highlighted, that is, we also act out the world we want to inhabit, and in so doing we taste it now. I use the metaphor of taste for the way art allows us to experience the envisioned and hoped-for future, because there is a vital sensibility called forth by artistic representation of the ends of struggle. To be sure, the artfully rendered future is not completely or directly present now. There is still much for which to be in struggle. There can be no avoiding the organizers' nitty-gritty work, day in, day out, and art is no substitute for that work. Nonetheless, the artful acting out of that world, through an aesthetics of resistance that enables activists to taste the world for which they work, is essential for sustaining movements of resistance, for nurturing the sense of connection between acts of protest now and the future worlds for which activists work.

Camus, too, noted how art enabled us to reach for the future. He wrote of the artist's "presentiment" of what the future perpetually only promises. Art gives a present form to the elusive goal of the future. Art has a power "to snatch from the grasp of history."[37] The importance of an aesthetic dimension to resistance was memorably put by Emma Goldman: "If I can't dance, it's not my revolution."

The third contribution of creativity, this theatricality, if you will, is its ability to unlock an actual world-making power in social and political settings. The world that is tasted aesthetically, acted out, especially when done repeatedly, issues in an enactment of new worlds, of new patterns of social and political interaction. This acting out and acting up sets in motion new ways of being in the world. So strong can these new patterns become that powerful systems can be provoked to overextend themselves, and so they can be subverted, even when they now can marshal the kind of imperial power we see in U.S. domestic and global arenas. A theatrics builds strength against imperial power not only by artfully giving form to an elusive future but now also by enacting new worlds of political practice. Art, as expressed in creative drama and theatricality, does what resistance and rebellion so need: it constructs a "substitute universe." It "reconstructs the world."[38]

This is one of the places where Christian communities can use some of their distinctive resources to make a significant contribution. I have in mind their liturgical resources. Many movements today have their own world-making "liturgies" in a whole host of ritual actions and ceremonies. It would bode well for the future if politically conscious churches would begin to reshape their liturgies and offer these arts as modes of drama and theater, allowing all oppressed people to rehearse themselves in resistance and flourishing within lockdown America. Liturgies of various movements, together with the churches, might thereby begin a joint dramatic effort to reconstruct the world.

But what kind of world? What kind of universe? It is at this point, I believe, that the necessity of nonviolence becomes most evident. Nonviolence is the creative, strategic practice that marks the alternative newness of the worlds sought by those resisting systemic terror. Nonviolence is the crucial feature of the world creatively envisioned, acted out, and being enacted by resisters. Whether nonviolence is cultivated between individuals or between groups, it is both a strategy employed by the movement against the violent worlds of empire and a value practiced within a movement of diverse activists.

Neither of these two embraces of nonviolence—as strategy against external terror or as practice within movements of resistance—is easy. Nonviolence is always to be preferred, however, because it is the only real break from the normal, a real subversion of the reigning assumption that change only comes by "unfolding the 'there' of violence."[39] To choose the way of nonviolence is not only to choose what works, a way to fight overwhelming and dominant power, it also is the truly new, the yet to be known. It is to nurture that which is not yet there.

When Christians, on behalf of or as oppressed peoples, find no option other than taking up arms (and I do not rule out the possibility in a world already structured by institutionalized violence), we will not realize even our own aspirations for change apart from some imaginative art form, some dramatic and aesthetic gesture that points toward the better way of nonviolence in human interaction. The example of the Maya Zapatistas of 1994, tying white strips of cloth around their gun barrels comes to mind. These dramatized, they said, their wish to discontinue use of those weapons. (Indeed, they have gone largely unused since the January 1994 Maya uprising for indigenous rights, which was quickly put down by the Mexican army at a cost of more than 150 Mayan lives.[40])

The preference for nonviolence, even amid necessary battle was evident in the Cuban revolution. When Che Guevara's band of fighters lost an especially dear comrade to the bullets of the forces of Fulgencio Batista (the U.S.-backed dictator in Cuba before Fidel Castro's leadership), Guevara's men wanted to execute a Batista soldier in immediate retaliation. Guevara forbid it, saying, "Do you think we're like them?"[41] Guevara's rebel forces triumphed against Batista's dictatorship, in part, because of this attitude and a regular practice by Cuban revolutionaries of medically treating the enemy's wounded as well as their own.[42] This is an example of the preference for nonviolence (even in a violent context), and it is a case that shows the newness and efficacy of that preference.

Although the preference for nonviolent modes of resistance and empowerment may often seem like an accommodation to terrorizing power, a bowing down to empire, it is this preference that allows the real alternative ways to be born. It is almost always the drama of nonviolence that is powerful enough to steal the strength from terrorizing power. It counters the established terror with a dramatic contrast to the habitual ways to institutionalized violence. Some say that violence is the only thing the violent understand. Yes, in fact they understand it so well that they often know how to deal with it, to crush it, to manipulate and manage it. Systems prone to violence may have to be dealt with best through what they do not understand, that is, an adversarial, surprising force of imaginative nonviolence.

We thus have a theatrics of counterterror made up of two impulses: bodily confrontation with established security forces and creative enactment of alternative worlds. We might call these a veritable pageant of empowerment for peoples in struggle and resistance, and we can consider precisely this to provide a new understanding of a triumph of God in lockdown America and *Pax Americana.* To this we now turn.

Stealing the Show in Lockdown America: A Triumph of God

When I speak of the triumph of God, I speak of no Christian triumphalism. The *triumph* of which I speak, as the etymology of the word suggests, is that of a this-worldly public celebration or spectacular pageant. Such a pageant is made up of an array of dramatic actions that, through bodily confrontation and creative building of nonviolent worlds, are eroding the empire at work today. In these ways, dramatic action is at work, stealing the show from the political theatrics of terror in which we live.

What this triumph entails may remain somewhat vague at this point. It will become clearer in the final chapter, where particular dramatic actions and movements are identified. Before making those identifications, permit me here to reflect on how the discussion of dramatic action in this chapter enriches the understanding of God developed in this volume. How is dramatic action, with its pageants of empowerment, a force we can say is of God?

Recall the senses of the term *God* as presumed in this book's phrase, the executed God.[43] This term refers to that power that is greater than all those structures entailed in imperially situated lockdown America. It achieves that greatness, however, by being a deeper power (emerging as a force pervasive of the nature of things) and by being also a wider power (flourishing in an array of peoples' movements).

I here want to show how dramatic action, as a theatrics of counterterror described in the previous section, can be a triumph of God in these senses. How does dramatic action unleash the greater power that is also a deeper power and then a wider power?

The answer lies in understanding more fully the two traits of dramatic action: bodily confrontation and creative enactment. It is bodily confrontation that helps unlock the depth of this greater power as a veritable force of nature. It is creativity in dramatic action that unleashes the width of that power, as a force flourishing amid social and political movements. So let us return to these two traits of dramatic action, this time with a view to how they unlock a depth and width of power for transforming lockdown America.

Deeper Power and Lockdown America

When Ziyon Yisrayah (Tommy Smith) was executed in 1996 after many appeals to prevent it, a thunderstorm erupted during the execution and prompted Sadiki, another prisoner in an adjoining cell block, to pen this lament.

> With every spark of Blak rage from our hearts, came deep flashes of lightning from Motha—then came de rain. As We grieved de best way We knew how, de whole earth seemed to shake. Soon you could not tell de difference between our grief and de universe's: Her pain was our pain; Her rain and our tears were inseparable. We had all become one-verse (uni-verse).
>
> I recall wondering as I kicked and shook de bars, if Ziyon cold hear or feel us. Diz made me put all my energy into it, b'cuz I wanted him to hear and feel us, in spite of distance between Us and de murder room. . . . It was as if We were trying to send a message out to Ziyon and We were all writing with de same pen. De message read: "We luv you Bro, and We will continue to struggle for liberation."[44]

What is particularly noteworthy about this is the way this creative lament yearning to connect with Ziyon's suffering uses language that invokes natural forces. "As it stormed outside the tombs, so too did it storm outside. For Blak Motha called 'Universe' was also found moaning de murder of her souljah."[45] This is just one example of people in struggle within lockdown America invoking the power of earth and nature when their natural bodies are pressed and oppressed within imperial systems.

We might also recall the way Barbara Curzi-Lamaan looked for power over lockdown America by looking down between the cracks of prison concrete for an earthy, blossoming growth.

> Seizing—with unbindable Hope
> we take the future
> and shower with care
> the blossoms of optimism.
>
> Life bursts forth
> even from the cracks
> between the concrete blocks.[46]

Here the imprisoned poet looks for power and hope in fledgling natural growth. In her other poems, the turn is to the strong bodies of her children and of her comradely friends, to the resources of the sky and its storms—all to tap some natural power for carrying on resistance. It may sound meager to some, but I have known residents of the Bronx, New York, who recall days as children seeing a few blades of grass in their concrete worlds of urban trauma and feeling that they were stubborn and wonderful signs of hope.

When we undergo a bodily confrontation with organized physical force (being handcuffed, forced to the ground, receiving police blows or long-term incarceration) something unexpected happens, and it is crucial to resistance. Those suffering this physical force in their bodies are driven to seek a power resident in the way their bodies remain connected to the power of nature. Bodies in a physical confrontation with imperial forces may be very vulnerable at times of dramatic action, but those bodies seek a greater power by "reaching deeper," we might say, into earth's own power.[47]

Sadiki and Curzi-Lamaan, at the heart of lockdown America, are giving expression to that in their prose and poetry. In this, there lies a kind of earth mysticism, a sense that nature is a friend to the body's resistance to unjust, imperial repression. This is not an abstract mysticism. It is a concrete sense of the earth's own dynamic power to sustain life in spite of repressive human systems.

When a policeman puts his knee in your back and is putting handcuffs on you, your face to the ground or pavement, you may have a sense that you are closer to real power in that moment than you are to the arresting officer, who thinks he is the powerful one. In my experience of arrest in this way, I have had the surprising sense that I was not simply being put to the ground in another act of subjugation. I am put to the earth where there is power. For the demonstrator open to it, there can be in that moment of bodily subjugation a discovery of a confidence and power believed to come from the depths of the earth. As Puebla-Laguna novelist Leslie Marmon Silko has said so well in interviews about her work, the earth and the land are protagonists in history.[48] The earth itself, all of nature, can be respected as an agent of resistance, as a source of empowerment.

Understandably, this kind of earth mysticism should not be romanticized. Obviously, this power of the earth is little comfort to the many victims of police brutality, who are often surprised with a police violence that throws them to the ground, where they receive the kind of verbal and physical abuse that usually is not present in intentional actions of civil disobedience or dramatic action. Historian Robin D. G. Kelley's account of his abuse at the hands of police is a case in point.[49] Yet, in the earth mysticism I tentatively envision, these abuses on the urban ground can be viewed as collecting and adding to the already teeming cries of the land. They might be interpreted as rising up, being heard, and galvanizing people's resistance to the official violence that throws so many down still today. Every abuse, whether on a country field or on police-patrolled pavements, leaves a powerful spirit that relentlessly presses for justice, especially when remembered in story.[50]

Dramatic actions, then, whether the voluntary movements of protestors to the ground (in sit-ins, die-ins, prostrations) or involving the forcing of demonstrators to the ground by police (during arrest and handcuffing), can be interpreted and celebrated as actions whereby demonstrators align themselves with the earth's power.

One of the most impressive examples of physically suffering peoples finding this greater power in nature comes, again, from the pen of Mumia Abu-Jamal. In 1995, this journalist on Pennsylvania's death row had just been transferred to Phase II of death row, given a date to die on August 18, locked up around the clock in a cell with lights blazing twenty-four hours a day, every day. Journalist Abu-Jamal sets the scene on one hot humid night: "The sun had set behind the hills of West Virginia amid ominous thunder heads, and now the forces of nature struck like a divine assault team. Lightning stabbed the earth as if in the throes of celestial passion, and so powerful were the bolts that the lights in the block—indeed, the whole jail—flickered out." As lightning played over his darkened sector of the American Gulag, Abu-Jamal pondered:

> There I sat in the darkness with less than a month to live, yet I felt better than any other night I spent on Phase II. I felt better even than I did a few weeks later, the night my stay [of execution] was granted.
>
> I saw, then, that though human powers sought to strangle and poison me and those around me, they were powerless. I saw that there is a Power than makes man's power pale. It is the power of Love; the power of God; the power of Life. I felt it surging through every pore. Nature's power prevailed over the man-made, and I felt, that night, that I would prevail. I would overcome the State's efforts to silence and kill me.[51]

A "divine dance," Abu-Jamal writes elsewhere, playing out through "the veins of nature" with a power to overcome the state's efforts to silence and kill—this is the power of earth.[52] It is the deep power that bodies seek amid physical confinement and punitive force and that they often find when they resist imperial power in all their bodily vulnerability.

When I say there now is a power of God at work to rival lockdown America and the *Pax Americana,* I say it because within our burgeoning prisons there are many among the incarcerated who have not succumbed to spirit death but who have tapped this deeper power of the earth. It is a crucial part of the greater power that can rival lockdown America. Moreover, there are the protestors and organizers working outside the prisons, against the political addictions to prison construction and death penalties; against also that police brutality pervading our social times. All these as well, some of whom I will present in the final chapter, tap into these deeper powers of earth.

This should not be seen as a new thing. The activists who remember the power in bodies connecting to nature as loci of spiritual power are rooted in long-standing indigenous traditions of both Africa and Native America. People of Euro-American descent don't need to extract this sense of nature from African and Native American descendants; they can turn to the indigenous people of Europe, such as the Sami peoples of northern Scandinavia and Russia.[53] The deep power of the earth is still believed by many Indian peoples of North America to be the ultimate power, one that renders the U.S. state power and its imposed seemingly intractable sufferings to be an interim power at best. The deep power of earth to rival state power is very much alive. "Blast it open, dig it up, or cook it with nuclear explosions: the earth remains. Humans desecrate only themselves. The earth is inviolate."[54]

John Trudell, indigenous activist and poet, has fleshed out the meaning of this deeper power. In meditating on the legacies of U.S.-forced removals and massacres, Trudell noted: "They can't stop the Wind and they can't stop the Rain. They can't stop the Earthquake and the Volcano and the Tornado. They can't stop Power. We are a Spiritual connection to the Earth. . . . Only by understanding our connection to the Earth can we create a fair system that's going to be good to the People." Time and again, Trudell sought to point activists toward this earth-source of spirit, which is also a political power for peoples' movements. "One of the things I hope you all learn . . . is the energy and power that the elements are: that of the sun and the wind and the rain. This is the only real power. . . . There is no such thing as military power; there is only economic exploitation. That is all it is. We are an extension of the earth; we are not separate from it. The earth is spirit, and we are an extension of that spirit. We are spirit. We are power."[55] In sum, the trait of bodily confrontation in dramatic action awakens (and keeps to the fore) our sense of the deeper power of earth as a spiritual and material force greater than what any empire can inflict.

The call to acknowledge the unifying power of earth, as a force to rival what human empires do, was made by Abu-Jamal on another occasion. When he found the water in his death row prison cell contaminated one day, Abu-Jamal paused to note that he was suffering this wound to nature along with the nearby suburban families whose kitchen sinks were alive with the same toxic odors that lurked in his steel basin.

> I think of white well-fed families who survive and thrive off houses of pain like this, in rural enclaves across the country, under the illusion of

> otherness. . . . Despite the legal illusions erected by the system to divide and separate life, we the caged share air, water, and hope with you, the not-yet-caged. We share the same breath. . . .
>
> The earth is but one great ball. The borders, the barriers, the cages, the cells, the prisons of our lives, all originate in the false imagination of the minds of men.[56]

The deep power of earth helps unleash the greater power needed. It is a kind of deeper power that makes for the oneness so necessary in a unified struggle against oppressive power.

Wider Power and Lockdown America

The pageant of empowerment, however, the triumph of God, will be not only deep, it will also be wide, galvanizing an array of diverse forces. To catalyze this width, dramatic action's trait of bodily confrontation needs that other trait, creative enactment. In other words, dramatic action thrives not just through a bodily confrontation that unlocks a deeper power of nature but also through that cultivation of creativity that generates collective width. The unifying deep power from an earth that is "one great ball," as Abu-Jamal put it, creates a collective unity that is also wide. Actions that are creative, then, bring more persons, more groups into an action of resistance. It is shared aesthetic delight in the drama of walking, marching, and dancing, in song, poetry, and chant, that builds the wider power. Creativity in art, to recall Camus again, opens up the "We are."[57] Moral commitment alone and organization alone do not build breadth. Shared delight, heavy laden with creative signs of a coming alternative future—this is what invites the many, encourages them to stand up in new solidarity to powers that rule by their spectacles of terror.

Are there new bursts of this creativity under the conditions of *Pax Americana* today? I believe there are. It was evident in the stunning success of some sixty thousand demonstrators in the civil disobedience actions and accompanying marches in Seattle, Washington, which in 1999 closed the World Trade Organization meetings and sent a clear message to global managers that unrestricted so-called free market principles were not acceptable to masses of working peoples who care about humane labor conditions, about limiting corporate greed, and about healthy environments. Seattle marchers employed a stunning array of creative slogans, costuming, and vivid display of their values. Their dressing up like the pollution-threatened sea turtles was just one example. Their positioning of their civil disobedience in front of Nike, Starbucks, and McDonald's establishments also evidenced the creativity at work.[58]

As U.S. society imbibes more immigrant populations, especially from the Caribbean, strategies of protest and organizing will take on still other aesthetic means of resistance. The protest marches of Haitians give a vivid example of this. As Haitian and other African diaspora groups, together with Latinos/Hispanics, press their demands, this country will most certainly see a mode of action that lifts the creativity of resistance to new levels of drama and effectiveness.[59]

I remember Haitians marching on the White House in 1994 to press their claims to relieve Haiti from the military tyranny it suffered after President Jean-Bertrand Aristide had been illegally ousted by strongman junta leader Raoul Cedras. Mounted police in Washington, D.C., tried to keep the demonstrators a block away from the White House. Many a leftist group of marching protestors might have paused in front of the phalanx of mounted enforcers and pondered when, how, or if they should press on forward into the wall of police. On this occasion, though, the Haitians simply stopped and went into a dancing, chanting, and drumming mode of creative celebration. Soon the horses reared up, turned aside, went the other way, leading the crowd of protestors up to the White House gates, carrying the mounted police with them.

Antonio Benítez-Rojo, Cuban literary critic, termed this kind of militant use of the arts against overwhelming forces, a "magico-militarism."[60] The term refers to the use in battle or other conflicts of belief systems that use amulets, prayers, rituals, oblations, and other symbolic actions. These were used throughout the Haitian revolutionary campaigns that eventually repelled Napoleon's forces from the Haitian country. Cultural strategies from Haitian immigrant populations and from many others will be crucial for building the breadth of movement we need in our theatrics of counterterror.

In the widening movement of youth, who find repugnant today's cultures of corporate greed, one can also see something like this magico-militarism at work, at least in the ways militant activists often depend on dramatic symbolism in their street actions. Alli Starr, for example, drives the streets of Santa Monica, California, and teaches workshops on nonviolent demonstrations for the Ruckus Society. This thirty-two-year-old, cell-phone-toting activist teaches others how to use music and dance "to defuse a violent vibe" in encounters with police. "'When we sing *Amazing Grace,* it has this powerful effect,' she says, recalling the moment in Seattle when police closed in on the crowd occupying an intersection. 'We did a slow-motion dance in unison—a prayer—and the whole energy changed. People started singing, the police stopped spraying [their pepper spray], and the sun broke through the clouds.'"[61]

Haitians marching on the White House and Alli Starr singing into police violence are examples of the galvanizing power of a protest culture's ethos of creativity. When it is displayed for others to see, it can invite other participants. As all the artistic styles of diaspora peoples from African, Asian, Latina/o worlds—as well as from Anglo and European traditions—build up their presence in the United States, the creativity of resistance will grow. Ruling elements of *Pax Americana* will do all they can to deny the value and beauty of those alternative cultural aesthetics, precisely because in them, especially under conditions of oppression, there resides potential to create the wider power that overcomes imperial power. Haitian voudou aesthetics will be dismissed by some as weird, as pagan, as only something that can be seen through Hollywood caricatures of Haitian religion as "voodoo." Anglo youth's puppeteering and street dancing against corporate greed will bring many paternalistic smiles. Meanwhile, popular forces against arrayed corporate, imperial forces will broaden and grow stronger.

As long as lockdown America continues to work its terror on communities, communities of resistance will draw strength from their arts. They will march the streets and bring their Yoruba priestesses to pour libations at the intersections. The Christian preachers with courage will come to read their scriptures and preach prophetically. Caribbean peoples will come to dance the rhythms of the sea and earth in ways to make crumble the walls of empire. The many who are either terrorized or mesmerized by lockdown America will take note. They will wake up, and the wider power will join the deeper power in one pageant of empowerment, in a kind of triumph of God most needed.

With the gathering of this wider power, we are prompted to consider the place of organizing peoples' movements in relation to the way of the cross. Thus, we move to the final chapter to discern how these movements are at work today resisting the seemingly intransigent repressions of lockdown America.

5. way of the cross
as Building Peoples' Movements

Both the popular messianic movements and the Jesus movement were interested in establishing the people's autonomous life free of domination by the alien and domestic rulers and, presumably, under the direct rule of God. . . . There is no indication, however, that people in the Jesus movement thought of theocracy in terms of hierocracy, however egalitarian.
—Richard A. Horsley, *Sociology and the Jesus Movement*

Central doctrines of Christianity prompted and sustained attractive, liberating and effective social relations and organizations.
—Rodney Stark, *The Rise of Christianity*

A theatrics of counterterror comes to its dynamic culmination in the building of peoples' movements. The power of the way of the cross is an eruption of adversarial politics, of dramatic action, and now, of organizing movements to rival the powers of lockdown America and *Pax Americana*.

Countering Rome with the theatrics of dramatic action, as the Gospel writers depict a Galilean Jesus movement to have done, was action also prefiguring a new way to organize human relations. When Paul spoke the unthinkable, claiming to "know nothing . . . except Jesus Christ, and him crucified" (1 Cor. 2:1-2), he not only was announcing the topic of a message but also beginning the startling process of building human solidarity and community around one who was seditious enough to be contrary to and condemned by empire.

The way of the cross, then, as adversarial and dramatic, prefigures new community. It is kinetic, moving, organizing, dynamic. Hence, the way of the cross, as a theatrics of counterterror, involves the building of peoples' movements. This chapter points to the peoples' movements that ultimately are the scenes for not just living against empire but also for flourishing and pressing beyond it. These movements catalyze the power we need to go through lockdown America—resisting and going beyond the forces of police brutality, the terror of today's prisons and of the death penalty.

While this chapter will focus on movements in lockdown America, against police brutality, prison injustice, and the death penalty, these do not occur apart from the equally important movements against the U.S.-led imperium that anchors the "predatory globalization" laying waste to so many of the world's poor and common folk today.[1] At the turn of the millennium, the most impressive of these movements include those so evident at trade meetings in Geneva, Switzerland, and Seattle, Washington, in 1999; in 2000, at Washington, D.C.; and at the Republican and Democratic National Conventions in Philadelphia and Los Angeles. Many participants in these actions also planned to appear in demonstrations in Melbourne, Australia, and Prague, Czechoslovakia.[2] These movements are integrally related to those working against the punitive regime of lockdown America. The punitive regime has been necessary, as I argued in Chapter 2, because of massive accumulations of corporate capital, often extracted from working poor the world over, and often with callous disregard for the environment. As the money goes up into the holdings of a new burgeoning elite (nationally and internationally), an elaborate apparatus of military power, paramilitary policing, prisons, and execution protocols are all needed to control the restless many. Movements, such as those I present in this chapter as resisting this punitive apparatus, are also engaging the complex network of forces confronted by protestors of corporate domination and the market policies of the International Monetary Fund, the World Bank, and the World Trade Organization. These movements reinforce one another.

Just as we began the previous chapter with commentary on dramatic action as part of Jesus' way of the cross, so here we begin by noting how the building of peoples' movements is also embedded in Jesus' way of the cross.

Jesus and Peoples' Movements

Jesus' life and words have been so spiritualized by Christendom that it is difficult for many to stop thinking of the spiritualized, saintly individual in order to behold the ways this Jesus prefigured and gave rise to dynamic social and political movements. In order to establish that the building of peoples' movements is not extraneous to the way of the cross, but in fact intrinsic to it, we must begin by noting how the way of the cross, as exemplified in the life and work of Jesus, bears some connection to political and social movements.

The mere fact that Jesus' most dramatic encounter, his execution, occurred during a religious and political festival like the Passover, where he intentionally positioned himself in the last tumultuous week of his life, suggests the orientation of his person and work to movements. Paula Fredriksen, who sees the historical Jesus as neither primarily a social reformer with a revolutionary message nor as a religious innovator of his tradition, nevertheless emphasizes that the message embodied in his person is part of what moved the crowds at the politicized tumult of the Jerusalem Passover.[3]

Jesus' message was frequently about the building of new relations, laden with talk about problems of hatred, oppression, anxiety, as well as about love, justice, and righteousness. This focus on the restoration of relationships, expressed in the political and social metaphor of kingdom, realm, or reign (*basileia*) of God, together with his own formulation of a group of disciples, clearly implicates Christianity's founding figure and savior (the new *sōtēr,* and hence a kind of anti-Caesar) in the nurturing and building of movements. All the more would this be the case, given his connections to the land, the travail and turbulent movements for which his Galilee was renowned.

The Galilean Jesus, who dared (in all likelihood, more than once[4]) to situate his person in Jerusalem during the politically and religiously turbulent social worlds of peoples' festivals, suggests a Jesus who was hardly above the fray or who could have been seen as apolitical. He risked having his message heard and acted upon where movements and social forces were in conflict. Indeed, it is perhaps due to "the crowds" in Jerusalem, more than anything, that Jesus was finally executed, by orders of a nervous Pontius Pilate with the support of religious elites.[5] Jesus risked presenting his adversarial themes and dramatic presence amid a festival of expectation where imperial powers were always on watch for resistance, subversion, and unrest. Note the kinetic qualities of the scene of Passover as Fredriksen describes it. The crowds met him "during the pilgrimage feast in the city of David at Passover, in all the excitement, panoply and ritual enactment of the holiday that commemorated the liberation and redemption of their people."[6]

The kinetic dimension of Jesus' life and work, his penchant for being implicated in peoples' movements, is an obvious trait in the way of the executed Jesus. Christendoms that eschew political movements and see them as somehow contrary to what being a follower of Jesus is all about thus miss the mark badly. Moreover, Christendoms whose effect is to shore-up entrenched imperial powers of the day are also out of step with the Jesus who was dramatically adversarial to imperial power, even to the point of being subject to torture and execution by it.

If Fredriksen's recent historical analyses of Jesus' presence in Jerusalem at Passover are correct, Pontius Pilate, the reigning Roman authority of the time, really did not expect much of a threat from this Jesus of Galilee. Although simply one's origins from Galilee, with its long tradition of resistance to Rome, could be enough to arouse some Roman suspicion, Pilate apparently had been sufficiently aware of Jesus' work to dismiss him as generally harmless.

Yet Jesus' message and presence apparently excited the crowds enough, and aroused the already offended religious elites, so that Pilate was led to deploy the always-ready machinery of crucifixion against him. Jesus, perhaps unexpectedly in Pilate's mind, presented an adversarial and dramatic presence within an already dramatic scene. His presence was enough to spike the brew of popular unrest and expectation. We must hear Fredriksen at length:

> The excitement of the crowds around Jesus that Passover might easily have spilled over into riot, or been perceived as about to do so by the Roman troops staring down at them from the roof of the Temple stoa. . . .
>
> His teachings about the coming Kingdom, like the Baptizer's before him, were well known. His pinpointing the arrival of the Kingdom for *this* particular Passover was the spark that ignited all the rest. The tinder had long been laid: hopes for the coming Kingdom, the message of liberation woven into the story of Passover itself, the excitement of pilgrimage, the swollen city population, the singular authority with which Jesus taught and acted in proclaiming his message And more fundamental to all this: the biblical traditions and pilgrim psalms lauding Jerusalem forever as the city of the Great King, the city of God and of his chosen one, his beloved son, scion of David's line, the Messiah. . . . Jesus' closest followers, and Jesus himself, never claimed this title or role for him. The crowds whose hopes he fanned and fed did. Their fervor led directly to his death.[7]

Moving into the tumult of peoples' movements, engaging their expectation for religio-political liberation from imperial powers, all this is intrinsic to the way of the cross. It is also essential to the way of the executed God, a way that catalyzes a greater, deeper, and wider power for challenging empire. Jesus' life and message were movement oriented. Not only were they adversarial and dramatic, they were kinetic. It is fully appropriate to see the way of the cross of this Jesus as bound up with the meanings of the political and social movements of the day.

It also needs to be noted, however, that kinetic qualities did not characterize only his entry toward the Jerusalem Passover scene or his experience there. The way of the executed God also entails the Jesus movement(s) that came after Jesus' death and were catalyzed by his life and death.

The Jesus Movements: Those Impious Galileans

The way of the executed God prompts us to consider movements because devotion to Jesus, especially after his execution, catalyzed political movement and resistance. This is implied by the postexecution traditions, oral and written, especially as they issued in the anti-imperial posture of the apostle Paul but also in the critiques of empire and imperial ways that we find in the gospel of Mark.[8]

The texts of Paul and Mark, pointing as they do to historically existent anti-imperial communities, are signs of a broader movement that grew up in the wake of Jesus' execution. Memory and devotion persisted and grew, especially because of the adversarial and dramatic action that were linked to this Galilean. It nurtured what scholars have called "the Jesus movement(s)."[9] There was considerable impetus for the growth of such movements, if for no other reason than that imperial systems of repression continued after his death. Indeed, from Jesus' execution to the destruction by Rome of Jerusalem in 70 C.E., it can be argued that imperial domination and repression only increased, especially in Judea. It is not surprising, then, that among the many Jewish movements, this one born of the adversarial and dramatic ways of this carpenter from Nazareth, would continue in force after his death. His way of the cross, entailing execution by state power, seemed a way of power and empowerment, a resource for living in and beyond the imperial ethos of the day. His presence and way, as a power challenging both the political and religious claims of empire, easily carried connotations suggesting that this way was a power of the source of life itself. It was a way of the reign of God, of an executed God, it turns out.

The Jesus movement was a messianic movement that "spread throughout the villages of Judea and the Galilee," running up the coast to cities ringing the Mediterranean through the network of Greek-speaking synagogue communities of Asia [M]inor."[10] This movement has many characteristics that, in our time, would be seen as otherworldly. And so scholars of the Jesus movements have described them as apocalyptic: vibrant with a cosmological vision that took the end of the world order to be imminent and that largely expected a return of the risen Christ.

As I have stressed throughout this book, however, such an otherworldly vision is not without political import. In fact, the Jesus' movements' apocalyptic orientations shared with the Roman imperial cultus a tendency to mix political and religio-cosmic concerns. The imperial establishment had, as often today, its otherworldly meanings. In this, it is similar to the Jesus movement, even if its God and consequent sociopolitical practice are most certainly different.

I do not deny that the Jesus movements were more than a political or social phenomenon. But their success as movements that endured empire, that forged its beliefs and practices into institutions that had staying power in history, was rooted in its uniqueness as a this-worldly phenomenon, a sociopolitical movement. In the words of sociologist Rodney Stark, the Jesus movement proved to be one of the "most successful revitalization movements in history." Stark argues that Christianity succeeded, in large part, because of its capacity to foreground central doctrines that "prompted sustained and attractive, liberating and effective social relations and organizations."[11]

We can remember this truth, that Christianity's success was due to its being a liberating movement, even while we simultaneously indict Christianity for becoming the Christendom that made friends with, and even became, imperial power. The indictment of Christianity's own imperialist and dominating ways must be made, whether those ways are evident in the Christian emperor Constantine of the fourth century or in North American missionary work that often consolidated European and then U.S. political ambitions in Asia, Africa, and the Americas across the nineteenth, twentieth, and twenty-first centuries.[12] This necessary indictment of Christendom, however, need not cancel out our appreciation for the Jesus movements pointed to by contemporary research into the first century and by the writings of Paul and Mark. (The appreciation of Jesus *and* Paul has been advocated even by a contemporary Marxian scholar.[13])

Early Christianity was a movement, revolutionary in its ideas, foregrounding radical ideas of divinely sanctioned practices of love that rarely were lifted up by the imperial cult. Christianity, with teachings rooted in Jewish traditions but forged by Paul and the memories of Jesus into a new adversarial and dramatic gospel, unleashed movements of powerful effect. A simple list of examples of such teachings would include: "I am my brother's keeper," "Do unto others as you would have them do onto you," and "It is more blessed to give than to receive."[14]

These teachings stood certain tests of history, particularly the devastating epidemics that raged across the Roman empire in the second and third centuries. When impoverished urban areas of empire were laid waste by devastating plagues, the Hellenistic and Roman officials and moral leaders thought nothing of leaving, running to preserve their own lives. Christians had an ethic of remaining, of staying on-site, to minister to the sick. So effective were their efforts that many developed immunities to the epidemic, even though many others died. Politically and economically, the effect was even more historically consequential. Such a comprehensive practice of care, both in its spontaneous and organized forms, gave rise, according to Paul Johnson, to "a miniature welfare state in an empire which for the most part lacked social services."[15]

In our own time, we may be accustomed to attributing such care as an act of great piety and moral virtue. In the context of empire, within which early Christianity emerged, such caring was seen as an act of political disobedience to the other, supposedly better way, that of imperial Rome. In fact, when the emperor Julian of Rome, in the fourth century, tried to reverse the empire's embrace of Christianity and to restore the pagan (Hellenic and Roman) charities and cults, Julian labeled the disciples of Jesus as "impious" in the same breath that he grudgingly gave respect to the ways they cared for the poor. In a letter to his own high priest in Galatia in 362, Julian admonished his priests to match the virtues of Christians, even if their "moral character" is "pretended." "I think that when the poor happened to be neglected and overlooked by the priests, the impious Galileans observed this and devoted themselves to benevolence. . . . The impious Galileans support not only their poor, but ours as well; everyone can see that our people lack aid from us."[16]

I suggest that there is still a need for followers of the executed Jesus to earn this label from imperial powers, to become impious Galileans. Christians must recover, especially amid lockdown America, a reputation for adversarial and alternative practice to the ways of empire, ways that neglect and exploit the poor.

Princeton political scientist Michael Doyle points out that this kind of "saintly calling" in Christians might have actually "sapped the military and civic power" of the ancient world's imperial aspirations.[17] In Emperor Julian's fourth-century lament about the Galileans and in the twentieth-century historical observation by Doyle, we have a crucial theological implication: Christians are often most pious in a positive sense, most faithful to the energizing spirit and teachings of their founder, Jesus, when they earn from empire the reputation of being unfaithful to the pieties of the powerful. When Christians organize in ways that question the claims to ultimacy made by imperial powers and organize in a way that resists empire on a practical level, then they are faithful to the ways of their executed Jesus.

In short, the executed God is a force moving within and against empire. A theatrics of counterterror, such as I have explored across the pages of this book, is to be found not just in occasional, adversarial events, even if rendered in the dramatic acts of resistance, but in these events as organized social movements. The way of the executed God, the way of the cross that is a greater, deeper, and wider power of transformation should be discerned today, yes, in adversarial stances of activists challenging imperial orders. Yes, indeed, it also can be found manifest in dramatic action. Nevertheless, to be an effective manifestation of the way of the executed God as defined by the Jesus movement(s) emergent after Golgotha, it will also need to culminate in organized forms of political and social movements.

The great Protestant theologian Karl Barth once discussed the need to oppose nuclear armament by Western nations, the incessant anti-Semitism of his own Germany, and the Vietnam War as pursued by the United States and its allies, and then he asked his fellow Christians, "Are you ready to organize a movement?" To underscore the importance of doing so, he added this:

> If your just confession of Christ dead and resurrected for us such as it is witnessed in Holy Scripture includes this and expresses it, then your confession is a good and precious one that will bear its fruits; if it does not include this and does not express it, *such confession is no good despite its justness;* on the contrary, it is a dead, cheap confession that

strains off the midge and gulps down the camel just like the Pharisees of Jesus' times.[18]

Impious Galileans Today?

Where are these organized movements today? Where are those in resistance to the forces of empire explored in this book as lockdown America and *Pax Americana?* Who among us still risks denunciation as impious Galileans? Can they be found today?

For answering these questions, there is a certain logic employed by theologians and Christians that prompts us to look to the church. This logic, following the apostle Paul's teachings, routinely stresses that the church is the body of Christ, the collective living organism embodying the messianic founder, Jesus of Nazareth. There, in that social world of love and practice, in the community of Christians, we allegedly will find a continuation of what Jesus was about. If Jesus was an impious Galilean with respect to empire, as were many of his subsequent followers, we might expect the church today to continue that tradition.

Alas, each of the elements of the theatrics of counterterror—adversarial practice, dramatic action, organized peoples' movements—are sadly lacking from established churches as defining traits. There are precious few impious Galileans to be found in the church today. Let us consider each element of a theatrics of counterterror, beginning with that theatrics' organizing of peoples' movements, and then look at its adversarial politics and dramatic action. How do today's churches stand in these terms?

In relation to organizing peoples' movements, the U.S. churches' dynamism, growth, and institution building often are ecclesiocentric, centered on the churches' own internal community and rarely engaged in the political and social dynamics of community and world. Even less, then, do the churches show themselves to be organized around the issues of lockdown America, police brutality, the growth of the prison-industrial complex, and the death penalty. In fact, the churches' way of organizing their internal functioning often serves existing orders more than it resists them.

Churches in the United States remain powerful institutions, and they do shape movements and social forces. This is evident from the way churches structure the aspirations and values of youth raised in their care and the way they often channel adult energies in various forms of neighborhood and charitable involvement. Unfortunately, those institution-building powers are rarely pointed in the direction of being on the move to redress the sufferings spawned by lockdown America. Usually, the churches apply themselves to these tasks only within the mainstream political policy channels established and legitimated by official structures.

How do the churches stand today regarding the adversarial politics sketched in this volume? Churches, indeed, have not been without their adversarial practices. Their leaders, for example, have routinely issued judgments, critiques, and denunciations of a wide array of cultural practices and political policies that they consider out of keeping with church teachings and Christian faith. This is true of leaders on both the Christian left and the Christian right. There often have been courageous, principled, and prophetic stands taken by the churches. It must be acknowledged that these adversarial stands have often played an important role in the shaping of progressive social movements.[19]

Rarely, however, have the adversarial practices of U.S. churches been the kind that characterized that of Jesus and Paul, that is, vibrant with a critique of empire, with a witness to a way of living and being that are alternatives to the routines of imperial practices. To the contrary, the adversarial stances of most churches have been accommodated to fit within the purview of standing political powers. Moreover, this accommodation is not simply that stealthy kind that oppressed groups often need to practice in order to survive and later resist. In the United States today, it is as if *Pax Americana,* that mighty and efficient empire, is simply accepted by the churches as a kind of stage upon which church ministries are to be acted out. That stage will rarely tolerate Christians and their members living and organizing as impious Galileans. So it is that the churches' adversarial politics is hardly like that demanded by a theatrics of counterterror.

Consider the notion in a theatrics of counterterror that I have termed dramatic action. The churches also have creative resources for displaying dramatic action, but there has been a similar failure here when it comes to marshaling the kind of theatrics of counterterror we need today. The churches' pageantry—so evident in procession, scriptural readings, sermons, song, liturgy, and ritual—offers a great wealth of dramatic resources. Moreover, these dramatic tools are often wielded with impressive effect within church communities, expressing their adherents' sense of the numinous and divine, enabling them to live their lives mindfully and regularly with a sense of that something more that men and women name God, spirit, or mystery.

And yet, because its critiques of culture rarely become the kind of adversarial stance that challenges imperial politics, the church's dramatic repertoire rarely generates dramatic action that wields bodily confrontation and creative resistance against the complex and repressive powers of our day. Hence, the church also often fails to generate organized movements against the terror of lockdown America.

Those church members who wish to be impious Galileans, who wish to live out the way of the cross as adversarial to empire, dramatically acting up and organizing against it, often find themselves in closer and more intense community with activists outside their churches than they do with members in their own churches. The other activists may be from other church groups or from no Christian group at all. They may be from other religions or embrace none. What makes them potential communal partners is that they show the traits of the theatrics of counterterror. They are impious Galileans, if you will, because they manifest an adversarial politics to imperial terror, seek ways of dramatic action against it, and are organizing movements to transform the social order. All this does not make them "anonymous Christians,"[20] but insofar as they share in a way of action trusting to and embodying that greater, deeper, and wider power of life that can rival imperial terror, they are participants in the communal movement of impious Galileans.

Those who enact a theatrics of counterterror today, and who thereby are like impious Galileans, may wish to (and often should) preserve their ties to existing church institutions. Those in this number, however, and I count myself one of them, will find ourselves drawing our most significant sense of communal belonging from a dynamic place of tension, that is, between the world of the church and that of extrachurch or nonchurch colleagues. This is the world where diverse people of different faiths find their way into resistance, employing a theatrics of counterterror. Christians live in this liminal space, that is, a space betwixt and between, flourishing in dynamic tension between, on the one side, church groups that invoke the name of Jesus yet manifest little of his anti-imperialist way, and, on the other side, the larger movements that form adversarial, dramatic, and organizing movement communities.

In closing this book, I want to direct attention to places of movement in the United States where a theatrics of counterterror is now at work. I want to point out how some are wielding the way of the cross to bring flourishing amid the political theatrics and practice of terror today. I wish to show where the executed God, as a power greater, deeper, and wider than the power of lockdown America, is clearly at work. Here you will find impious Galileans on the move, whether they emerge from the churches or from some other social grouping. It is to be hoped that more and more church people who claim to belong to the way of Jesus will actually situate themselves along such a Galilean way of resistance and enter the full community of impious Galileans who fight to form a better world amid lockdown America and *Pax Americana.*

Impious Galileans today are challenging the three powerful forces of terrorizing power in lockdown America: police brutality, the prison-industrial complex, and capital punishment. Increasingly, they are also seeing the need to direct the power of their adversarial politics, dramatic action, and organized movements toward the globalized corporate gambits that combine ruthless economic policy with military backing, as we studied in Chapter 2.

In considering peoples' movements against police brutality, prison industries, and the death penalty, I cannot give full attention to every movement or organization. Happily, there are more than I could summarize in this text. What I can and will do, however, is to select those movements in which we can discern the three distinctive traits of a theatrics of counterterror: an adversarial politics, dramatic action, and organizing that sustains peoples' movements and puts new structures in place. In each example, churches and their leaders have played some important roles, even though they certainly were not the only players, and rarely the initiating ones.

Dismantling the Police Function As We Know It

Across the United States today, there is a vigorous movement to end police brutality, the use of excessive force against residents that results in injury and often death. The movement is anchored in urban experiences of police violence in communities of color (especially African American and Latino communities). As we have seen, the problem of police violence reaching epidemic proportions has been argued in studies by Amnesty International,[21] Human Rights Watch,[22] and the Center for Constitutional Rights.[23] Empirical and social analyses and historical perspective, which confirm the extent of the problem, have been provided by important book-length studies like Jerome G. Miller's *Search and Destroy: African-American Males in the Criminal Justice System* and Jill Nelson's edition of *Police Brutality: An Anthology.*[24]

Every region of the United States now shows police violence to have reached problematic levels,[25] but New York City at the turn of the century has become something of an epicenter of the problem and of organized resistance to it. On that urban site can be seen not only an organized peoples' movement but also its traits as adversarial and as employing dramatic action. Hence, it is a prime example of impious Galileans in organized movement.

New York City, referred to by many as the "capital of police brutality," has become notorious in the turn-of-the-century United States, largely due to the announced aggressive acts of Mayor Rudolph Giuliani, who seemingly has given his police department unusual latitude in intimidating and controlling urban youth and others (especially in communities of color), who are seen as threats to the mayor's views of what makes for quality of life in the city.[26] Residents of other cities, such as Philadelphia, Los Angeles, and Chicago, might wish to nominate their own municipalities to the status of police brutality capital, but New York City has been the undeniable focus of national attention on the problem.

In particular, the torture and beating of Haitian American Abner Louima in 1997 and the shooting death of the Guinean man Amadou Diallo in 1999 forced New York City's police brutality problem into the national limelight and so foregrounded the national problem. Louima was brutalized by New York City police officers in a Brooklyn nightclub rest room, as they used the end of a toilet plunger to destroy his rectum and teeth. Amadou Diallo was struck by nineteen bullets in a hail of forty-one shots fired by the New York Police Department's (NYPD) infamous Street Crime Unit (the officers involved were found not guilty of all charges).

These are just two of the many other notorious New York cases. There is the case of Anthony Baez, a Puerto Rican youth, who died in a choke hold by police after his football accidentally struck a squad car. Anthony Rosario and Hilton Vega are two others, both killed "execution style by officers of the NYPD as they lay face down on the floor."[27] The mothers of these latter two victims became leaders of a grassroots movement throughout the East Coast, as many citizens rose up to contest police violence. The Center for Constitutional Rights has been one organization especially active in mobilizing and unifying the movement, but working alongside that center, just in the New York–New Jersey region, have been other organizations: the National Congress for Puerto Rican Rights, the Committee against Anti-Asian Violence, the Black Panthers, the December 12 Movement, Black Cops against Police Brutality, the Malcolm X Grassroots Movement, Jews for Racial and Economic Justice, the New York chapter of the National Lawyers Guild, Refuse and Resist, the NAACP Legal Defense and Education Fund, and the Asian American Legal Defense and Education Fund.

The movement has generated numerous street actions numbering often in the thousands of marchers at different events between 1996 and 2000. Conferences have frequently been held on the problems of police brutality, such as the one held at Hunter College in New York City in 1997 (drawing over seven hundred people). The April 3, 1999, National Emergency March for Justice/Against Police Brutality drew over five thousand people from all over the nation to Washington, D.C.[28]

The peoples' movements became so notable that populist singer Bruce Springsteen showcased a new song in ten concerts at New York City's Madison Square Garden, which referred to Amadou Diallo's shooting and the policemen's claim about why they unleashed the forty-one shots at the African, a man in whose hand was a wallet that police thought was a knife or gun. Springsteen's song provoked widespread rage in the establishment circles and denunciation by police union leaders.[29] Springsteen's was not the first song about Amadou Diallo's shooting,[30] but because it came from a popular singer who reaches large white audiences, the impact was particularly forceful. The words left no doubt about where Springsteen stood:

41 shots and we'll take that ride
Across this bloody river to the other side
41 shots they cut through the night
You're kneeling over his body
in the vestibule
Praying for his life
Is it a gun?
Is it a knife?
Is it a wallet?
This is your life
It ain't no secret
It ain't no secret
No secret my friend
You can get killed just for
living in your American skin.[31]

Springsteen's audience has remained supportive of their singer, though some, closely identified with police establishments, have renounced him. That the problem of police violence could reach such a level of popular audiences signals how widespread the problem is. Movement activists are pressing, therefore, for no mere tinkering with police institutions. This is no movement that will be placated by a few sensitivity training sessions for police or by another civilian review board or two. No, the movement is clearly characterized by a spirit of the adversarial politics that is so crucial to a theatrics of counterterror today. Ron Daniels, from the Center for Constitutional Rights, minces no words in asserting that the paramilitary models for policing "must be eliminated."[32] With a similar force, historian and activist Robin D. G. Kelley, after reviewing the way today's crisis in police violence is rooted in the whole history of institutionalized violence in the United States, including slavery and centuries of racist degradation, articulates an adversarial politics with a clarion call.

> Indeed, I would go so far as to propose the complete dismantling of police departments (and consequently the entire criminal justice system) as we know it. Perhaps we might return to the long-standing radical proposal for community-based policing. Imagine institutions for public safety structured along nonmilitary lines and run by elected community boards! I am not simply proposing that community members be employed to do the work of policing; rather, I am suggesting that the very job itself be reinvented.[33]

This is an adversarial politics issuing forth from peoples' movements. Its adversarial nature is marked by its insistence on dismantling the structures, the models, the paradigms of paramilitary-style policing that make police violence and terror such routine realities in lockdown America. Such a call, especially in its challenge to paramilitary models in the neighborhoods, strikes directly at the heart of the way the theatrics of terror is institutionalized and operative in the United States and abroad. The adversarial stance at work in peoples' organizing calls for an end to what we have seen as crucial to both lockdown America and *Pax Americana.*

Note, however, that being adversarial to paramilitary police powers and their violent propensities involves also an imaginative call for an alternative way. The quote from Kelley called for a fresh burst of imagination to establish community-based models. In fact, numerous others have been experimenting with these for some years.[34] Ron Daniels also details a number of key structural changes. Daniels insists that the U.S. government must mobilize all its levels to root out racial and economic justice in policing. He urges the elimination of the paramilitary "war" paradigm for U.S. policing, the ending of mass sweeps in urban neighborhoods, mandating that police reside in the jurisdictions in which they work, and that topics of "antiracism and diversity training" be substantially addressed in police academies.[35]

Today's movement against police brutality, in fact, allows the imagination to flourish in a manifestation of what I have called the kind of dramatic action that is also central to an effective theatrics of counterterror. The penchant for dramatic action, where bodies move into contestation with police forces, and do so creatively, is clear. The struggle around Abner Louima's case is an example. After Louima was sodomized by police, upwards of ten thousand marchers, largely Haitian and Haitian American, flowed across the Brooklyn Bridge and marched on NYPD headquarters and city hall. It was a nonviolent protest, but it was made especially dramatic by Haitian activists drawing on all the resources of their dramatic cultural traditions.

Haitians marching against and amid police forces used art to mimic and mock, to express their rage, and to break down the terrorizing ways they saw around them. Marchers showed up with toilet plungers, not as tools for vengeful brutality but as props in moving street theater: wearing them as hats, marching with them as mock police billy clubs, or brandishing them as pathetic-looking phalluses. The powers were impressed and intimidated by the creative march. The spectacle of this march was especially influential in keeping the Louima case from disappearing from public attention, as have many other police brutality cases. The dramatic march also helped ratchet up the entire country's concern about police brutality and to force the issue onto the front pages of some national magazines.[36]

There could hardly be a better example of the kind of dramatic action so direly needed today in a theatrics of counterterror than this 1997 march of the Haitian American community. Clearly, even though it was not a civil disobedience action resulting in massive arrests, it did feature bodies in public contestation and a heightening of drama through artistic creativity. The dramatic action of this event was crucial for further galvanizing the organized peoples' movements against police brutality and misconduct, and for focusing and forging their adversarial politics into a force to be reckoned with.

Dramatic action was just as powerfully unleashed by adversarial peoples' movements responding to the death of Amadou Diallo. Less than a month after the killing of this young, unarmed, and innocent victim of forty-one bullets, pastors and others mobilized a civil disobedience action against police brutality in the heart of Wall Street. Hundreds were mobilized by the Reverend Al Sharpton in a demonstration that occurred on March 3, 1999. In an especially dramatic moment, eleven demonstrators—among them the Reverend Herbert Daughtry from the House of the Lord Church in Brooklyn, New York; Charles Barron of the Unity Party; and Reverend Wyatt Tee Walker, pastor of the Canaan Baptist Church in Harlem—"locked arms with the Reverend Sharpton, walked to the center of Wall Street, and kneeled down for prayer."[37] This dramatic move, for which they were arrested, unleashed a series of additional moves that received some local press coverage, but the full dimensions of which were not reported in the mainstream press.

At the church building of Reverend Daughtry, plans were laid for daily civil disobedience actions to be held at the headquarters of the NYPD, modeled after the Free South Africa Movement actions. Beginning six days after the original march, therefore, notable activists and personalities showed up at the headquarters to be arrested. These included several pastors. On subsequent days, hundreds came forward to be arrested at daily demonstrations, among them leaders and members of numerous coalitions against police brutality, women's and youth groups.[38] Students from Christian and Jewish seminaries crossed the police lines to be arrested, as did dignitaries from many walks of life, in the New York–New Jersey area and across the country. This dramatic action, beginning with the public act of kneeling to pray on Wall Street and extending into daily actions at the NYPD headquarters again focused and forged the adversarial stance of this peoples' movement into a new force to be heard on the national scene.

This is exemplary of the theatrics of counterterror that can be seen at work today. It is a movement in which Christian leaders and church folk have played crucial roles, as is evidenced by the role of the Reverends Sharpton, Daughtry, Walker, and others. Nevertheless, it must be said that it was the work of countless activists, many outside of established churches, who formed the coalition of organizers who forged the adversarial stance and dramatic action of these forces. It is the families and neighbors who are the heart of this peoples' movement, and even if some of them, like Tony Baez's mother, would frequent rallies with Bible in hand and numerous references to her Christian faith, the bulk of the movement can hardly be said to be a Christian one.

Nevertheless, these organized movements, with their adversarial politics and dramatic action, embody the theatrics of counterterror that, as I have argued in this book, can be seen in the way of the cross that takes on imperial power. The organizations on the move against police brutality exemplify that way. They embody it and call those Christians not yet participating in the movements to follow and find their Galilean Jesus along the way of this movement for justice and peace in order to counter the terrors of lockdown America. In so doing, they may take on the mantle of being those impious Galileans so needed today.

No More Prisons!

There also exist vigorous peoples' movements to end the prison system as we know it today. As we have seen, the prison-industrial complex, with a confined population nearly quadruple that of 1980, has become a staple of the social, political, and economic landscape of life in the United States in the twenty-first century. We now risk becoming a nation whose effective governance depends not on a shared system of values but on the maintenance of a vast prison colony, in and out of which increasing numbers of our populace rotate on a regular basis.

Fortunately, there is an ethos and practice of struggle at work among those who resist this destructive development, and it is yielding organized, concrete movements that inspire hope. This ethos of struggle and supportive movements are scattered all across the country—in various community organizations; among those who have family members imprisoned; among some chaplains who work in prisons but not for prisons; in the efforts of teachers and writers, most notably, perhaps, Angela Y. Davis,[39] who tours the country analyzing the startling rise of the prison-industrial complex.

In discussing the movements making this effort, I will once again select those that exemplify the three crucial elements of a theatrics of counterterror, which I have argued forge the way of the cross, not only peoples' movements as such but those as adversarial and employing dramatic action. Once again, too, the people leading and constituting these movements are those impious Galileans, who may have important connections to some church but often have none at all. Regardless, each movement, each voice is essential given the crisis we face. Right now, however, it must be said that the movements manifesting a theatrics of counterterror in resistance to the prison terror of the day are not arising from church-connected communities. There are, as I will show, church-related folk playing key roles, but in the main, we are still awaiting the church communities who will make "No More Prisons!" part of their proclamation and enactment of the gospel.

One source of hope for church involvement is the striking text written by a college instructor, campus minister, and long-time activist, Lee Griffith. His 1993 work, *The Fall of the Prison: Biblical Perspectives on Prison Abolition,* still awaits the large-scale embodiment in Christian action for which it calls. As the title suggests, Griffith clearly manifests the trait of an adversarial politics. His text seeks to show why a Christian theological perspective warrants and why society needs "the fall of the prison." Using Protestant Christianity's most important normative source, the Bible, Griffith argues that prisons nowhere in the scriptures are presented as necessary institutions, vehicles of divine will, grace, or even judgment. Prisons, he says with adversarial vigor, are not simply "one of the many social institutions that may be more or less effective in pursuing the various goals assigned them."[40] No, they are, according to Griffith, identical in spirit and practice to the violence and murder they pretend to combat.

We might recall the psalmist of Hebrew scriptures who offered up lament alongside "prisoners in misery and in irons" and dwelling in darkness (Ps. 107:10), or another psalmist who urged us not to neglect God's own, not to despise "his own that are in bonds" (Ps. 69:33). The prisons, insists Griffith, function in the Scriptures as symbols of the power of death toward which both the law and gospel of God are adversaries. Prison cells of confinement and death are like the entrance holes to Sheol and the underworld. Indeed, today's prison vernacular seems to bear witness to the biblical portrayal: prisoners refer to the intensive-control units of maximum security in today's prisons as the hole.

Echoing the themes of the anti-imperial gospel of Paul and Jesus, Griffith and others have reminded us that the church was born amid the imprisoned and lived on the edge of constant threat or suffering of confinement. As we already noted, Karl Barth, in a sermon preached in Basel, Switzerland, told listening prisoners that "the first Christian community" was that between Christ and the crucified prisoners with him.[41]

Given the Scriptures' near-total adversarial stance regarding prisons, given their tendency to see the prison as symbol of the death power that the gospel contests and redresses, and given also early Christians' suffering in prisons, Griffith makes clear the adversarial stance Christians must take, and he makes reference to Jesus to do it. When Jesus of Nazareth proclaimed "liberty for the captives," this was not just a mere metaphor. Surely it was not just an isolated saying. No, against the backdrop of the whole of Scripture, "it stands as a renunciation of the power of death."[42]

Griffith's text shows not only the trait of adversarial politics but also the penchant for dramatic action. In the first place, he himself has been a long-time activist contesting prisons and other social injustices by putting his body on the line. He has, by his own admission, not "done time" in the truly horrific conditions of many of today's confined doing long sentences, but he has had his jail time.[43]

Most striking, however, is the way Griffith's text displays dramatic action in his call to a certain kind of creativity that is lived on the personal level of confronting violent crime. Griffith concludes his text with various examples of activists against prison injustice who themselves become victims or near-victims of crime. Drawing from several examples—a potential home robbery and rape, a potential stabbing, another robbery—Griffith highlights persons who used various strategies of "evoking wonder" in their would-be assailants, and so effectively avoided the criminal act with which they were threatened.[44]

Responding to a potential crime in a way that evokes wonder in the violator is a creative way to break the power of fear and anger that are often so destructive. One woman quickly asked a home intruder what time it was, noted a contrast between his watch and her own clock, started a human conversation, and offered him a couch to sleep on downstairs.[45] Griffith gives other examples as well, showing how imaginative retorts and responses evoke wonder and defuse situations of criminal conflict. This is, for Griffith, to "live the fall of the prison," because it contests the whole ideology upon which prisons are founded, that is, that we as common citizens have no defense from crime apart from the unimaginative phone call to police and the warehousing and imprisonment of threatening people. Griffith points to the power of creativity, of imaginatively evoked wonder, of dramatic action. To see this is to see through the usual ideological justifications for massive prison construction.

Griffith does not, however, discuss the way an adversarial politics and dramatic action fuse on the level of the peoples' movements we need today. To see this emphasis better, we might turn to the effort being forged by longtime social activist and Christian pastor Reverend Lucius Walker. He and his organization, the Interreligious Foundation for Community Organizing (IFCO), are organizing a movement against the present prison-industrial complex that ably reflects the adversarial and dramatically active elements of the theatrics of counterterror we need. Walker is a Christian pastor who preaches routinely in a New York City church, but his IFCO as an interreligious and broadly public movement appropriately does not foreground Christian perspectives. Nevertheless, because he and his organization mobilize peoples' movements with an adversarial politics and dramatic action, the basic rubric of a way of the cross is present here in an exemplary fashion. Followers of the Galilean Jesus would do well to lend support to his group.

IFCO manifests a definite adversarial stance vis-à-vis today's prison archipelago. Their most recent efforts are not grounded in typical prison reform actions. Most of such actions, historically, have simply strengthened the endurance of prisons and their devastating effects.[46] No, in the manner of an adversarial stance demanded by the theatrics of counterterror today, Walker has forged a position that challenges the entire country's reliance on professionalized, corporate-guided prison terror. In a letter calling for new action, Walker has referred to today's prison buildup as nonjustifiable. It is, he says, a "malignant disease that is eating away at the core of our entire society."[47]

In the context of the people's movement Walker projects, it is the dramatic action that he and IFCO propose that is especially striking. His action, as in the case of Griffith, is one that again marshals creativity and evokes wonder as a way of mobilizing broad public interest in transformation. Unlike Griffith, however, the focus falls more on foregrounding a broad, social movement.

Walker and IFCO are organizing, at this writing, an inspiring and potentially quite dramatic movement amid Gulag America, a movement they have named Prison Justice Caravans. In its work over the past two decades, IFCO has used the caravan approach as a mode of sending across the United States cadres of activists, who then go on to take supplies and friendship to refugee populations in Central America and to the embargoed population in Cuba. Now, they plan to take this concept and apply it to a wide array of issues that bear upon the criminal injustice suffered by so many. Two to four caravans will snake their way across prison-land America for a five-day encampment in Washington, D.C., to culminate and consolidate their witness to a new vision amid present prison injustice.

The caravans traversing the land give powerful, dramatic expression to the adversarial stance against prisons today. The drama will be heightened and sustained by the presentation of children and parents of the needlessly imprisoned, including a mother of a son among the five hundred on Texas' death row; the father of a child killed in the Oklahoma City bombing who speaks out against the death penalty; clergy, teachers, and laity challenging the ethical foundations of our lock 'em up and throw away the key policies; and labor activists challenging the no-pay or low-pay prison labor practices of today.

Putting these people and many others on the road caravan-style is a kind of dramatic action that truly helps to build a theatrics of counterterror. It remains to be seen if these caravans can steal the show, to constitute an alternative spectacle that interrupts and reorients the media and pundits of the day, whose racial stereotypes and get tough on crime rhetoric often produce the major show for people on our airwaves.

It is the No More Prisons! movement, however, that is already under way and displays most forcefully the fusion of adversarial politics and dramatic action in organized political movement. It features only the slightest of connection to any Christian church influence, yet its contribution to a theatrics of counterterror is significant. Christians who really care about countering today's prison injustice must make common cause with the impious Galileans taking on empire in this striking movement.

No More Prisons! is a special project designed to mobilize youth and others around the problems posed by today's prison industry. It is a part of an umbrella organization called the Prison Moratorium Project (PMP). The PMP was founded in 1995 when progressive student activists associated with the Democratic Socialists of America met with former prisoners in the Harlem-based Community Justice Center. The PMP became a youth-led grassroots organization dedicated to halting prison expansion, empowering youth and other constituencies, and advocating for a fair, effective, and humane criminal justice system.

Clearly this movement is expressive of an adversarial politics. No More Prisons! (NMP), working within the PMP, advises its volunteers to argue for the position that "building more prisons will not significantly reduce crime," and that "there are alternatives which work at least as well as prison."[48] Its analysis of the prison-industrial complex makes clear that the system is not simply one that sports imperfections; more seriously, it is so flawed that a moratorium is in order and it is time to say that prisons should be built no more.

The NMP movement has carried its adversarial posture into the realm of building movements. It seeks to express creativity in its very way of organizing, which puts the emphasis on "people educating one another" and building "non-traditional collaborations" (for example, youth–adult, criminal justice activists–labor activists). They have collaborated with a variety of associations of youth and students in California and New York.[49] Their collaborations have included a project called Education Not Incarceration, which exposes the shift in funding of many states from educational needs to prison warehousing. Most recently, NMP and PMP have launched a campaign called No Punishment for Profit, which exposes particular corporations whose design on profit contributes to prison expansion.

The heart and soul of No More Prisons!, however, has become its recent release of a compact disc (CD) publicized by a tour, and which has also been coordinated with a book written by William Upski Wimsatt, *No More Prisons.*[50] Although his book has only a few chapters directly on the issues of prison injustice, Wimsatt coordinated its publication with the release of a CD of hip-hop music out of a conviction that "if there is one evil force at a state and national level that can unite Americans of different races and classes, across sex, religion and sexual orientation, it's the expansion of the prison industry."[51] Wimsatt is happy to link his "punk rock book publisher" (Soft Skull Press) with the hip-hop label Raptivism because he sees it as a way to support the growing grassroots movement in this country against the prison system, which he likens to the movements against the Vietnam War.[52]

Indeed, the link from book to hip-hop is significant. Hip-hop is now the musical genre that outsells all others, recently surpassing the popular country music category.[53] Moreover, hip-hop, in spite of its compromises with commercial instincts, has from the beginning been about an organizing impulse, an active element. Wimsatt recalls the four elements of hip-hop listed by Afrika Bambaataa in the early 1970s: MCing (rap), b-boying (dance), writing (graffiti), and Djing. All were rooted in the foundation of Bambaataa's founding of the Zulu Nation, a youth organization. "The *Active Element* has been the foundation of hip-hop."[54]

Those of us committed to developing creatively and dramatically our adversarial stance toward today's prison system must acknowledge and actively support the No More Prisons! movement. It is forged and led by many of those most vulnerable to and victimized by today's prisons. The No More Prisons! hip-hop CD features over seventy artists. At this writing in 2000, the artists are touring against prisons not only to give concerts but also to raise awareness and provide workshops and educational opportunities about the prison industry. The present Raptivist tour is visiting forty cities. The magazine *Rap Pages* announces, "This will be the spark that reignites a conscious movement."[55]

No matter how extensive the movement proves to be, those seeking a vigorous movement displaying the kind of theatrics of counterterror needed today amid the government-led and corporation-sponsored prison boom in lockdown America need the hip-hop movement of No More Prisons! The adversarial and dramatic Lee Griffith needs it. Reverend Walker and IFCO need it. All in the churches and any would-be impious Galileans can only come closer to their goals by making common cause with No More Prisons!

The No More Prisons! movement is in fact reaching out to churches and other religious institutions.[56] NMP is well aware that churches (African American, Latina/o, white progressive churches and synagogues) have had prison ministries and "concern," but often not forthright activism. The hip-hop-oriented NMP knows also that many of these religious institutions have qualms about the entire musical genre of rap and hip-hop. Nevertheless, NMP is reaching out to them. Churches, especially, representing all traditions, must transcend differences of musical taste and moralist concerns about offensive lyrics (concerns that are only partly justified) and embrace a musical genre such as raptivism, and thereby display some of the most powerful virtues of anti-imperial orientations of Paul and Jesus, that is, of any Christians who dare to follow the Galilean Jesus through lockdown America and *Pax Americana.*

The place to which the raptivist movement of No More Prisons! invites us all is to "a real place" that even these "raptivists" dare to call "a sacred place."[57] From the perspective of this book, at least, they are right to employ the language of the sacred. In the space(s) opened up by this kind of movement, we will find part of the power of the executed God to rival the forces of lockdown America. From those spaces, we participate in the unleashing of the greater, deeper, and wider power we need now for rivaling the executing ways that lockdown America builds up against us.

The Death of the Death Penalty

We come again to the death penalty, which I have already treated as the "paradigmatic action" of the political theatrics of terror in lockdown America.[58] It is these state-sanctioned, ritual killings that dramatize the spectral awe of state power that officials take to themselves and by which they try to create a generalized compliance with imperial ethos. All the more is it crucial for the state to ritually display the specter of its power over life and death, when surplus populations and dissident activists may be especially prone to challenge state power. A theatrics that counters today's political theatrics of the state needs a way of the cross through lockdown America that can take on the death penalty, dreaming and working for a time when it is no more, a time when no more prisons means also no more capital punishment.

The organizing effort against the death penalty today is made up of movements distinguishable from one another in terms of two kinds of focus. First, there are abolitionist and moratorium movements, focusing on the general reality of the death penalty and the need to abolish it or to call a moratorium on executions. These movements feature abolitionist societies in different states, such as Pennsylvania Abolitionists United Against the Death Penalty. It includes various groups in religious institutions that labor to stop the death penalty. Most prominent here are the Quakers, whose efforts to end capital punishment have been expressed in the tireless work of the American Friends Service Committee. Various human rights organizations also have put forward strong campaigns to end the death penalty, most notably Amnesty International, which has lobbied the world over for the eradication of capital punishment and in 1999 ratcheted up its efforts against the United States' stubborn practice of the death penalty. All of these organizations work out of a sense that the death penalty is wrong in some fundamental sense; for example, it does not deter; it condones violence and feeds a vicious cycle of violence; it violates the Universal Declaration of Human Rights; it is racist, biased with respect to the poor, unfairly used against juveniles, people with mental retardation, and the innocent; it is unconstitutional (cruel and unusual) in the United States. Some religious groups argue that it is a social sin violating tenets of religious faith, and so on.

There are other movements, however, with another kind of focus, deriving from advocacy for specific prisoners on death row. These advocacy-based movements should not be seen as contrary to or separate from the more general abolitionist and moratorium movements. In fact, successful organizing against the death penalty usually requires the mutual interaction of general calls for abolition or a moratorium, on the one hand, with a particular advocacy for individuals among the thirty-six hundred facing execution on U.S. death rows, on the other. Several of the current Web sites that support the movements against the death penalty display the two foci of the struggle: foregrounding arguments and criticisms of the death penalty as a general practice and highlighting the particular struggle of named individuals on death row.[59]

In the last decade of the twentieth century, there came to prominence a movement that united organizations with an abolitionist focus with those based on advocacy of particular cases. The movement was one of advocacy for one death row prisoner, Mumia Abu-Jamal, whose case and writings have already been referred to in this book. The people's movement for Abu-Jamal was one of advocacy for this particular figure, but it was a kind of advocacy that reignited the vigor of broader abolitionist efforts against the death penalty. The rise of the movement for Abu-Jamal, beginning in 1994 and continuing into the next century, went hand in hand with the increasing vigor of movements against the death penalty. By mid-year 2000, Francis X. Clines was writing in the *New York Times* that the movement for Mumia Abu-Jamal was clearly flourishing and entwined with a reinvigorated movement to organize against the death penalty.[60]

It is no accident that there sprang up a vigorous synergy between the particular case of Abu-Jamal and the general abolitionist movement on behalf of many. Abu-Jamal is a skilled communicator and was a practicing print and radio journalist before his arrest and sentencing. Even though many, ranging from Amnesty International to *American Lawyer* magazine, branches of the NAACP and the ACLU, have contested the fairness of his original trial, Abu-Jamal himself rarely writes about his own case. Beginning with his 1995 book, *Live from Death Row,* and continuing across the pages of two other books and over four hundred columns and essays (compiled within Internet sources), Abu-Jamal has specialized in exposing a large number of issues and the general structure of institutionalized violence in the United States, of which his own case is but one example.

PEN/Faulkner award–winning novelist John Edgar Wideman commented on the uniqueness of Abu-Jamal's struggle in the introduction he wrote for Abu-Jamal's 1995 book. It is a peculiar kind of "uniqueness," writes Wideman, because it mobilizes meanings beyond its own sphere. In this respect, Wideman contrasted Abu-Jamal's story and witness with many of the "classic" slave narratives that sell so well. In these latter: "The fate of one black individual is foregrounded, removed from the network of systemic relationships connecting, defining, determining, undermining all American lives. This manner of viewing black lives at best ignores, at worst reinforces, an apartheid status quo. . . . The idea of a collective, intertwined fate recedes."[61] The contribution of Abu-Jamal's voice, whether on radio or in print, is that it functions to question the narratives about individualized black mythic heroes that decorate bookstores today. Abu-Jamal has long been termed "the voice of the voiceless," and about the character of this voice, Wideman continues: "His essays are important as departure and corrective. He examines the place where he is—*prison,* his status—*prisoner, black man,* but refuses to accept the notion of difference and separation these labels project. . . . Although dedicated to personal liberation, he envisions that liberation as partially dependent on the collective fate of black people."[62]

It is this capacity that has meant that advocacy mobilized around Abu-Jamal's case has had effects that ripple outward to throw attention on the large numbers of others who are on death row but also onto a whole host of issues that concern the violence done by criminal justice systems today and economic exploitation in general. If one peruses Abu-Jamal's many essays, one encounters writings on the many themes characterizing lockdown America (capital punishment, police brutality, the prison-industrial complex, paramilitary policing, unfair court processes), but also on the politics of twenty-first-century *Pax Americana* (the recent bombings of Iraq and Serbia; the crime bills; the cuts in social services for the poor; U.S. callousness about the struggle of the Maya Zapatistas in Chiapas, Mexico; the bias of mainstream media in the United States; and more).

The growth of the movement for Abu-Jamal, arguably the strongest ever seen for a prisoner on America's death row, has galvanized movements to end the death penalty in this country. Moreover, I argue that the movement for Abu-Jamal has been effective because it carries the key features of a theatrics of counterterror, that is, not only is it an organized people's movement, it also includes an adversarial politics in resistance to imperial state terror, and it clearly has a penchant for dramatic action. In embodying a theatrics of counterterror, those in the movement for Abu-Jamal, which include a growing number of religious and Christian participants,[63] can be counted among those we have identified in this chapter as impious Galileans.

The adversarial politics of the movement for Abu-Jamal is evident in the rhetoric of many of his writings and that of activists in the movement for him. There is, for example, the language about the "Rehnquistian Court," referring to the U.S. Supreme Court, with Chief Justice William H. Rehnquist, a court that has allowed the resurgence of capital punishment and paved the way for some of the most vigorous supports for unchecked law enforcement and criminal justice proceedings. There are the references to "State power,"[64] "the system," "white supremacism," and a "ruling class" in the United States.[65] This is markedly different from many in the abolitionist movement generally, whose discourse of opposition to the death penalty is marked by a tendency to see capital punishment as a barbaric holdover, strangely persisting in an otherwise civilized order. Abu-Jamal's well-chosen words make clear that the death penalty is inscribed in a larger social order that is also marked by barbarity. His words, and those of the movement for him, regularly throw the focus of resistance on the entire state system that maintains the ritual killing conducted on death row U.S.A.

Abu-Jamal's adversarial politics are clear, even though at times he can argue on behalf of police officers who have been wrongfully convicted.[66] Exemplary of his adversarial politics, focused at the violations of U.S. empire building, we might cite this portion of his work: "Imagine the most violent nation on earth, the heir of Indian and African genocide, the *only* nation ever to drop an atomic bomb on a civilian population, the world's biggest arms dealer, the country that napalmed over ten million people in Vietnam to 'save' it from communism, the world's biggest jailer, waving the corpse of [Martin Luther] King, calling for nonviolence!"[67] With this kind of language, the movement for Abu-Jamal has become a comprehensive movement against not only the death penalty but also against the assumptions and structures of all of lockdown America's draconian so-called criminal justice procedures and against the imperial pretensions of *Pax Americana.* This has enabled the movement for Abu-Jamal to function as the epicenter for a wide diversity of movements working on key structural problems in the United States.[68] This has been strikingly evident in the way demonstrators for Abu-Jamal have constituted one of the strongest contingents among protestors marching against corporate dominance in the year 2000.

The penchant for dramatic action is markedly evident in what the movement has become as a whole, as well as in particular strategies it has embraced. As a whole, the movement has pushed itself onto the level of media spectacle in a way that death row prisoners' cases rarely do. The entire movement has become a kind of counterspectacle, challenging the political theatrics of terror. The usual spectacles glorify state power and its political theatrics, or they distract with sports, comedy, the lives of the rich and famous. Here, in the movement for Abu-Jamal, is a death row prisoner getting publicity and support from famous people, Nobel laureates, world leaders, and others. Here is a prisoner in a faraway rural corner of Pennsylvania who has had thousands of people turn out to support his quest for a new trial every year for a six-year period. Abu-Jamal has been invited to send commencement addresses to graduating classes at four of the nation's colleges (Evergreen State College in 1999; in 2000, at Antioch College, Kent State University, and at Merrill College of the University of California, Santa Cruz; and more are being planned at this writing). All this interrupts the spectral power of the theatrics of terror, which puts so many citizens in a kind of trance that permits power to have its way in defining who is respectable and who is not.

The Mumia movement has built its own theater, in other words, a theater of counterterror. It is a militant but peaceful people's movement for marshaling a theatrics to counter the terrors of lockdown America, an America that has built itself up, in part, by a series of law and order spectacles or other kinds of shows designed to distract the populace. The Mumia movement has broken into the popular symbolics of the spectacular media and has presented the claims to humanity and justice of a death row prisoner who has also succeeded in getting a hearing for his more comprehensive critique of lockdown America and *Pax Americana.* All this is no small feat.

If the movement as a whole has created this kind of counterspectacle, this is because it also embraces dramatic action in many other ways. Artists, both within prisons and without, have been vigorous in developing their poetry, music, and painting in support of his case and to highlight the comprehensive issues he has analyzed.[69] These efforts have been continually cycled in and out of media outlets.

Activists for Abu-Jamal have undertaken a wide array of dramatic actions through civil disobedience throughout the nation and world. The first such action was by youth with Refuse 'n Resist!, who blocked traffic in downtown Philadelphia in 1995. Since then, activists the world over have occupied banks, corporations, embassies, museums, and government buildings in order to dramatize their organizing efforts to stop Abu-Jamal's execution. On July 3, 1999, nearly one hundred activists were arrested after closing down the Liberty Bell in Philadelphia, many of them ringing bells and chanting, "Let freedom ring for Mumia!" In February of 2000, another mass action of nearly two hundred people occurred in front of the U.S. Supreme Court, as it deliberated on important cases relating to death penalty litigation in this country. Activists sat and lay down in the street in front of the building, or mounted the Supreme Court steps with banners saying, "Stop the Racist Death Penalty/New Trial for Mumia!"

This embrace of dramatic action—ranging from regular use of the peoples' various creative arts, to the dramatics of bodily confrontation in civil disobedience—accounts for much of the success of the Mumia movement. It also makes the movement a primary embodiment of the theatrics of counterterror needed today. Being a peoples' movement with an adversarial politics, as well as one of dramatic action, it is also a group with all the marks of those impious Galileans who find themselves wielding a theatrics to counter imperial terror in the tradition of the Galilean Jesus and the anti-imperialist Paul.

Indeed, as the movement moves into the twenty-first century, a growing number of Christian clergy and members of churches have dared to link their faith in the Galilean Jesus to this growing movement of impious Galileans. In April 2000, "Call for a New Trial for Mumia Abu-Jamal" was featured in the pages of *The Christian Century*, featuring many Christian leaders and members. The African Methodist Episcopal denominational publication *The Christian Recorder* featured the same call as a full-page ad in April 17, 2000. The call, signed by one hundred church leaders and members, contained this statement about Abu-Jamal:

> We have chosen him in our demand for justice, because his uniquely inspiring voice and insistent call for justice—on behalf of the poor, the imprisoned, the marginalized—carries special authority, coming as it does from one in prison and on death row. . . . Our faiths mandate that we stand with Mumia Abu-Jamal in his struggle for justice for all, even as he is punished in retaliation by the authorities for his uncompromising stand.[70]

Whether this movement will be successful in saving Mumia Abu-Jamal's life, many still cannot say for sure. As an activist myself in that movement, I refuse to articulate any other outcome other than the release of Mumia Abu-Jamal so that he may join us in what will be a long and ongoing struggle in resisting, redirecting, and reorganizing power amid and against the forces of lockdown America and *Pax Americana*.

Regardless of the exact nature of future developments, it is clear that the Mumia movement has invigorated the movement against the death penalty with a new strength. Its power to do that lies, I believe, in the success of grassroots organizers to put in place a people's movement on death penalty issues, which also fuses a courageous and cogent adversarial politics with a flair for imaginative dramatic action. Because of the work of this movement, the death of the death penalty is brought nearer to hand; and a broad landscape of social flourishing can be seen beyond the lockdown America that looms so large at the present time.

Conclusion: People on the Move with an Executed God

In the face of lockdown America, much more organizing of peoples' movements will be necessary. These movements will not come forth without work. Many people will be given to despair and resignation. Champions of a domestic realpolitik will insist that the police are too many, too strong, and too well equipped for people to challenge. The prisons will seem too massive and so thoroughly intertwined with the warp and woof of the United States in the twenty-first century that it will seem ludicrous to even think No More Prisons! Criminals and murderers will always be scary, and politicians will feed the fear of the populace. Thus, it will be tempting to keep on trusting the system's executioners.

The way of the executed God, however, allows the executioner neither the last word nor the final act. The way of the executed God, the way of the cross through lockdown America, is still under way, still making a way. Whether in the mother of the slain son, Anthony Baez, rising another day to speak at the next meeting and rally against police brutality, whether in Yoruba priestesses pouring libations to remember the deaths of youth of color slain at urban crossroads in the United States, whether in the courage of a few protesting pastors who kneel to pray in front of traffic on Wall Street, whether in a Mumia Abu-Jamal who pens his 451st treatise from an 8 1/2 ft. x 10 ft. death row cell, whether in the next movement of coalitions gathering to hold up Abu-Jamal's name and cause—in all these, the finality of the state's executing ways is challenged. Those who pray, worship, and act in the way of the executed God know that the days of exploitative imperial power are numbered. At best, today's empire is an interim state; it is not final. It is only a frail challenger to the greater, deeper, and wider way of the executed God.

epilogue
Christian Living: Toward a Fullness of Rebellion

> [Rebellion's] most profound logic is not the logic of destruction; it is the logic of creation.
> —Albert Camus, *The Rebel*

This book, *The Executed God,* has abounded with the rhetoric of opposition. Opening with a lament regarding Christendom's betrayal of faith in the Jesus of Galilee and Golgotha, I moved to a critique of lockdown America as a political theatrics of terror, seeking to show how it serves interests of empire and *Pax Americana.*

Indeed, the rhetoric of opposition was especially strong when, throughout Part Two, I presented the way of the cross (with its three dimensions of adversarial politics, dramatic action, and organizing movements) as a theatrics that can counter terror. The way of the cross, it may seem, all takes place under the sign of resistance or of a rebellion against lockdown and empire.

Is Christian living thus a complex practice of negation, a nay-saying, only a practice of continually positioning ourselves against things? Does not Christian living entail more than this? What, we might ask in a more positive vein, do Christians live *for?*

I close this book by responding to these questions. I will not do so, however, by simply identifying some positive traits, some positive sense of the good to arrange on some other side, in order to create balance for an otherwise allegedly negative situation.

No, resistance and rebellion, especially pursued along the way of the cross, reveals its good from within the process of resistance. Resistance is not some evil to be counterposed to the good. Resistance as struggle amid institutionalized evil of our time is a point of suffering that is dialectically related to the good. Resistance, when embraced fully, is a practice of negation that yet expresses, embodies, and gives rise to practices of affirmation and celebration. The good, the positive that is worth celebrating, is not something other than the practice of resistance, not some alternative to the theatrics of counterterror. The good is revealed by exploring the various textures and implications of rebellion, which are entailed in the way of the executed God.

So it is that Christian living can be viewed as the fullness of rebellion. It would take another book to examine this fullness in its many dimensions. In this brief epilogue, though, permit me to point toward some basic features of this fullness of rebellion.

Rebellion and Revelation

The affirmation and celebration that are entailed in resistance can be seen in investigations into the experience of rebellion. Albert Camus' 1956 book, *The Rebel*, still stands as one of the most thorough and eloquent treatises on rebellion. His analysis makes clear how inaccurate it is to see rebellion as purely negative, something that is only oppositional. Quite to the contrary, there is, as Camus shows throughout the work, a fruitfulness to rebellion, a creativity, a power to birth the good we most need to understand and withstand the terrors of inhuman conditions.

Rebellion, in other words, has a revelatory capacity. As revelatory, rebellion initiates certain insights, and unveils a fullness of meanings that go beyond what is seen as a negative act of rebellion. The kind of Christian living entailed in a practice of resistance or in the way of the cross must acknowledge this revelatory capacity of rebellion in both senses, as initiating insights and as unveiling a fullness of meanings.

Why is rebellion an initiator of insight? Why does it have a certain priority in the order of human insight? This is a difficult question to answer because in several parts of Camus' book he suggests that rebellion is not prior. There seems, in other words, to be something before, or more basic than, rebellion. Camus refers, for example, to the "human condition" that rebellion protests or to some "concept of a complete unity" that functions as an ideal to "motivate" rebellion.[1] In another place, Camus writes that rebellion does not have itself as its own source but rather has something else as its "fountainhead," something he calls a "principle of superabundant activity and energy."[2] This all suggests that rebellion is not first, not the initiator. For Camus, however, it is our being in a state of rebellion that creates awareness of these prior conditions. Any prior knowledge (about the world, God, nature, humans, or whatever) is not really had until one rebels. It sounds like a contradiction, but Camus is saying that whatever it is that exists before rebellion is not known until after you rebel. Thus Camus can insist on the initiating role of rebellion, as initiating all insight and revelation, without claiming that there is nothing before rebellion. Rebel first, and then you will know what was there to see and enjoy all along.

This book has worked with something of this sensibility about rebellion's initiating role. It has worked largely from a stance of resistance, which can look purely negative but now can be discussed as revealing something more positive. We must ask now about what, precisely, is it that is revealed. We can answer this question by returning, yet again, to the dimensions of the theatrics of counterterror, to see what each might reveal about human flourishing and Christian living.

Rebellion Today and the Rising of the Executed God

Rebellion today—especially as it is lived out as participation in organized peoples' movements, as an adversarial politics against imperial oppression and as dramatic action—entails a positive flourishing. In this final section, I want to sketch what that flourishing might look like, and I will interpret this flourishing as a rising of the executed God, a kind of resurrection, if you wish to use that term, that can become real for those working along the rebellious way of the cross through lockdown America.

Many will find what follows to be a rather minimalist notion of resurrection, but the writer of the Gospel of Mark could be charged in a like manner. That writer left readers with little more than an inspiring report from an empty tomb that Jesus had gone on back to Galilee, to that place crossed by empires but always generating rebellion. That may seem like less than what most Christians have looked for in their resurrection faith, but given what Christian resisters are up against today, Mark's witness to a certain undying quality in people to return to "Galilee," to a place of ever new struggle, may be a lot. It may be everything.

Organizing Movements: A New Social Life

What is the flourishing we might note amid rebellion's work in the organizing of peoples' movements? I suggest that what is to be found is a distinctive way of having a social life. It is characterized by forging communal interaction and love, in a social milieu marked by the vigorous and emphatic pursuit of justice. The drive toward an alternative good practice, designed to rival the injustices of lockdown America, leaves a distinctive mark upon those involved in that struggle and upon the ways they seek and craft relations of love.

Love in its many modes—as equal regard, respect, affection, friendship, the eros of mutual sexual attraction—can be found in nearly all sites of our social and political order. Along the way of the cross that practices a theatrics of rebellious counterterror, however, these adventures in love and loving receive a distinctive focus by reason of their intense relation to contemporary struggles for justice. Given the enormity of the challenges faced along the way of the cross, love within the community of struggle will be challenged, intensified, goaded on to craft modes of human relation that in other settings might not be considered appropriate, necessary, or possible.

Again, I cannot here go into this in depth, exploring relations between love and justice generally or into the new modes of being family, of forging diverse friendship, of the many modes of relating—all of which arise in the communities of struggle that embody a theatrics of counterterror. Suffice it to say that when love must flourish amid the concrete communal tasks of organizing peoples' movements, focused on challenging the kind of systemic violence that abounds today, then it is born anew. Then one is in an adventure of love and loving that entails not just resistance and rebellion but also an honoring and affirming of love.

In short, in the organizing movements against lockdown America, as in other grassroots political movements, living out our rebellion means being challenged and invited to nothing less than new modes of love and relation. Challenging the system as fundamentally as these movements do, frees the participants from the forms of love and relation that are dependent upon a political order buttressed by dynamics of lockdown and repression. Participants in movements organized for justice amid imperial lockdown will be sent into an invigorating search for new modes of love and relation that often are not available when one is ensconced in the established orders that are dependent upon imperial force.

We need not fool ourselves into thinking that the matrix of struggle is some new locale where love can always work and relations achieve some ideal state. Far from it. In fact, it may well be the case that the rigors of struggle subvert relationships or make it necessary to lay certain partnerships aside and shoulder certain burdens of aloneness. That being said, there is nothing about rebellion and struggle against institutionalized repression that should mean the end of good loving, good friendships, and community.

If, as Alice Walker writes, "love is *the* revolutionary emotion,"[3] it may grow into its most true and powerful forms when cultivated in movements of resistance to reigning injustices. If, as poet Martín Espada muses, "Rebellion is the circle of a lover's hands / that must keep moving / always weaving,"[4] then movements of resistance and rebellion may be the valuable spaces where friends and lovers are challenged to grow continually toward their fullest mobile communions.

Living along the way of the cross, the way of the executed God, which situates us in these powerful movements against lockdown America, can be undertaken, then, in the hope of flourishing in new communities and new whole relationships. It is, yes, a process of entering into a set of demanding social practices but in a way where the fullness of rebellion might blossom as new ways to love.

Adversarial Politics: A New Mystery in Struggle

Especially in the dimension of adversarial politics, we may discern nothing but resistance and rebellion that is all negative in nature. What might be the mode of human flourishing, something to be affirmed and celebrated, which is revealed in such a politics?

To begin with, recall that the kind of adversarial politics presented in this volume is one that is resistant to empire, to the ordered peace imposed perhaps by a Rome or by some other transnational power that poses as if it is the only existing order. Empire presents itself as the most powerful order and is often seen as such in the minds of many. It appears so formidable that it becomes the given order of things. It is seemingly unchallengeable.

Participants who embrace an adversarial politics, by positioning themselves as adversaries to empire, evoke a greater power than the one many collectively assume to be the greatest. In doing so, the rebels' struggle must occur in a transcending mode. It presumes a power that is somehow more than all powers known. Yet, unlike many notions of transcendence, which orient us to some plane above history, politics, and culture, this transcending mode is more radical precisely because it goes down to the roots, is more concrete. It positions itself in empire's own domain (of history, politics, and culture) and finds there a greater power.

In resistance amid and against empire, there is available to Christian living something worth celebrating indeed. You can taste it and sense it in the bodily actions of civil disobedience when protestors raise their chant, "Ain't no power like the power of the people / And the power of the people don't stop!" It is also known when in the middle of the night, or at the end of a long workday, a resister rises to write one more press release, to make a few more phone calls, to stuff a few more envelopes about the next march, to send one more fax transmission for widening the network of resistance, or gets the inspiration for just the right symbol to paint on tomorrow's banner.

In these ways and more, those adhering to an adversarial politics are driven to invoke a transcending power, one that is marked not by spatial transcendence (that moves away from or outside of history, politics, and culture) but by a qualitative one (moving into a new configuration within history, politics, and culture).

There will be no challenging the powers of lockdown America without a countervailing power. The practice of an adversarial politics invokes that countervailing power. It is this power, always a mystery to the established ones who live by domination and exploitation, that is the greater power this text has described as the way of God. More particularly, as revealed in the one from Nazareth who ever returns to a Galilean resistance in spite of execution on a Roman cross, it is the mysterious power of the executed God.

As with transcendence, so the term *mysterious* is not used by me here to catapult us onto some suprahuman terrain or transpose us into some supernatural domain. No, the mystery abides in a new qualitative configuration of forces that rival imperial power in a mode that the given order cannot fathom.

To experience this transcending and mysterious power is a mode of human flourishing into which the practitioner of an adversarial politics is drawn. His or her adversarial politics, then, for all its this-worldly risk and conflict, is a terrain upon which the deepest wells of spiritual power open up to us, brimful of a new kind of transcendence and mystery. The rebellion traced by the theatrics of counterterror, especially in its dimension of adversarial politics, is hardly only a practice of negation. It is to be surprised by, to invoke, to need, to bask in that greater power of which empires know not. Ultimately, it leads protestors to go dancing, because they know they are released by the greater, deeper, and wider powers, the ones that liberate them from the weighty bonds of oppressive worlds.

Dramatic Action: Toward Festivals of Resistance

Finally, turn now to the dimension of a theatrics of counterterror that I have termed dramatic action. Dramatic action, too, is not only a matter of acting up against something. It is not just a practice seeking to negate the powers of empire. It is also a portal through which dramatic actors enter a mode of human flourishing. In particular, it is a way to discover and nurture an aesthetic delight. Especially as I have construed dramatic action in this text, as both confrontational bodily action and as a creativity to birth new worlds, the actor is taken into an aesthetic realm. The movement of rebellion and resistance, when presented as theatrics, steeps us in a realm of aesthetic celebration.

This is crucial because it gives to the struggle for justice a component of play, a ludic quality (from the Latin, *ludere,* to play). Unlike many postmodern aspects of the ludic, where play, difference, and carnival proliferate, often creating sophisticated *in*difference regarding systemic oppression, the play I advocate here is generated by the dramatic actions that counter empire. This doesn't just make play serious (although there always is an element of seriousness in play[5]), it also allows play to blossom into forms that spill over into all sectors of human social life. In contrast to usual patterns that consign play and the arts to the margins of society (as mere entertainment, distraction, ornament, as belonging to enclaves of classical and elite so-called good taste), the play of dramatic actions that challenge empire belongs potentially to all sectors of society.

Indeed, it is especially necessary to invoke strategies of play and all of its creative art forms because the present global empire is working through a colonization of the arts. It appropriates them as new modes of control and reinforcement of the ways of empire. Use of the arts for repression and bonding between elites is nowhere more evident, perhaps, than in the way many poor neighborhoods in urban waterfront areas have been closed up, with their residents moved out, so that arts and entertainment complexes, funded by corporations, can be developed for catering to higher-income groups. It is strategically important, therefore, that ways of political struggle against empire seize play and aesthetic delight to be celebrated within movements of resistance.

Beyond the value of play in strategies of resistance, for which I have already argued, my main emphasis here is upon the fruitfulness that accrues to resisters themselves, when they are given to play and aesthetic delight. We need more of the kind of sensibility reflected in Elaine Scarry's book *On Beauty and Being Just,* which argues that admiring the beautiful fosters the spirit of justice.[6] This is not always emphasized sufficiently by proponents of political rebellion, whose styles of confrontation often are dominated by disseminating the flyer, making long speeches, or planning the next organizer's meeting, rally, or march. All this, of course, is essential, but without the aesthetic delight, without resistance becoming festival and a scene of play, participants can become stagnant, burned out, unable to galvanize the multitudes they seek. The Maya Zapatistas' penchant for sponsoring festivals of resistance is a healthy instinct and an instructive example. For them, the festival is no mere addendum to real resistance but intrinsic to resistance.

Without creativity, nurtured by our celebrations and festivals of rebellion, resistance and struggle can easily collapse in two very familiar ways. Struggle without dramatic creativity can collapse, on the one hand, into the perennial cynicism and despair that have been the end of many a "rebel." Without creativity, the protracted struggle of the rebel, against often intractable forces, becomes more and more a drudgery that turns hope into a caustic and bitter cynicism. Amid the terrors of lockdown America, especially, despairing cynicism will always be near to hand. We will need drama and dancing more than ever, to help us envision the future we dream of but cannot see on the horizons of our history.

On the other hand, struggle and resistance can also collapse into hyperbole and exaggerated claims about "the revolution around the corner" or about "the fundamental crisis now promoting total change." Radical change might come in our time (we must work and hope for it!), but it cannot be forced. Often hyperbolic claims about revolution are actually the flip-side of burned-out rebels' despairing cynicism. Paradoxically, a celebration of creativity can enable rebels to grow stronger, helping them to taste and envision the revolutionary future in today's celebration without embracing exaggerations that claim revolutionary changes to be more concretely present than they are. So, drama and dance, all the arts practiced now, are crucial to saving rebels as much from their hyperbole as from their cynicism.

If there is some good news on the scene of resistance and rebellion against lockdown America and *Pax Americana* today, it lies in the actions of many youth and others whose demonstrations of bodily confrontation and creative enactment include a cultivation of a whole host of new aesthetic styles of acting up. Such aesthetic sensibilities have always accompanied the successful movements of confrontation,[7] but they are multiplying in movements of resistance that today seek new artistic conventions.[8]

I have already pointed out how musicians and artists of diverse stripes are finding their way into movements of resistance against police brutality, prison injustice, and the death penalty. In addition to these efforts that target lockdown America very specifically, there is now also a wide array of movements resisting the global market that serves corporations more than it does common folk and the environment. These movements, especially, are targeting the First World military powers and the multilateral and transnational monetary powers like the World Trade Organization, the International Monetary Fund, and the World Bank. With a striking array of puppetry, costuming, masks, street dancing, imaginative marching, and more, these young activists shut down the November 1999 meetings of executive powers in Seattle, Washington, and forced the topic of intransigent world poverty into the news media during the meetings of the International Money Fund and World Bank in April 2000. All of these forces, intentionally and forthrightly, are employing a wide array of artistic forms as a mode of resistance and protest. They also focused this aesthetic strategy in the streets of Philadelphia and Los Angeles during protests at the Republican and Democratic National Conventions.

Such a theatrics, with all its new forms, joins a long history of resistance through art. It continues the "theatric imperatives" discovered by many a slave in the United States past who had to find some creative way to forge his or her rage into a resistance that could be survived and be effective.[9] It is an embrace of aesthetic beauty that recalls the inspiring strains of choruses and hymns sung by marchers and protestors in the civil rights struggle of the 1950s and 1960s. It is to remember that struggle is always for bread but "for roses too."[10]

These dramatic actors are not only resisting, they are playing. In this, rebellion is again opening into a fullness in which aesthetic delight is replete with celebration and affirmation. When youth who have just been arrested in front of the Supreme Court for Mumia Abu-Jamal are rocking a full-size bus with their rhythmic chants, tell me that there is not both serious confrontation and delight. Both are most certainly present. Both are as crucial to human flourishing as they are to effective resistance.

It is through this dramatic action, especially as acted out bodily, that actors find that qualitative, anti-imperial power that resides in earth itself, that deeper power of nature that enhances the struggle.[11] Moreover, when actors' creativity is gifted enough to galvanize participants in resistance, then they also unlock that wider power that lives from the creative gathering up of diverse peoples and groups into the struggle.

This opening into aesthetic play through dramatic action is part of the fruitfulness of rebellion, just as much as were the opening into a new kind of transcending power through adversarial politics and the opening into new adventures in love and friendship through organizing peoples' movements.

All this is part of living along the way of the cross. It is part of the human flourishing that is known along the way of the executed God. When and if Christians dare to own this way, through these times of lockdown America, it will become a Christian living. Then, Christians might help foment the fullness of rebellion dramatized by their Galilean Jesus.

notes

Preface

1. Christian Parenti, *Lockdown America: Police and Prisons in the Age of Crisis* (New York: Verso, 1999).

2. Stephen Donziger, ed., *The Real War on Crime: The Report of the National Criminal Justice Commission* (New York: Harper Perennial, 1996), 31.

3. Abu-Jamal is a journalist and author who has been confined on Pennsylvania's death row for nearly twenty years. He languishes there in spite of some of the most impressive and most extensive support ever shown for a confined person in the United States. As I write in the year 2000, he is still sentenced to execution for the 1981 shooting death of a Philadelphia police officer, Daniel Faulkner, even though Amnesty International has issued a formal study calling for a new trial, and both the NAACP and the (ACLU) feature branches that have submitted a special "Memorandum of Law" arguing that Abu-Jamal's death sentence violates the U.S. Constitution. As is typical of Abu-Jamal's many writings (three books and over four hundred essays, from which quotations are made throughout this volume), the quotation at the outset of this Preface focuses our attention not upon his own controversial case, important as it is, but onto issues that impact all of us.

4. Martin Hengel, *Crucifixion* (Philadelphia: Fortress Press, 1977), 32.

5. For the comparison between transnational empire in the United States and Roman empire, which we will discuss in depth in Chapter 3, see Richard Hardt and Antonio Negri, *Empire* (Cambridge, Mass.: Harvard University Press, 2000), 166, 314–16.

6. Karl Barth, *Deliverance to the Captives: Sermons and Prayers* (New York: SCM, 1961), 76–78.

7. Ibid., 76.

8. John Dominic Crossan, *Who Killed Jesus? Exposing the Roots of Anti-Semitism in the Gospel Story of the Death of Jesus* (San Francisco: HarperSanFrancisco, 1996), 133–35; John Dominic Crossan, *The Historical Jesus: The Life of a Mediterranean Jewish Peasant* (San Francisco: HarperSanFrancisco, 1993), 171–72; and Hengel, *Crucifixion,* 49–63, 79.

9. Hengel, *Crucifixion,* 78.

10. Parenti, *Lockdown America,* 163–69.

11. For one insider's account of this brutalization, while working as a prison guard, see Ted Conover, *New Jack: Guarding Sing Sing* (New York: Random House, 2000).

12. Michael Doyle, *Empires* (Ithaca and London: Cornell University Press, 1986), 19.

13. On the contemporary viability of this notion of empire, see Hardt and Negri, *Empire,* xiv.

14. Felix Greene, *The Enemy: Notes on Imperialism and Revolution* (London: Jonathan Cape, 1970), 96.

15. The full quote, given on the opening page of this Preface, is from Leo Tolstoy, *Resurrection,* trans. Louise Maude (Moscow: Progress, 1953), 186. The quoted lines are extracted from a narrative about a visit to a Russian prison made by the leading character, Nekhlyudov.

Introduction: The Executed God

1. James Baldwin, *The Fire Next Time* (New York: Modern Library, 1995), 46.

2. Jürgen Moltmann, *The Crucified God: The Cross of Christ as the Foundation and Criticism of Christian Theology* (Minneapolis: Fortress Press, 1993), 131.

3. Frank Graziano, *Divine Violence: Spectacle, Psychosexuality, and Radical Christianity in the Argentine Dirty War* (Boulder, Colo.: Westview, 1992), 205.

4. Jon Sobrino, *Christology at the Crossroads: A Latin American Approach* (Maryknoll, N.Y.: Orbis, 1976), 72.

5. E. P. Sanders, *Jesus and Judaism* (Philadelphia: Fortress Press, 1985), 332–33.

6. David Tombs, "Crucifixion, State Terror, and Sexual Abuse," *Union Seminary Quarterly Review* 53, nos. 1–2 (1999): 89–109.

7. Albert Camus, *The Rebel: An Essay on Man in Revolt,* trans. Antony Bower (1956; New York: Vintage, 1961), 24.

8. Thomas Aquinas, *Summa Theologica,* pt. 1, ques. 44, art. 1, in Anton C. Pegis, ed., *Basic Writings of Saint Thomas Aquinas,* (New York: Random House, 1945), 1.427.

9. Alice Walker, *The Color Purple* (New York: Harcourt Brace, 1982), 190.

10. On the nature of God-language and its relations to "limits," and as "odd," see Paul Ricoeur in "The Specificity of Religious Language," *Semeia* (1975): 107, 131, and 142. Ramsey's older work is still a lucid and clear treatment of the issues. See Ian Ramsey, *Religious Language* (New York: Macmillan, 1957).

11. Christian Smith, *Disruptive Religion: The Force of Faith in Social Movement Activism* (New York: Routledge, 1996), 1–2.

12. Paul Tillich, *The Shaking of the Foundations* (New York: Scribner's, 1948), 57.

13. For an early discussion of the notion of *Pax Americana,* see Ronald Steel, *Pax Americana: The Cold War Empire the United States Acquired by Accident—and How It Led from Isolation to Global Intervention* (New York: Viking, 1967). While Steel is critical of U.S. imperial formations, he is insufficiently critical in seeing U.S. policy as "accidental" and "benign" in its attaining of imperial power.

14. Michael Doyle, *Empires* (Ithaca and London: Cornell University Press, 1986), 93–97.

15. Paula Fredriksen, *Jesus of Nazareth, King of the Jews: A Jewish Life and the Emergence of Christianity* (New York: Knopf, 1999), 72–73.

16. Ibid., 243.

17. Crossan is surely correct to see this passage in John as a piece of nonhistorical "Christian propaganda," designed to tag all Jews as responsible for Jesus' death, hence, the charge of "Christ-killers." It is also possible to interpret this text, as I do here, as a literary example of the historical tendency of religious elites to deliver an upstart like Jesus over to political authorities. See Crossan, *Who Killed Jesus: Exposing the Roots of Anti-Semitism in the Gospel Story of the Death of Jesus* (San Francisco: HarperSanFrancisco, 1996), 11–13, 151–52.

18. Jürgen Moltmann, *The Crucified God: The Cross of Christ as the Foundation and Criticism of Christian Theology* (New York: Harper & Row, 1973), 128–35.

19. Ibid., 131.

20. Sara Diamond, *Roads to Dominion: Right-Wing Movements and Political Power in the United States* (New York: Guilford, 1995), 246–49.

21. This point is made clear, with numerous examples, in the works of James C. Scott, *Weapons of the Weak: Everyday Forms of Peasant Resistance* (New Haven and London: Yale University Press, 1985) and *Domination and the Arts of Resistance: Hidden Transcripts* (New Haven and London: Yale University Press, 1990).

22. Fredriksen, *Jesus of Nazareth, King of the Jews,* 257ff.

23. Audre Lorde, *Sister Outsider: Essays and Speeches* (Trumansburg, N.Y.: Crossing, 1984), 110–13.

24. Richard Hardt and Antonio Negri, *Empire* (Cambridge, Mass.: Harvard University Press, 2000), 299.

25. Ibid., 150–53.

26. See the tendency in Michael Harrington, *Socialism* (New York: Saturday Review/Dutton, 1970, 1972), 234–36.

27. Ibid., 236.

29. Mumia Abu-Jamal, *Death Blossoms: Reflections from a Prisoner of Conscience* (Farmington, Penn.: Plough, 1997), 39.

1. Lockdown America: A Theater of Terror

1. Jonathan Kozol, *Amazing Grace: The Lives of Children and the Conscience of a Nation* (New York: Crown, 1995), 32.

2. Ibid., 32–39.

3. Ibid., 73.

4. Ibid.

5. Ibid., 142.

6. This figure is from Vincent Schiraldi and Jason Ziedenberg, *The Punishing Decade: Prison and Jail Estimates at the Millennium* (Washington, D.C.: Justice Policy Institute, 2000), 1. Compare Joy James, ed., *States of Confinement: Policing, Detention and Prisons* (New York: St. Martin's, 2000), x.

7. Stephen R. Donziger, ed., *The Real War on Crime: The Report of the National Criminal Justice Commission* (New York: HarperPerennial, 1996), 36–37.

8. Christian Parenti, *Lockdown America: Police and Prisons in the Age of Crisis* (New York: Verso, 1999), 167.

9. Donziger, *Real War on Crime,* 31.

10. Michel Foucault, *Discipline and Punish: The Birth of the Prison* (New York: Vintage, 1977), 301.

11. Kozol, *Amazing Grace,* 143.

12. Parenti, *Lockdown America,* 211–12.

13. Matthew Purdy, "One Community's Lawbreakers Are Another's Growth Industry," *New York Times* (June 25, 2000): 25.

14. Parenti, *Lockdown America,* 213.

15. Ibid.

16. Donatella Lorch, "The Utmost Restraint and How to Exercise It: The Incarceration-Minded Meet to Buy Mobile Cells, Ballistic Batons and More," *New York Times* (August 23, 1996): B1.

17. Ibid.

18. Angela Y. Davis, "Race and Criminalization: Black Americans and the Punishment Industry," in *The House That Race Built: Black Americans, U.S. Terrain,* ed. Wahneema Lubiano (New York: Pantheon, 1997), 264–79.

19. Tom Wicker, "The American Gulag," *Earth Time* (April 16–30, 1999). The strongest case against the supposition that more prisons are helping to reduce crime can be found in Marc Mauer, *The Race to Incarcerate: The Sentencing Project* (New York: New Press, 1999), especially Chapter 5, "The Prison-Crime Connection," 81–99.

20. Wicker, "The American Gulag."

21. Hans-Georg Gadamer, *Truth and Method,* trans. and rev. Joel Weinsheimer and Donald G. Marshall, 2d ed. (New York: Crossroad, 1989), 110–15.

22. Mumia Abu-Jamal, *Live from Death Row* (Reading, Mass.: Addison-Wesley, 1995), 65.
23. Mumia Abu-Jamal, "Killing Time," *Forbes Magazine* (November 30, 1998): 106.
24. Abu-Jamal, *Live from Death Row,* 65.
25. Peter Matthiessen, *In the Spirit of Crazy Horse* (New York: Penguin, 1991). World religious leaders, over sixty U.S. congressional representatives, Amnesty International, and many others have called for clemency and unconditional release to be granted him. For the most detailed documentary of Peltier's case, in the context of the U.S. government's war on the American Indian Movement, Matthiessen's book is still the most detailed.
26. Leonard Peltier, *Prison Writings: My Life Is My Sun Dance,* ed. Harvey Arden (New York: St. Martin's, 1999), vi.
27. For an excellent study on the conviction of innocent people in the United States, see Barry Scheck and Jim Dwyer, *Actual Innocence: Five Days to Execution and Other Dispatches from the Wrongly Convicted* (New York: Doubleday, 2000).
28. For more information on these movements, see Peltier, *Prison Writings,* 218–21, and Mumia Abu-Jamal, *All Things Censored,* ed. and prod. Noelle Hanrahan (New York: Seven Stories, 2000).
29. Parenti, *Lockdown America,* 211.
30. Ibid., 167.
31. James, *States of Confinement,* x.
32. Ibid., xii.
33. Donziger, *Real War on Crime,* 42.
34. Ibid., 102.
35. James, *States of Confinement,* xvi. For two excellent studies of the burgeoning numbers of women in U.S. prisons, see Phyllis Jo Baunach, *Mothers in Prison* (New Brunswick, N.J., and London: Transaction, 1988), and Kathryn Watterson, *Women in Prison: Inside the Concrete Womb* (Boston: Northeastern University Press, 1973, 1996).
36. Parenti, *Lockdown America,* xii.
37. See "Race and Criminal Justice," in Donziger, *Real War on Crime,* 99–129.
38. Abu-Jamal, *Live from Death Row,* 92–93.
39. Donziger, *Real War on Crime,* 108, and 288–89 n.16. See also the Bureau of Justice statistics cited at the Death Penalty Information Center's Web site: http://www.deathpenaltyinfo.org.
40. "Developments in the Law—Race and the Criminal Process," in *Harvard Law Review* 110, no. 7 (1988): 1473–641.

41. Donziger, *Real War on Crime,* 114–20. See also Randall Kennedy, "Race, Law and Suspicion: Using Color as a Proxy for Dangerousness," in his *Race, Crime and the Law* (New York: Pantheon, 1997), 136–67. See also the study by Georgetown University law professor David Cole, *No Equal Justice: Race and Class in the American Criminal Justice System* (New York: New Press, 1999).

42. Donziger, *Real War on Crime,* 106, 288 n.14.

43. See Lawrence Friedman, *Crime and Punishment in America* (New York: Basic, 1993), and C. George Caffentzis, *After Such Knowledge, What Forgiveness?: Foucault, Racism and the Death Penalty* (Portland, Maine: Anti-Death Penalty Project of the Radical Philosophy Association, 1998). An overall and thorough history of the connections between slavery and U.S. prisons can be found in Scott Christianson, *With Liberty for Some: Five Hundred Years of Imprisonment in America* (Boston: Northeastern University Press, 1998).

44. Donziger, *Real War on Crime,* 129.

45. Parenti, *Lockdown America,* 185.

46. Ibid., 190–93.

47. Ibid., 188. *Fordist* in this quote is a reference to an efficient mode of manufacturing, developed in twentieth-century industrial culture. See David Harvey, *The Conditions of Postmodernity* (London: Basil Blackwell, 1989), 125–97.

48. Parenti, *Lockdown America,* 185.

49. James Gilligan, M.D., *Violence: Reflections on a National Epidemic* (New York: Vintage, 1996), 164.

50. Parenti, *Lockdown America,* 198–210.

51. Ibid., 186.

52. Ibid., 185–88.

53. Lee Griffith, *The Fall of the Prison: Biblical Perspectives on Prison Abolition* (Grand Rapids, Mich.: Eerdmans, 1993).

54. Marguerite Feitlowitz, *A Lexicon of Terror: Argentina and the Legacies of Torture* (New York: Oxford University Press, 1998), 8–12.

55. As dramatic as this genocidal war was, it was well hidden by media and public relations ploys. See Joyce Nelson, *Sultans of Sleaze: Public Relations and the Media* (Monroe, Maine: Common Courage, 1989).

56. For further discussion of these figures, see *Nunca Más: Informe de la Comisión Nacional sobre la Desaparición de Personas (1998),* 4th. ed. (Buenos Aires: Eudeba, 1998), and Heikki Patomäki and Teivo Teivainen, *Critical Responses to Globalization in the Mercosur Region* (Helsinki: Network Institute for Global Democratization, 2000), 13.

57. General Iberico Saint-Jean, quoted in Eduardo Galeano, *Memory of Fire,* vol. 3, *Century of the Wind* (New York: Pantheon, 1988), 233.

58. Frank Graziano, *Divine Violence: Spectacle, Psychosexuality, and Radical Christianity in the Argentine Dirty War* (Boulder, Colo.: Westview, 1992), 241.

59. Ibid., 77.

60. Ibid., 164–66.

61. Ibid., 38, 241ff.

62. For a general introduction to this dynamic, see Gabriel Torres and David A. Love, "The Militarization of the Police in the United States," in James, *States of Confinement,* 222–29.

63. Parenti is indebted to the exceptional work of a few sociologists who have been exploring connections of U.S. police to military models of action. See especially Peter Kraska, "Enjoying Militarism: Political/Personal Dilemmas in Studying U.S. Police Paramilitary Units," *Justice Quarterly* 13, no. 3 (1996): 405–29, and Peter G. Kraska and Victor E. Kappler, "Militarizing American Police: The Rise and Normalization of Paramilitary Units," *Social Problems* 44, no. 1 (1997): 1–18.

64. Colonel Nicholas D. Rudziak, "Police-Military Relations in a Revolutionary Environment," *Police Chief,* September 1966. Cited in Parenti, *Lockdown America,* 18.

65. See John Anderson and Hilary Hevenor, *Burning Down the House: MOVE and the Tragedy of Philadelphia* (New York: Norton, 1987), and Robin Wagner-Pacifici, *Discourse and Destruction: The City of Philadelphia versus MOVE* (Chicago: University of Chicago, 1994).

66. Parenti, *Lockdown America,* 22.

67. Ibid., 58–60.

68. Ibid., 58.

69. Mike Davis, *City of Quartz: Excavating the Future in Los Angeles* (New York: Vintage, 1990), 268.

70. Cited in Parenti, *Lockdown America,* 135.

71. Lenora Todaro, "It Takes a Global Village," *The Village Voice* (July 25, 2000): 10–41, and Michael Elliott, "The New Radicals," *Newsweek* (December 13, 1999): 36–39.

72. Parenti, *Lockdown America,* 144.

73. Amnesty International, *United States of America: Rights for All* (London: Amnesty International USA, 1998), 87–98.

74. Parenti, *Lockdown America,* 152.

75. Robert Meeropol, cited in James, *States of Confinement,* 7.

76. This ratio is based on comparison of the figures of the number executed since 1977 with that of the number released in the same period. Figures taken from the Death Penalty Information Center Web site at http://www.deathpenaltyinfo.org.

77. Senator Feingold of Wisconsin speaking on the Federal Death Penalty Abolition Act of 1999 to the United States Senate, *U.S. Congressional Record* (November 10, 1999), Proceedings and Debates of the 106th Congress, Second Session, vol. 146, no. 163.

78. See philosopher and abolitionist Jeffrey Reiman, "Why the Death Penalty Should Be Abolished in America," in Louis Pojman and Jeffrey Reiman, *The Death Penalty: For and Against* (Lanham, Md.: Rowman & Littlefield, 1998), 87–107.

79. Ibid., 67–87.

80. William J. Bowers and Glenn L. Pierce, "Deterrence or Brutalization: What Is the Effect of Executions?," *Crime and Delinquency* 26, no. 4 (1980): 453–84.

81. See how New Jersey doctors, for example, helped service the lethal injection apparatus in the state of Texas. Stephen Trombley, *The Execution Protocol: Inside America's Capital Punishment Industry* (New York: Crown, 1992), 26–31, 67–68, 76–78.

82. Scheck and Dwyer, *Actual Innocence,* and Michael L. Radelet, Hugo A. Bedau, and Constance E. Putnam, *In Spite of Innocence: The Ordeal of Four Hundred Americans Wrongly Convicted of Crimes Punishable by Death* (Boston: Northeastern University Press, 1992).

83. Reiman, "Reply," in Pojman and Reiman, *Death Penalty,* 118–32.

84. On this historical legacy as the key matrix for the use and persistence of capital punishment, see the excellent study by Peter Linebaugh and Marcus Rediker, *The Many-Headed Hydra: Sailors, Slaves, Commoners and the Hidden History of the Revolutionary Atlantic* (Boston: Beacon, 2000), 30–31, 51–52, 118, 316–17. They cite numerous cases of capital punishment used in European and U.S. history as "class discipline."

85. Cited from Peter Linebaugh, "Aesop and Abolition: Some Materials Concerning the Death Penalty, with Particular Reference to Northern Ohio," March 5, 1998. Independently published pamphlet. For the novel, see Brand Whitlock, *The Turn of the Balance,* illus. Jay Hambridge (Indianapolis: Bobbs-Merrill, 1907).

86. Trombley, *Execution Protocol,* 276.

87. For a prison warden's account of why he quit the execution business, which raises issues that many others who have roles in our nation's execution rituals also face, see Donald A. Cabana, *Death at Midnight: Confessions of an Executioner* (Boston: Northeastern University Press, 1996).

88. In Texas, where former Governor George W. Bush oversaw more than 150 executions during his tenure in office, the Texas Department of Corrections tends to revel in such details, mounting them regularly on an official Web site, listing "last meal," "last statement," and other data. See http://www.tdcj.state.tx.us/stat/grahamgarylast.htm.

89. David Carrasco, *City of Sacrifice: The Aztec Empire and the Role of Violence in Civilization* (Boston: Beacon, 1999), 75–76, 85.
90. Foucault, *Discipline and Punish,* 301.
91. My summary of Foucault's thought is taken primarily from Foucault's last chapter of *Discipline and Punish,* "The Carceral," 293–308.
92. Ibid., 298–300.
93. Ibid., 301–3.
94. Christopher C. Taylor, *Sacrifice as Terror: The Rwandan Genocide of 1994* (New York: Oxford International Publishers, 1999), 182–83.
95. See above, pp. 29–31.
96. Gerry Spence, *Give Me Liberty! Freeing Ourselves in the Twenty-first Century* (New York: St. Martin's, 1998), 77–78.
97. Ibid., 78.
98. Ibid., 31–39.
99. Derrick Bell, *Faces at the Bottom of the Well: The Permanence of Racism* (New York: Basic, 1992).
100. For just one example, see The Roots' song, "Clones," on *Illadelph Halflife,* Uni/Geffen, 1996.
101. Caffentzis, *After Such Knowledge, What Forgiveness?,* 3.
102. On the connections of the death penalty to the past lynching cultures, see ibid., 12–13.
103. Robert Meeropol, cited in James, *States of Confinement,* 7 (emphasis added).
104. James S. Liebman, Joseph Fagan, and Valerie West, *The Broken System: Error Rates in Capital Cases, 1973–1995,* available only on the Internet: http://www.law.columbia.edu/news/PressReleases/liebman.html.
105. Marcus Rediker, "Democracy and the Death Penalty? The Press Conference," public statement, August 1, 2000, The Old First Reformed Church, Philadelphia, Pennsylvania.
106. Ibid.

2. Theatrics and Sacrifice in the U.S.-Led Imperium

1. Cited in Jonathan Kozol, *Amazing Grace: The Lives of Children and the Conscience of a Nation* (New York: Crown, 1995), 142.
2. James Madison, "Publius" [*The Federalist X,* 22 November 1787], in *Debate on the Constitution: Federalist and Anti-Federalist Speeches, Articles and Letters during the Struggle over Ratification: In Two Parts,* ed. Bernard Bailyn (New York: Library of America, 1993), 1.406.
3. Ward Churchill, *Struggle for the Land: Indigenous Resistance to Genocide, Ecocide and Expropriation in Contemporary North America* (Monroe, Maine: Common Courage, 1992).

4. Richard Hardt and Antonio Negri, *Empire* (Cambridge, Mass.: Harvard University Press, 2000),117.

5. Derrick Bell, *Faces at the Bottom of the Well: The Permanence of Racism* (New York: Basic, 1978), 1–6.

6. Hardt and Negri, *Empire,* 122.

7. Enrique Dussel, *The Invention of the Americas: Eclipse of "the Other" and the Myth of Modernity* (New York: Continuum, 1995), 12.

8. Edward W. Said, *Orientalism* (New York: Vintage, 1978), 1–6.

9. Eduardo Galeano, *The Open Veins of Latin America: Five Centuries of the Pillage of a Continent* (New York: Monthly Review, 1973).

10. Gudrun Lenkersdort, "La resistencia a la conquista espanola en Los Altos de Chiapas," in *Chiapas: Los rumbos de otra historia,* eds. Juan Pedro Viqueira and Mario Humberto Ruiz (Mexico City: UNAM, 1998), 71–85.

11. *Archivo General de Indias* (Seville: Audiencia de Charcas), 313, cited in Dussel, *Invention of the Americas,* 47.

12. Dussel, *Invention of the Americas,* 164 n.51.

13. Ibid., 48.

14. Ibid., 64, 66–67.

15. Ibid., 64.

16. On the dynamics of female sacrifice, see Mark Taylor, "Of Monsters and Dances: Masculinity, White Supremacism, Ecclesial Praxis," in Elisabeth Schüssler Fiorenza and M. Shawn Copeland, eds., *Violence against Women* (New York: Continuum, 1994), 88–94, and Anne McClintock, *Imperial Leather: Race, Gender and Class in the Imperial Contest* (New York: Routledge, 1996).

17. On these mortality rates, derived from UNICEF's mortality data, see Anthony Arnove, *Iraq under Siege: The Deadly Impact of Sanctions and War* (Cambridge, Mass.: South End, 2000), 161. On Americans' rationalization of these deaths, see Eric S. Margolis, "High Oil Prices: The Curse of Saddam," *Foreign Affairs,* September 24, 2000. Margolis not only points out the inhumanity suffered by Iraqi children, but also portrays this as an affront to consumers in the United States who assume cheap oil to be "theirs by divine right," and to be had no matter what the cost to others.

18. Radio talk-show caller, heard on 101.5 FM, in Princeton, New Jersey, March 20, 2000.

19. Franz J. Hinkelammert, *Sacrificios humanos y sociedad occidental: Lucifer y la bestia* (San José, Costa Rica: DEI, 1991), 43–49.

20. Hardt and Negri, *Empire,* 115, 124–26.

21. Christopher C. Taylor, *Sacrifice as Terror: The Rwandan Genocide of 1994* (New York: Oxford International, 1999), 181.

22. Richard W. Stevenson, "In a Time of Plenty—the Poor are Still Poorer," *New York Times* (January 23, 2000).

23. William Julius Wilson, *The Bridge over the Racial Divide: Rising Inequality and Coalition Politics* (Wildavsky Forum Series 2; Berkeley: University of California Press, 1999), 1–8.

24. Kevin Phillips, *The Politics of Rich and Poor: Wealth and the American Electorate in the Reagan Aftermath* (New York: Harper Perennial, 1990), 14.

25. Wilson, *The Bridge over the Racial Divide,* 25.

26. Ibid., 26.

27. Ibid., 27.

28. Doug Henwood, "The Nation Indicators," *The Nation* (December 6, 1999): 10.

29. Keith Bradisher, "Widest Gap in Incomes? Research Points to the U.S.," *New York Times* (October 27, 1995): D2.

30. Richard Jolly, *The Human Development Report 1998* (New York: Oxford University Press, 1998), 2.

31. Arloc Sherman, *Extreme Child Poverty Rises Sharply in 1997* (Washington, D.C.: Children's Defense Fund, 1999).

32. Wilson, *The Bridge over the Racial Divide,* 23–25.

33. Stevenson, "In a Time of Plenty—the Poor are Still Poorer," 3.

34. John Bodley, "The American Industrial State," in *Cultural Anthropology: Tribes, States and the Global System* (Mountain View, Calif.: Mayfield, 1997), 347–49.

35. William Julius Wilson, *When Work Disappears: The World of the New Urban Poor* (New York: Knopf, 1996), 29ff.

36. Phillips, *Politics of Rich and Poor,* 114.

37. Brian Knowlton, "Cabinet Issue Intrudes as Bush Aides Meet on Military," *International Herald Tribune* (January 9, 2001), 1, 4.

38. Christian Parenti, *Lockdown America: Prisons and Policing in the Age of Crisis* (New York: Verso, 1999), 45–46. Parenti is citing Steven Spitzer's "Toward a Marxist Theory of Deviance," *Social Problems* 22 (1975): 638–51.

39. Parenti, *Lockdown America,* 46.

40. Ibid.

41. Ibid.

42. Howard Zinn, *A People's History of the United States: 1492 to the Present,* Twentieth Anniversary Edition (New York: HarperCollins, 2000), 211–52.

43. On Los Angeles gang life and social betterment of communities, see the many stories compiled in Yusuf Jah and sister Shah' Keyah, *Uprising: Crips and Bloods Tell the Story of America's Youth in the Crossfire* (New York: Scribner, 1995).

44. Parenti, *Lockdown America,* 46.

45. Kenneth O'Reilly, *Racial Matters: The FBI's Secret File on Black America* (New York: Free Press, 1989), 416 n.49.

46. Parenti, *Lockdown America,* 46.
47. Ibid., 45–66.
48. Tom Wicker, "The American Gulag," *Earth Time* (April 16–30, 1999).
49. David Barstow, C. J. Chivers, Juan Forero, Sarah Kershaw, and Nina Siegal, "View from New York Streets: No Retreat by Police," *New York Times* (June 25, 2000): 1, 28.
50. James Gilligan, M.D., *Violence: Reflections on a National Epidemic* (New York: Vintage, 1996), 45–85. Gilligan is a prison psychiatrist who has worked for many years with intractably violent criminals. He directed the Center for the Study of Violence at Harvard Medical School and was the director of mental health for the Massachusetts prison system.
51. Thomas Matthiesen, *Prison on Trial: A Critical Assessment* (London: Sage, 1990), 40, 70–72.
52. Gilligan, *Violence,* 139–294.
53. On the sinister turns such creativity can take, see Manning Marable, "Black Radicalism and an Economy of Incarceration," in *States of Confinement: Policing, Detention and Prisons,* ed. Joy James (New York: St. Martin's, 2000), 58ff.
54. Originally classified as top secret from February 24, 1948, this document was included in Thomas H. Entzold and John Lewis Gaddis, eds., *Documents in American Policy and Strategy 1945–1950* (New York: Columbia University Press, 1978), 226–28.
55. Zygmunt Bauman, *Globalization: The Human Consequences* (New York: Columbia University Press, 1998), 118.
56. For additional arguments of how prisons serve an economically bifurcated U.S. culture and economy, see Joel Dyer, *The Perpetual Prisoner Machine: How America Profits from Crime* (Boulder, Colo.: Westview, 2000), especially "Manufacturing Fear," 83–114.
57. The especially flagrant support and, then, betrayal of Saddam Hussein is ably documented across the pages of Said K. Aburish, *Saddam Hussein: The Politics of Revenge* (New York and London: Bloomsbury, 2000).
58. Arnove, *Iraq under Siege,* 137–48.
59. Peter Gowan, *The Global Gamble: Washington's Faustian Bid for World Dominance* (New York: Verso, 1977), 77.
60. On differences and similarities between these different historical manifestations of imperial powers, see Michael W. Doyle, *Empires* (Ithaca and London: Cornell University Press, 1986), 82–138, 257–305. On the remarkable similarities between Roman empire and U.S.-led global empire today, see Hardt and Negri, *Empire,* 161–64, 166.
61. President George Bush, "State of the Union," *New York Times* (January 29, 1992): A16.

62. Patrick E. Tyler, "Excerpts from Pentagon's Plan: 'Prevent the Emergence of a New Rival,'" *New York Times* (March 8, 1992): sec. 1, p.14.
63. Ibid.
64. Thomas L. Friedman, "What the World Needs Now: A Manifesto for the Fast World," *New York Times Magazine* (March 28, 1999).
65. Doyle, *Empires,* 96, 372.
66. Hardt and Negri, *Empire,* 183–204.
67. Doyle, *Empires,* 305.
68. David Korten, *When Corporations Rule the World* (San Francisco: Berrett-Kohler and Kumarian, 1997).
69. John R. MacArthur, *The Selling of "Free Trade": NAFTA, Washington and the Subversion of American Democracy* (New York: Hill and Wang, 2000), 100.
70. For further confirmation of these statistics, see Alexander Cockburn, "New Century, Old Crime," *The Nation* (January 31, 2000): 9.
71. Paul Richter, "No End in Sight to U.S. Air Campaign over Iraq," *Los Angeles Times* (March 3, 1999): A1.
72. Quoted in Arnove, *Iraq under Siege,* 111.
73. On Iraq as oil supplier to the United States in particular, see Andrea Gerlin, "Iraq Now a Top Oil Supplier to U.S.," *Philadelphia Inquirer* (August 6, 2000): A1.
74. Martin Luther King, Jr., "A Time to Break Silence," in *A Testament of Hope: The Essays, Writings and Speeches of Martin Luther King, Jr.,* ed. James M. Washington (New York: HarperCollins, 1986), 233. Compare this to another sermon, reprinted on page 637 of the same volume, to find King repeating the statement.

3. Way of the Cross as Adversarial Politics

1. Howard Thurman, *Jesus and the Disinherited* (1976; reprint, with a foreword by Vincent Harding, Boston: Beacon, 1996), 91.
2. Richard A. Horsley, *Galilee: History, Politics, People* (Valley Forge, Penn.: Trinity Press International, 1995), 276.
3. Richard A. Horsley, *Archaeology, History, and Society in Galilee: The Social Context of Jesus and the Rabbis* (Valley Forge, Penn.: Trinity Press International, 1996), 15–42.
4. Horsley, *Galilee,* 276.
5. Luke 23:3-5; cf. John 11:48; 19:12; and Mark 15:2, 26. See the discussion of this charge against Jesus in Sean Freyne, *Galilee from Alexander the Great to Hadrian, 323 B.C.E. to 135 C.E.: A Study of Second Temple Judaism* (Notre Dame, Ind.: University of Notre Dame, 1980), 226–27.
6. See pp. 13–14.

7. Marianne Sawicki, *Crossing Galilee: Architectures of Contact in the Occupied Land of Jesus* (Harrisburg, Penn.: Trinity Press International, 2000), 12. See also her notion of "flexible strategies of resistance," 8f.

8. Horsley, *Galilee,* 278.

9. On the temple-state, see Richard A. Horsley and J. Hanson, *Bandits, Prophets, and Messiahs: Popular Movements in the Time of Jesus* (Minneapolis: Winston, 1985), 61.

10. Freyne, *Galilee from Alexander the Great to Hadrian,* 261ff.

11. In the Gospel of Mark, especially, the frequently found term for "the crowds" around Jesus (*Eacles*) refers to masses of people, often those differentiated from elite groups. See Ahn Byung-Mu, "Jesus in the Gospel of Mark," in *Minjung Theology: People as the Subjects of History* (Maryknoll, N.Y.: Orbis, 1971), as discussed in Ched Myers, *Binding the Strong Man: A Political Reading of Mark's Story of Jesus* (Maryknoll, N.Y.: Orbis, 1988), 156–57.

12. Sawicki, *Crossing Galilee,* 203.

13. Horsley, *Archaeology, History, and Society in Galilee,* 36–42.

14. Rodney Stark, *The Rise of Christianity: A Sociologist Reconsiders History* (Princeton, N.J.: Princeton University Press, 1996), 84.

15. John Dominic Crossan, *The Historical Jesus: The Life of a Mediterranean Jewish Peasant* (reprint; San Francisco: HarperSanFrancisco, 1993), 261–64.

16. Crossan's very notion of the peasantry includes this awareness, and the point is emphasized also by Sawicki regarding Jesus: "It would seem that if Jesus knew how to recline, to dine in a *trikline* [dining rooms with couches for leisurely dining], then he was not a simple peasant villager" (*Crossing Galilee,* 182).

17. Horsley, *Galilee,* 278.

18. Ibid., 207–18.

19. Myers, *Binding the Strong Man,* 176–77.

20. Sawicki, *Crossing Galilee,* 7.

21. Ibid., 172.

22. Virgilio Elizondo, *Galilean Journey: The Mexican-American Promise* (1983; reprint Maryknoll, N.Y.: Orbis, 1998), 49–53.

23. Sawicki, *Crossing Galilee,* 194.

24. Recall the senses in which I am using the term *God* in this text. See the Introduction, pp. 4–7.

25. John Dominic Crossan, *The Birth of Christianity: Discovering What Happened in the Years Immediately after the Execution of Jesus* (San Francisco: HarperSanFrancisco, 1998), 411.

26. Crossan, *Who Killed Jesus? Exposing the Roots of Anti-Semitism in the Gospel Story of the Death of Jesus* (San Francisco: HarperSanFrancisco, 1998), 1–4.

27. Ibid., 17.

28. Crossan, *The Birth of Christianity,* 462–76.

29. Christian Smith, *Disruptive Religion: The Force of Faith in Social Movement Activism* (New York: Routledge, 1996).

30. On resistance to empire as intrinsic even to Christian worship (ideally!), see my "Worship in a Caribbean Key: Toward an Effective Fullness of the Word of God," in *Making Room at the Table: Multicultural Worship,* eds. Brian K. Blount and Nora Tubbs Tisdale (Louisville: Westminster John Knox, 2000).

31. Again, I use the term *anti-imperial* instead of *anti-imperialist* because the Rome resisted by Jesus and Paul, as with the U.S.-led empire we must resist today, were imperial efforts very different from the imperialist ventures of the European nation-states of modernity whose *imperialis* have been studied and rightly criticized. The imperial dominations of Rome and of the U.S.-led global empire of today, both of which warrant critique and resistance, are a different, more complex abuse of transnational power. See Richard Hardt and Antonio Negri, *Empire* (Cambridge, Mass.: Harvard University Press, 2000), xii–xiii, 9, 166–67, 374.

32. On this notion, see *The Encyclopedia of Religion,* XX ed., s.v., "orientation."

33. See Richard A. Horsley, ed., *Paul and Empire: Religion and Power in Roman Imperial Society* (Harrisburg, Penn.: Trinity Press International, 1997).

34. Paula Fredriksen, *Jesus of Nazareth, King of the Jews: A Jewish Life and the Emergence of Christianity* (New York: Knopf, 1999), 136.

35. This succinct summary of the kerygma (the basic early preaching) was offered by Thomas Cahill, *Desire of the Everlasting Hills: The World before and after Jesus* (New York: Nan A. Talese/Doubleday, 1999), 122–23.

36. Sawicki, *Crossing Galilee,* 154–75, 197–98, 221–24.

37. Ibid., 154, 162, 174.

38. Debates among scholars of this period (that of the paleochurch), for Sawicki especially, center around whether paleochurch resistance to empire featured "egalitarian" structures (Richard A. Horsley, *Sociology and the Jesus Movement* [New York: Crossroad, 1989], 146, and John Dominic Crossan, *The Historical Jesus,* 347f.), "democratic" impulses (as suggested by Elisabeth Schüssler Fiorenza's notion of the Jesus movement exhibiting a "democracy of equals" in *In Memory of Her: Reconstructing Christian Origins* [New York: Crossroad, 1984], 209), or invoked key notions of "liberation" as have been important to twentieth- and twenty-first-century theologies of liberation. As I write, this matter is much in debate and far from being settled. As just one way of entering into that debate, see Sawicki, *Crossing Galilee,* 154ff.

39. Horsley, *Sociology,* 96–99.

40. Rom. 13:1-2. *The New English Bible with the Apocrypha* (London: Oxford University Press, 1970).

41. See the discussions in Neil Elliott, *Liberating Paul: The Justice of God and the Politics of the Apostle* (Maryknoll, N.Y.: Orbis, 1994).

42. Sawicki, *Crossing Galilee,* 162, 166.

43. Dieter Georgi, "God Turned Upside Down," in Horsley, *Paul and Empire,* 148.

44. Klaus Wengst, *Pax Romana and the Peace of Jesus Christ* (Philadelphia: Fortress Press, 1987), 46ff.

45. Theological Dictionary of the New Testament, s.v. "euangelion," cited from Myers, *Binding the Strong Man,* 123.

46. Georgi, "God Turned Upside Down," in Horsley, *Paul and Empire,* 141, 149.

47. Ibid., 149.

48. Ibid.

49. Karl P. Donfried, "The Imperial Cults and Political Conflict in Thessalonians," in Horsley, *Paul and Empire,* 217.

50. Michael Doyle, *Empires* (Ithaca and London: Cornell University Press, 1986), 93–95.

51. Georgi, "God Turned Upside Down," 153.

52. Helmut Koester, "Imperial Ideology and Paul's Eschatology in 1 Thessalonians," in Horsley, *Paul and Empire,* 162.

53. Ibid., 160, 165–66.

54. Neil Elliott, "The Anti-Imperial Message of the Cross," in Horsley, *Paul and Empire,* 180–81.

55. Martin Hengel, *Crucifixion* (Philadelphia: Fortress Press, 1977), 32.

56. Ibid., 2.

57. David Dow, "The Real Scandal on Death Row Is Inept Lawyers," *Houston Chronicle* (February 23, 2000).

58. Apuleius, *Antologia Latina* 794.35, translated and cited from Hengel, *Crucifixion,* 60.

59. Hengel, *Crucifixion,* 54, 59.

60. Ibid., 7–8.

61. Ibid., 22ff.

62. On the problem of crucifixion and the lack of burial, see Crossan, *The Historical Jesus,* 391–94.

63. Ibid., 392.

64. John Dominic Crossan, *Jesus: A Revolutionary Biography* (New York: HarperCollins, 1989), 127.

65. Cahill, *Desire of the Everlasting Hills,* 120.

66. Elisabeth Schüssler Fiorenza, "The Praxis of Coequal Discipleship," in Horsley, *Paul and Empire,* 234.

67. Ibid., 233 (emphasis added).

68. Cahill, *Desire of the Everlasting Hills,* 125.

69. Schüssler Fiorenza, "The Praxis of Coequal Discipleship," 225.

70. From the perspective of this well-known text from Galatians, Paul's admonitions elsewhere, in his letter to Philemon, that a runaway slave, Onesimus, be returned to his master, Philemon, seems a troubling act of compliance and capitulation. Yet this letter, which seems so accommodating to empire and to institutions of slavery, is a very difficult text to interpret. Was Paul really, here, only condoning slavery? Was he somehow speaking a coded language, suggesting one thing for imperial censors, something else to the desperate slave? Was Onesimus really a slave? some historical scholars ask. Others ask: was the accommodating interpretation of this letter, perhaps, a later move of Christendom to impose a slaver's interpretation on a Pauline text? For the whole problematic of interpreting Paul's letter to Philemon, see Allen Dwight Callahan, "Paul, Ekklesia, and Emancipation in Corinth: A Coda on Liberation Theology," in Richard A. Horsley, ed., *Paul and Politics* (Valley Forge, Penn.: Trinity Press International, 2000), 216–23.

71. Daniel Boyarin, *A Radical Jew: Paul and the Politics of Identity,* Contraversions: Critical Studies in Jewish Literature, Culture, and Society I (Berkeley: University of California Press, 1994), 106. Crossan takes Boyarin to task for theorizing only gender and ethnicity from this Galatians formula and not class (the "slave or free" clause). See Crossan, *Birth of Christianity,* xxiv–xxvi.

72. Richard A. Horsley, "I Corinthians: A Case Study of Paul's Assembly as an Alternative Society," in *Paul and Empire,* 246.

73. Ibid., 244.

74. Ibid., 245.

75. Ibid., 246.

76. Walter Mosley, *Workin' on the Chain Gang: Shaking off the Dead Hand of History,* The Library of Contemporary Thought (New York: Ballantine, 2000), 25–29.

77. Horsley, "I Corinthians," 250.

78. Ibid., 251.

79. Stephen Patterson, "Paul and the Jesus Tradition: It Is Time for Another Look," *Harvard Theological Review* 84 (1991): 23–41. See especially 39–40.

80. Georgi, "God Turned Upside Down," 157.

81. Ibid.

82. Elizondo, *Galilean Journey,* 53.

83. For more recent appraisals of the communal matrix of Mark's Gospel, see Myers, *Binding the Strong Man,* 40–42, 417f., and Crossan, *Who Killed Jesus?,* 17–18. Compare William L. Lane, *The Gospel According to Mark: The New International Commentary on the New Testament* (Grand Rapids, Mich.: Eerdmans, 1974), 24–25, and Howard C. Kee, *Christian Origins in Sociological Perspective* (Philadelphia: Westminster, 1980).

84. Crossan, *Who Killed Jesus?* 17.

85. On Herod Antipas over the Galilee, see Fredriksen, *Jesus of Nazareth, King of the Jews,* 190–91. On the economic positioning of agrarian Galilee as breadbasket for urban powers, see Horsley, *Galilee,* 163–85.

86. Doyle, *Empires,* 93–95.

87. Cited in Cahill, *Desire of the Everlasting Hills,* 110.

88. Richard A. Horsley, "Caesar the Savior," in *The Liberation of Christmas: The Infancy Narratives in Social Context* (New York: Crossroad, 1989), 25–26.

89. Horsley and Hanson, *Bandits, Prophets, and Messiahs,* 61. Cited in Myers, *Binding the Strong Man,* 79.

90. S. R. F. Price, *Rituals and Power: The Roman Imperial Cult in Asia Minor* (Cambridge: Cambridge University Press, 1984), 207–33.

91. Fredriksen, *Jesus of Nazareth, King of the Jews,* 176, and Price, *Rituals and Power,* 221.

92. For explication of the political motivations in John's arrest and beheading, see Myers, *Binding the Strong Man,* 214–17, and Fredriksen, *Jesus of Nazareth, King of the Jews,* 153.

93. On the ways that sacrifices for forgiveness of debt had to be made, and especially by those with certain kinds of blemish and impairment, see Joachim Jeremias, *Jerusalem in the Time of Jesus: An Investigation into Economic and Social Conditions during the New Testament Period* (London: SCM, 1969), 271–344.

94. Myers, *Binding the Strong Man,* 155.

95. Ibid., 152–56.

96. Ibid., 161.

97. On the problem of "anti-Semiticism" in Christian interpretation of the Gospels, see Crossan, *Who Killed Jesus?*

98. Ibid., 190.

99. J. Duncan M. Derrett, "Contributions to the Study of the Gerasene Demoniac," in *Journal of the Study of the New Testament* 3 (1979): 5ff, cited in Myers, *Binding the Strong Man,* 191.

100. Ibid., 191.

101. Ibid., 192.

102. Ibid., 192.

103. Ibid., 294.

104. Ibid., 299.

105. Fredriksen, *Jesus of Nazareth, King of the Jews,* 226–27.

106. Crossan, *Who Killed Jesus?,* 65.

107. Sawicki, *Crossing Galilee,* 197, compare 49.

108. William R. Telford, *The Barren Temple and the Withered Tree,* JSNT Supplementary Series I (Sheffield, Eng.: JSOT Press, 1980), 193–96. Cited in Myers, *Binding the Strong Man,* 297.

109. Mumia Abu-Jamal, interview by C. Clark Kissinger, *Revolutionary Worker*, no. 576, December 1994.

110. Robert Farris Thompson, *Flash of the Spirit: African and Afro-American Art and Philosophy* (New York: Random House, 1983), 108–10.

111. This phrase is from Jon Sobrino, writing from the perspective of the "crucified peoples" of Latin America, and particularly El Salvador, in his *Jesus the Liberator: A Historical-Theological View* (Maryknoll, N.Y.: Orbis, 1993), 255.

4. Stealing the Show: Way of the Cross as Dramatic Action

1. James C. Scott, "Domination, Acting and Fantasy," in *The Paths to Domination, Resistance and Terror,* eds. Carolyn Nordstrom and JoAnn Martin (Berkeley: University of California Press, 1992), 57, 66.

2. Angela Y. Davis, *Blues Legacies and Black Feminism: Gertrude "Ma" Rainey, Bessie Smith, and Billie Holiday* (New York: Pantheon, 1998), 127–29, 164.

3. W. E. B. Du Bois, *The Souls of Black Folk,* with an introduction by John Edgar Wideman (1903; reprint, New York: Vintage/Library of America, 1990), 180–90.

4. On the ways art and rage are orchestrated within and by subordinated groups, see Scott, "Domination, Acting and Fantasy," 66. Compare the older work: Abraham Kardiner and Lionel Ovesey, *The Mark of Oppression* (Cleveland: Meridian, 1962); Gerald W. Mullin, *Flight and Rebellion: Slave Resistance in Eighteenth-Century Virginia* (New York: Oxford University Press, 1972); and Mary Field Belenky, Blythe Clinchy, Nancy Goldberger, and Jill Tarule, *Women's Ways of Knowing: The Development of Self, Voice and Mind* (New York: Basic, 1986).

5. Scott, "Domination, Acting and Fantasy," 57.

6. André Trocmé, *Jesus and the Nonviolent Revolution,* trans. Michael H. Shank and Marlin E. Miller (Scottsdale, Penn.: Herald, 1973), 98–99.

7. Cited from Trocmé, *Jesus and the Nonviolent Revolution,* 99–100.

8. Paula Fredriksen, *Jesus of Nazareth, King of the Jews: A Jewish Life and the Emergence of Christianity* (New York: Knopf, 1999), 233.

9. Josephus, *The Jewish War,* 5:450.

10. Trocmé, *Jesus and the Nonviolent Revolution,* 99.

11. Jesus' penchant for hyperbole and "intensification" has been noted by scholars of the parables of Jesus. See, for one example, Paul Ricoeur, "The Specificity of Religious Language," *Semeia* 4 (1975): 129–31.

12. Ched Myers, *Binding the Strong Man: A Political Reading of Mark's Story of Jesus* (Maryknoll, N.Y.: Orbis, 1988), 162.

13. Simone Weil, *The Iliad, or The Poem of Force* (Wallingford, Penn.: Pendle Hill, 1956).

14. Lee Bernstein, " . . . 'Give Me Death': Capital Punishment and the Limits of American Citizenship," in *States of Confinement: Policing, Detentions and Prisons,* ed. Joy James (New York: St. Martin's, 2000), 11.

15. Richard Hardt and Antonio Negri, *Empire* (Cambridge, Mass.: Harvard University Press, 2000), 323, 339 (emphasis added). The authors are citing Thomas Hobbes, *Leviathan,* ed. C. B. Macpherson (1651; London: Penguin, 1968), 200.

16. Walter Mosley, *Workin' on the Chain Gang: Shaking off the Dead Hand of History,* Library of Contemporary Thought (New York: Ballantine, 2000), 25.

17. Frank Graziano, *Divine Violence: Spectacle, Psychosexuality and Radical Christianity in the Argentine Dirty War* (Boulder, Colo.: Westview, 1992), 241–42.

18. For a complex treatment of this myth and of the scapegoat mechanism see René Girard, *The Scapegoat,* trans. Yvonne Freccero (Baltimore, Md.: Johns Hopkins University Press, 1986).

19. On the history of this phenomenon in the United States, see Joel Kovel, *White Racism: A Psychohistory* (1979; reprint, New York: Columbia University Press, 1986); and Richard Delgado and Jean Stefancic, *Critical White Studies: Looking Behind the Mirror* (Philadelphia, Penn.: Temple University Press, 1997), especially "How Whites See Others," 49–136.

20. For a nearly classic statement and analysis of this projection of evil in European consciousness, see Frantz Fanon, *Black Skin, White Masks* (1952; reprint, New York: Grove, 1967), 190ff.

21. On scapegoating myths as one dimension of the 1994 Rwandan genocide, see Christopher C. Taylor, *Sacrifice as Terror: The Rwandan Genocide of 1994* (New York: Oxford International, 1999), 120–21.

22. This notion of scapegoating is evident in the most prominent understanding of what Christians often call their doctrine of atonement, and, as New Testament scholar Stephen Moore pointed out, it crops up in numerous student papers by Christians as follows: "Jesus was nailed to the cross instead of me. He took the punishment that was due to me on account of my sins." See Stephen D. Moore, *God's Gym: Divine Male Bodies of the Bible* (New York: Routledge, 1996).

23. For numerous examples of these strategies, see Kenneth O'Reilly, *Racial Matters: The FBI's Secret File on Black America* (New York: Free Press, 1989).

24. Note the Direct Action Network founded on the principles of decentralized democracy and nonviolent direct action, which has been especially operative in the years 1999 and 2000. See Joshua Lefkowitz, "Act Up! Here's How: A Selected List of Organizations," in *Village Voice* (July 25, 2000): 56.

25. Thomas L. Friedman, "What the World Needs Now: A Manifesto for the Fast World," *New York Times Magazine* (March 28, 1999).

26. On the values and ethos of globalization, see Fredric Jameson and Masao Miyoshi, eds., *The Cultures of Globalization* (Durham, N.C.: Duke University Press, 1998), especially 13–21.

27. For connections between the U.S. military and just one other nation, Mexico, see James Cockcroft, *Mexico's Hope: An Encounter with Politics and History* (New York: Monthly Review, 1998), 340–45. On military and paramilitary strategies, generally, in the context of U.S.-dominated global politics, see Noam Chomsky, *World Orders Old and New* (New York: Columbia University Press, 1994).

28. Martin Luther King, Jr., "Showdown for Nonviolence: The Only Road to Freedom," in *A Testament of Hope: The Essential Writings and Speeches of Martin Luther King, Jr.,* ed. James M. Washington (New York: HarperCollins, 1986), 58, 60, 66, 68.

29. Erik H. Eriksen, *Gandhi's Truth: On the Origins of Militant Nonviolence* (New York: Norton, 1969), 198.

30. Gabriel Torres and David A. Love, "The Militarization of the Police in the United States," *States of Confinement: Policing, Detention and Prisons,* ed. Joy James (New York: St. Martin's, 2000), 222–29.

31. Cited from Walter Wink, *Engaging the Powers: Discernment and Resistance in a World of Domination* (Minneapolis: Fortress Press, 1992), 248.

32. The references to Wink are to his seven-page list of selected acts of nonviolent action, taken in turn from Gene Sharp, *The Politics of Nonviolent Action* (Boston: Porter Sargent, 1973). See Wink, *Engaging the Powers,* 243–56.

33. Ibid., 250.

34. John Nichols, "Raising a Ruckus—Join a Caravan, Don a Turtle Costume—It's WTO Time in Seattle," *The Nation* (December 6, 1999): 18–19. See also Andrew Boyd, "Extreme Costume Ball: A New Protest Movement Hits the Streets in Style," *The Village Voice* (July 25, 2000): 46–47.

35. Albert Camus, *The Rebel: An Essay on Man in Revolt,* trans. Antony Bower (1956; New York: Vintage, 1961), 29.

36. For a summary of these issues and a Christian theological interpretation of them, see Robert Goss, *Jesus Acted Up: A Gay and Lesbian Manifesto* (San Francisco: HarperSanFrancisco, 1993).

37. Ibid., 258.

38. Ibid., 255.

39. Leonard Harris, "Foreword," in Greg Moses, *Revolution of Conscience: Martin Luther King, Jr., and the Philosophy of Nonviolence* (New York: Guilford, 1997), vi.

40. John Ross, *Rebellion from the Roots: Indian Uprising in Chiapas* (Monroe, Maine: Common Courage, 1995).

41. Paco Ignacio Taibo II, *Guevara Also Known as Che,* trans. Martin Michael Roberts (New York: St. Martin's, 1997), 246.

42. Ibid., 237.

43. See Introduction, 4–7.

44. Sadiki, "In De Storm," e-mail to author, July 30, 1996.

45. Ibid.

46. Barbara Curzi-Lamaan, "Winning Battle," in *Hauling Up the Morning/Izando la Mañana: Writings and Art by Political Prisoners and Prisoners of War,* eds. Tim Blunk and Raymond Luc Levasseur (Trenton, N.J.: Red Sea, 1990), 155.

47. I realize that the notion of deeper for referring to earth and nature is, in a sense, arbitrary. After all, nature might be viewed as also high or broad. Being from Kansas, I tend to associate nature with the prairie grass and sod under my feet; it's a simplification, to be sure, but it is what leads me to join those who talk of a deeper power of nature. On spatial imagery in references to experience, see David Abram, *In the Spell of the Sensuous: Perception and Language in a More-Than-Human World* (New York: Pantheon, 1996), 182–83.

48. Frederick Turner, "Voices out of the Land: Leslie Marmon Silko's *Ceremony,*" in *The Spirit of Place: The Making of the American Literary Landscape* (San Francisco: Sierra Club, 1989), 330.

49. Robin D. G. Kelley, "Slangin' Rocks . . . Palestinian Style: Dispatches from the Occupied Zones of North America," in *Police Brutality: An Anthology,* ed. Jill Nelson (New York: Norton, 2000), 21–24.

50. On this kind of vision, see Leslie Marmon Silko, *Almanac of the Dead* (New York: Simon & Schuster, 1991), 316.

51. Mumia Abu-Jamal, "Night of Power," in *Death Blossoms: Reflections from a Prisoner of Conscience* (Farmington, Penn.: Plough, 1997), 30–31.

52. Ibid., 31.

53. Odd Mathis Haetta, *The Sami: An Indigenous People of the Arctic* (Karsjok, Norway: Davvi Girji OS, 1999).

54. Leslie Marmon Silko, *Yellow Woman and a Beauty of the Spirit* (New York: Simon & Schuster, 1996), 125.

55. Cited in T. C. McLuhan, *The Way of the Earth: Encounters with Nature in Ancient and Contemporary Thought* (New York: Simon & Schuster, 1994), 424.

56. Mumia Abu-Jamal, "A Toxic Shock," in *Live from Death Row* (Reading, Mass.: Addison-Wesley, 1995), 62–63.

57. Camus, *The Rebel,* 275.

58. Richard Goldstein, "The Birth of a Movement," *The Village Voice* (July 25, 2000): 36–39.

59. For discussion of resources for creative resistance in the religious and cultural movement of Rastafarianism, emanating primarily from Jamaica, see Randal L. Hepner, "Chanting down Babylon in the Belly of the Beast: The Rastafarian Movement in the Metropolitan U.S.," in *Chanting down Babylon: The Rastafari Reader,* eds. Nathaniel Samuel Murrell, William David Spencer, and Adrian Anthony McFarlane (Philadelphia: Temple University Press, 1998), 199–216.

60. Antonio Benítez-Rojo, *The Repeating Island: The Caribbean and the Postmodern Perspective,* 2d ed. (Durham, N.C.: Duke University Press, 1996), 161–62.

61. Goldstein, "The Birth of a Movement," 37.

5. Way of the Cross as Building Peoples' Movements

1. Richard Falk, *Predatory Globalization: A Critique* (Oxford: Polity, 1999).

2. See Lenora Todaro, "It Takes a Global Village," *The Village Voice* (July 25, 2000): 41.

3. Paula Fredriksen, *Jesus of Nazareth, King of the Jews: A Jewish Life and the Emergence of Christianity* (New York: Knopf, 1999), 233.

4. Ibid., 240–41.

5. Ibid., 234. Fredriksen here directs readers' attention to "the crowds" for understanding Jesus' execution and the motives for it.

6. Ibid., 235

7. Ibid., 254, 257.

8. See Chapter 3.

9. Richard A. Horsley, *Sociology and the Jesus Movement* (New York: Crossroad, 1989), 105–29.

10. Ibid., 235.

11. Stark, *The Rise of Christianity: A Sociologist Reconsiders History* (Princeton, N.J.: Princeton University Press, 1996), 9.

12. On Constantine, see Stark, *Rise of Christianity,* 10–11. Christian missionaries can, at times, play roles resistant to exploitative domination, but their record is not good. For one account of their performance in the Americas, particularly in North America regarding indigenous populations, see George A. Tinker, *Missionary Conquest: The Gospel and Native American Cultural Genocide* (Minneapolis: Fortress Press, 1993), 112–23.

13. See Slavoj Zizek, *The Fragile Absolute, Or Why Is the Christian Legacy Worth Fighting For?* (New York: Verso, 2000), 1–2, 113–29.

14. Robert M. Grant, *Early Christianity and Society: Seven Studies* (San Francisco: Harper & Row, 1977).

15. Paul Johnson, *A History of Christianity* (New York: Atheneum, 1976), 75.

16. Cited from Stark, *Rise of Christianity,* 83–84.

17. Michael Doyle, *Empires* (Ithaca and London: Cornell University Press, 1986), 98.

18. Karl Barth, cited in George Casalis, "Théologie et socialisme: L'example de Karl Barth," in *Etudes theologiques et religieuses* 49, no. 1 (1974), 158.

19. Christian Smith, *Disruptive Religion: The Force of Faith in Social Movement Activism* (New York and London: Routledge, 1996), 1–23. See also the two studies by Christian Smith, *The Emergence of Liberation Theology: Radical Religion and Social Movement Activism* (Chicago: University of Chicago Press, 1991) and *Resisting Reagan: The U.S. Central America Peace Movement* (Chicago: University of Chicago Press, 1996).

20. This term was used somewhat condescendingly by some Christian theologians in their dialogues with other religions. It was problematic because the declaration that an adherent to another religious way was an "anonymous Christian" was often made without the dialogue partner's consent to the term. See Karl Rahner, "Christianity and the Non-Christian Religions," in *Christianity and Other Religions: Selected Readings,* eds. John Hick and Brian Hebblethwaite (Philadelphia: Fortress Press, 1990), 75–79.

21. Amnesty International, *The United States of America: Rights for All* (London: Amnesty International, 1999).

22. Allyson Collins, *Shielded from Justice: Police Brutality and Accountability in the United States* (New York: Human Rights Watch, 1998).

23. David A. Love and Gabriel Torres, *Police Brutality and Racism in the United States: Race Convention Report of the United Nations* (New York: Center for Constitutional Rights, 1998).

24. Jerome G. Miller, *Search and Destroy: African-American Males in the Criminal Justice System* (New York: Cambridge University Press, 1996), and Jill Nelson, ed., *Police Brutality: An Anthology* (New York: Norton, 2000).

25. Ron Daniels, "The Crisis of Police Brutality and Misconduct in America: The Causes and the Cure," in Nelson, *Police Brutality,* 242–43.

26. Ibid., 244.

27. Ibid., 241.

28. Ibid., 254.

29. Kelly-Jane Cotter, "N.Y.C. Cops Asked to Boycott the Boss: Police Protest Lyrics of Springsteen's 'American Skin,'" [East Brunswick, N.J.] *Home News Tribune* (June 10, 2000): B12.

30. See Will Villanova, *Devils in A Blue Dress,* DPI Music Group. The disc addresses not only the Diallo case but that of Mumia Abu-Jamal and police brutality in general.

31. Bruce Springsteen, "American Skin (41 Shots)," lyrics cited in full at Jon Pareles, "Born to Run, or at Least to Be Redeemed," *New York Times* (June 14, 2000): E1.

32. Daniels, "The Crisis of Police Brutality and Misconduct in America," 258.

33. Robin D. G. Kelley, "Slangin' Rocks Palestinian Style: Dispatches from the Occupied Zones of North America," in Nelson, *Police Brutality,* 51.

34. See, for example, the work of Eddie Ellis, the educational coordinator of the Neighborhood Defender Services of Harlem, discussed in Steven R. Donziger, ed., *The Real War on Crime: The Report of the National Criminal Justice Commission* (New York: HarperCollins, 1996), 258–59.

35. Daniels, "The Crisis of Police Brutality and Misconduct in America," 258–60.

36. See, for example, *Emerge* magazine, in which Louima was shown in a hospital bed after the assault, with a cover-story title, "Police Brutality: What Can Be Done?" *Emerge: Black America's News Magazine* 9, no. 2 (November 1997): 43–46, 48–49.

37. Daniels, "The Crisis of Police Brutality and Misconduct in America," 253.

38. Ibid., 254, 258.

39. For just one example of the kind of message Davis is bringing to her speaking engagements across the country, see Angela Y. Davis, "From the Convict Lease System to the Super-Max Prison," in *States of Confinement: Policing, Detention and Prisons,* ed. Joy James (New York: St. Martin's, 2000), 60–74.

40. Lee Griffith, *The Fall of the Prison: Biblical Perspectives on Prison Abolition* (Grand Rapids, Mich.: Eerdmans, 1993), 106.

41. Karl Barth, *Deliverance to the Captives: Sermons and Prayers* (New York: Harper, 1961), 78.

42. Griffith, *The Fall of the Prison,* 107.

43. Ibid., 71–78.

44. Ibid., 204–5.

45. Ibid., 205–6.

46. Griffith is one of the clearest for arguing this point. See his section, "Prison Reform/Prison Entrenchment," in ibid., 157–76.

47. Reverend Lucius Walker, "Letter of Invitation to the Movement of Prison Justice Caravans," Interreligious Foundation for Community Organizing, November 15, 1999.

48. No More Prisons! Web site: http://www.nomoreprisons.org/front.htm

49. Ibid.

50. William Upski Wimsatt, *No More Prisons: Urban Life, Home Schooling, Hip-Hop Leadership, The Cool Rich Kids' Movement, A Hitchhiker's Guide to*

Community Organizing, and Why Philanthropy Is the Greatest Art Form for the Twenty-First Century (New York: Soft Skull, 2000).

51. Ibid., 147.

52. Ibid., 146.

53. Christopher Farley, "Hip Hop Nation," *Time* (February 8, 1999): 54–64. For a fuller cultural analysis of hip-hop, see Nelson George, *Hip Hop America* (New York: Viking, 1998), 1–33.

54. Wimsatt, *No More Prisons,* 151.

55. No More Prisons! Web site: http://www.nomoreprisons.org/front.htm (emphasis added).

56. No More Prisons! Web site: http://www.nomoreprisons.org/involve.htm #build.

57. No More Prisons! Web site: http://www.nomoreprisons.org.

58. See Chapter 1, 36–41.

59. Two of the more important Web sites displaying these foci are the Death Penalty Information Center (http://www.deathpenaltyinfo.org) and the Canadian Coalition against the Death Penalty (http://www.ccadp.org).

60. Francis X. Clines, "The Poster Boy for and against the Death Penalty: Killer or Victim?," *New York Times* (May 21, 2000).

61. John Edgar Wideman, "Introduction," in Mumia Abu-Jamal, *Live from Death Row* (Reading, Mass.: Addison-Wesley, 1995), xxxiii.

62. Ibid., xxiv.

63. See "A Call by the Religious Community for a New Trial for Mumia Abu-Jamal," in *Christian Century* (April 5, 2000): 396, and in *The Christian Recorder: The Official Organ of the African Methodist Episcopal Church* (April 17, 2000): 9.

64. Mumia Abu-Jamal, *Death Blossoms: Reflections from a Prisoner of Conscience* (Farmington, Penn.: Plough, 1997), 7.

65. Abu-Jamal, *Live from Death Row,* 144, 148.

66. Ibid., 143. On his general view of police as an institution in the United States, see page 148 of the same work.

67. Ibid., 134.

68. For an analysis of these structural problems, which place the United States in various levels of human rights violation, see Amnesty International, *The United States of America: Rights for All.*

69. On prisoners' own support for Mumia, see *Sparks of Resistance for Mumia with Love: International Political Prisoners Unite to Save Mumia Abu-Jamal* (Jersey City, N.J.: Art and Writings against the Death Penalty, 1995). More recently there occurred an impressive outpouring of artistic creativity for Abu-Jamal around the "Mumia 911" effort in 1999. See the Web site at http://www.mumia911.org. See also the CD *Free Mumia: Reggae without Apology,* Without Apology Music, Inc., and the numerous references to

Mumia on the Rage Against the Machine CD titled *The Battle of Los Angeles,* Sony Music Entertainment.

70. No More Prisons! Web site: http://www.nomoreprisons.org.

Epilogue: Christian Living: Toward a Fullness of Rebellion

1. Albert Camus, *The Rebel: An Essay on Man in Revolt,* trans. Antony Bower (1956; New York: Vintage, 1991), 24.

2. Ibid., 17.

3. Alice Walker, *Anything We Love Can Be Saved: A Writer's Activism* (New York: Ballantine, 1997), 160.

4. Martín Espada, *Rebellion Is the Circle of a Lover's Hands/Rebelión es el giro de manos del amante* (Willimantic, Conn.: Curbstone, 1990), 26.

5. Hans-Georg Gadamer, *Truth and Method,* trans. and rev. Joel Weinsheimer and Donald G. Marshall, 2d rev. ed. (New York: Crossroad, 1989), 102.

6. Elaine Scarry, *On Beauty and Being Just* (Princeton, N.J.: Princeton University Press, 1999), 86–93.

7. See Chapter 4, 114–15.

8. See, for example, Michael Elliott, "The New Radicals," *Newsweek* (December 13, 1999): 36–39. Compare Andrew Boyd, "Extreme Costume Ball: A New Protest Movement Hits the Streets in Style," *The Village Voice* (July 25, 2000): 46–47.

9. James C. Scott, "Domination, Acting and Fantasy," in *The Paths to Domination, Resistance and Terror,* eds. Carolyn Nordstrom and JoAnn Martin (Berkeley: University of California Press, 1992), 57ff.

10. For one brief account of the Bread and Roses strike, led by women organizers, see William Cahn, *Lawrence 1912: The Bread and Roses Strike* (New York: Pilgrim, 1980).

11. See Chapter 4, 110–13.

Acknowledgments

1. Shaka Sankofa, last statement, see the Texas Department of Corrections Criminal Justice Web site at http://www.tdcj.state.tx.us/stat/grahamgary-last.htm.

2. S. E. Anderson, *The Black Holocaust for Beginners* (New York: Writers and Readers, 1996), vi.

3. Howard Zinn, *A People's History of the United States: 1492 to the Present,* Twentieth Anniversary Edition (New York: HarperCollins, 2000), 518–19, and José Lopez, "Political Incarceration," and Donna Willmott, "It's Time to Bring Our Political Prisoners Home," in *States of Confinement: Policing, Detention and Prisons,* ed. Joy James (New York: St. Martin's, 2000), 302–11

and 312–21. On theorizing the notion of political prisoners in the United States and identifying them, see former U.S. Senator Charles Goodell, *Political Prisoners in America* (New York: Random House, 1973), and Ward Churchill and J. J. Vander Wall, eds., *Cages of Steel: The Politics of Imprisonment in the United States* (Washington, D.C.: Maisonneuve, 1992).

for further reading:
A Select Bibliography

The following selection of volumes are arranged according to five basic categories, each reflecting the types of literature that have informed the writing of *The Executed God*. In most cases, the titles and subtitles clarify the contribution that each book makes. Although some Christian organizations have Web sites on criminal justice issues, I have limited the Web sites here listed to those that are focused around building broad interfaith and public movements.

I. The U.S. Prison Industrial Complex

Abu-Jamal, Mumia. *All Things Censored.* Edited and audio production by Noelle Hanrahan. New York: Seven Stories, 2000.

———. *Death Blossoms: Reflections from a Prisoner of Conscience.* Farmington, Pa.: Plough, 1997.

———. *Live From Death Row.* Reading, Mass.: Addison-Wesley, 1995.

Blunk, Tim, and Levasseur, Raymond Luc, eds. *Hauling Up the Morning/ Izando La Mañana: Writings and Art by Political Prisoners and Prisoners of War.* Trenton, N.J.: Red Sea, 1990.

Burton-Rose, Daniel. With the editors of *Prison Legal News*, Dan Pens and Paul Wright, *The Ceiling of America: An Inside Look at the U.S. Prison Industry.* Monroe, Mass.: Common Courage, 1998.

Christianson, Scott. *With Liberty for Some: 500 Years of Imprisonment in America.* Boston: Northeastern University Press, 1998.

Churchill, Ward, and Vander Wall, J. J., eds. *Cages of Steel: The Politics of Imprisonment in the United States.* Washington, D.C.: Maisonneuve, 1992.

Cole, David. *No Equal Justice: Race and Class in the American Criminal Justice System.* New York: New Press, 1999.

Donziger, Stephen, ed. *The Real War on Crime: The Report of the National Criminal Justice Commission.* New York: Harper Perennial, 1996.

Dyer, Joel. *The Perpetual Prisoner Machine: How America Profits from Crime.* Boulder, Colo.: Westview, 2000.

Gilligan, James. *Violence: Reflections on a National Epidemic.* New York: Vintage, 1996.

James, Joy, ed. *States of Confinement: Policing, Detention and Prisons.* New York: St. Martin's, 2000.

Mauer, Mark. *The Race to Incarcerate: The Sentencing Project.* New York: New Press, 1999.

Parenti, Christian. *Lockdown America: Police and Prisons in the Age of Crisis.* New York: Verso, 1999.

Peltier, Leonard. *Prison Writings: My Life Is My Sun Dance.* New York: St. Martin's, 1999.

Schiraldi, Vincent, and Ziedenberg, Jason. *The Punishing Decade: Prison and Jail Estimates at the Millennium.* Washington, D.C.: Justice Policy Institute, 2000.

Watterson, Kathryn. *Women in Prison: Inside the Concrete Womb.* Boston: Northeastern University Press, 1973/1996.

II. Police Brutality in the U.S.A.

Anderson, John, and Hevenor, Hilary. *Burning Down the House: MOVE and the Tragedy of Philadelphia.* New York: Norton, 1987.

Collins, Allyson. *Shielded from Justice: Police Brutality and Accountability in the United States.* New York: Human Rights Watch, 1998.

Love, David A., and Torres, Gabriel. *Police Brutality and Racism in the United States: Race Convention Report of the United Nations.* New York: Center for Constitutional Rights, 1998.

Miller, Jerome G. *Search and Destroy: African-American Males in the Criminal Justice System.* New York: Cambridge University Press, 1996.

Nelson, Jill, ed. *Police Brutality: An Anthology.* New York: Norton, 2000.

Stolen Lives, Killed By Law Enforcement. Second edition. This book, documenting over 2,000 cases, is a Project of the Anthony Baez Foundation, National Lawyers Guild, and the October 22nd Coalition to Stop Police Brutality, Repression, and the Criminalization of a Generation. New York: PO Box 2627, 10009.

III. The Death Penalty in the U.S.A.

Cabana, Donald A. *Death at Midnight: Confessions of an Executioner.* Boston: Northeastern University Press, 1996.

Haines, Herbert H. *Against Capital Punishment: The Anti-Death Penalty Movement in America, 1972–1994.* New York: Oxford University Press, 1996.

O'Shea, Kathleen. *Women on the Row: Revelations from Both Sides of the Bars.* Ithaca, N.Y.: Firebrand, 2000.

Pojman, Louis P., and Reiman, Jeffrey. *The Death Penalty: For and Against.* Lanham, Md.: Rowman & Littlefield, 1998.

Prejean, Helen. *Dead Man Walking: An Eyewitness Account of the Death Penalty in the United States.* New York: Random House, 1993.

Radelet, Michael, Bedau, Hugo A., and Putnam, Constance. *In Spite of Innocence: The Ordeal of 400 Americans Wrongly Convicted of Crimes Punishable By Death*. Boston: Northeastern University Press, 1992.

Scheck, Barry, and Dwyer, Jim. *Actual Innocence: Five Days to Execution and Other Dispatches from the Wrongly Convicted*. New York: Doubleday, 2000.

Trombley, Stephen. *The Execution Protocol: Inside America's Capital Punishment Industry*. New York: Crown, 1992.

IV. Jesus Movements and Roman Empire

Crossan, John Dominic. *The Historical Jesus: The Life of a Mediterranean Jewish Peasant*. San Francisco: HarperSanFrancisco, 1993.

———. *The Birth of Christianity: Discovering What Happened in the Years Immediately After the Execution of Jesus*. San Francisco: HarperSanFrancisco, 1998.

Elizondo, Virgilio. *Galilean Journey: The Mexican-American Promise* Maryknoll, N.Y.: Orbis, 1998.

Fredriksen, Paula. *Jesus of Nazareth, King of the Jews: A Jewish Life and the Emergence of Christianity*. New York: Knopf, 1999.

Hengel, Martin. *Crucifixion*. Philadelphia: Fortress Press, 1977.

Horsley, Richard. *Sociology and the Jesus Movement*. New York: Crossroad, 1989.

———. *Galilee: History, Politics, People*. Valley Forge, Pa.: Trinity Press International, 1995.

———. *Paul and Empire: Religion and Power in Roman Imperial Society*. Harrisburg, Pa.: Trinity Press International, 1997.

———. *Paul and Politics: Ecclesia, Israel, Empire*. Harrisburg, Pa.: Trinity Press International, 2000.

Moltmann, Jürgen. *The Crucified God: The Cross of Christ as the Foundation and Criticism of Christian Theology*. New York: Harper & Row, 1973.

Myers, Ched. *Binding the Strong Man: A Political Reading of Mark's Story of Jesus*. Maryknoll, N.Y.: Orbis, 1988.

Schüssler Fiorenza, Elisabeth. *Jesus—Miriam's Child, Sophia's Prophet: Critical Issues in Feminist Christology*. New York: Continuum, 1994.

Stark, Rodney. *The Rise of Christianity: A Sociologist Reconsiders History*. Princeton: Princeton University Press, 1996.

Wink, Walter. *Engaging the Powers: Discernment and Resistance in a World of Domination*. Minneapolis: Fortress Press, 1992.

V. Empire and Imperial Power Today

Bauman, Zygmunt. *Globalization: The Human Consequences*. New York: Columbia University Press, 1998.

Doyle, Michael. *Empires*. Ithaca and London: Cornell University Press, 1986.

Dussel, Enrique. *The Invention of the Americas: Eclipse of "the Other" and the Myth of Modernity*. New York: Continuum, 1995.

Gowan, Peter. *The Global Gamble: Washington's Faustian Bid for World Dominance*. New York: Verso, 1977.

Green, Felix. *The Enemy: Notes on Imperialism and Revolution*. London: Jonathan Cape, 1970.

Hardt, Michael, and Negri, Antonio. *Empire*. Cambridge, Mass.: Harvard University Press, 2000.

Korten, David. *When Corporations Rule the World*. San Francisco: Berret-Kohler and Kumarian, 1997.

VI. The Politics of Economic Injustice Today

Collins, Chuck, and Yeskel, Felice. *Apartheid in America: A Primer on Economic Inequality and Insecurity*. New York: New Press, 2000.

MacArthur, John R. *The Selling of "Free Trade": NAFTA, Washington, and the Subversion of American Democracy*. New York: Hill and Wang, 2000.

Phillips, Kevin. *The Politics of Rich and Poor: Wealth and the American Electorate in the Reagan Aftermath*. New York: Harper Perennial, 1990.

Sherman, Arloc. *Extreme Child Poverty Rises Sharply in 1997*. Washington, D.C.: Children's Defense Fund, 1999.

Wilson, William Julius. *The Bridge Across Our Racial Divide: Rising Inequality and Coalition Politics*. Berkeley: University of California Press, 1999.

VII. The Politics of Racial Injustice Today

Anderson, S. E. *The Black Holocaust for Beginners*. New York: Writers & Readers, 1996.

Bell, Derrick. *Faces at the Bottom of the Well: The Permanence of Racism*. New York: Basic, 1992.

Delgado, Richard, and Stefanic, Jean. *Critical White Studies: Looking Behind the Mirror*. Philadelphia: Temple University Press, 1997.

Kornweibel, Theodore, Jr. *Seeing Red: Federal Campaigns Against Black Militancy, 1919- 1925*. Bloomington: Indiana University Press, 1998.

McClintock, Anne. *Imperial Leather: Race, Gender and Sexuality in the Colonial Contest*. New York and London: Routledge, 1995.

Lubiano, Wahneema, ed. *The House That Race Built*. New York: New Press, 1999.

VIII. Essential Web Sites

1. The Canadian Coalition Against the Death Penalty: http://www.ccadp.org
2. The Death Penalty Information Center: http://www.deathpenaltyinfo.org
3. No More Prisons!: http://www.nomoreprisons.org/front.htm
4. International Concerned Family & Friends of Mumia Abu-Jamal: http://www.mumia.org

5. The Mobilization to Free Mumia Abu-Jamal: http://www.freemumia.org
6. Moratorium 2000 (working to get a U.S. moratorium on the death penalty): http://www.moratorium2000.org
7. Texas Department of Criminal Justice Home Page (monitor the execution machine in Texas): http://www.tdcj.state.tx.us
8. Refuse & Resist!: http://www.refuseandresist.org
9. The International Action Center: http://www.iacenter.org
10. The New Afrikan Movement: http://www.nalfnationtime.com
11. The Justice Policy Institute Publications: http://www.cjcj.org/jpi/publications.html
12. October 22nd Coalition to Stop Police Brutality, Repression, and the Criminalization of a Generation: http://www.October22.org

acknowledgments

Whether this book's rhetoric is raised in lament, denunciation, or in an announcement of hope and life, I must acknowledge those who suffer in lockdown America today. They have not only cried out, they have organized. They have invited those of us in the outer prison to think along with them while they labor within the belly of the beast that is America's carceral archipelago, its prison and death row system.

I send thanks, then, to Mumia Abu-Jamal, whose struggle for his own life and for others, has waged a resistance to empire exemplary to us all. As my quoting him at the outset of the Preface suggests, I consider him both leader and colleague in the struggle all of us must wage if we value real justice for all in the American lands of the twenty-first century. I remember, too, Ziyon Yisraya, executed in Indiana in 1996 (one of two black men executed for the death of a white detective in a predawn police raid, in which prosecutors still don't know whose bullet killed him). Those especially, who die in struggle, live on in our marching and organizing, giving power 'til the fight is won. We remember you, Ziyon.

I remember, too, Gary Graham (Shaka Sankofa, as he renamed himself) who was executed on June 22, 2000, maintaining an innocence that was supported by human rights activists the world over, and also by the *New York Times,* which devoted three editorials to him within the space of one week. Sankofa breathed his last while looking at the Reverend Jesse Jackson, Sr., and saying, "They know I'm innocent. . . . They are killing me tonight. They are murdering me."[1] Sankofa died on the lethal injection gurney, after putting up a fierce physical fight, and, according to witnesses, with one eye open.

I like to interpret that one open eye as the vigilance that the forever dead maintain in the world of the living. I take that open eye as a challenge to remember (the very idea, by the way, signaled by the African notion of *Sankofa*[2]) all the tormented ones, dead or alive, who have unjustly suffered lockdown America. These dead, through our remembrance and action, are a resource for the struggles we still must undertake.

Grateful thanks go out also to Reginald Lewis, also on Pennsylvania's death row, turning out stories and plays for children to perform at different times of the church year, for my worshiping community and for others. I am grateful to Lawrence Hayes, a one-time death row inmate in New York, who earned his master's degree from New York Theological Seminary while in prison and now, upon his exoneration and release, teaches every citizen who will listen about the draconian twists and turns of criminal justice and injustice in the United States.

I must acknowledge all those who have come to see that the prison system today is about much more than punishing violators, who know firsthand its intention to terrorize. I see this book as one of many texts in that diverse discourse called liberation theology, in which thinking about God follows and seeks to support liberating struggle for all. I have attempted to listen, think, and act in the way of those who have cried out from these places of suffering and oppression, to lament a lockdown America that threatens us all.

This book does not claim to be any simple rendering of their voices. Their voices live in the street and rally speeches of activists, in the newsletters circulating among those struggling in support of them, through the mail, the Internet. Their voices cannot be replaced by any of the words I formulate for this book. Their voices, and the movement of many others' voices and lives of resistance, create a milieu for this book, a veritable power of people on the move who hold this book in a dynamic place. While I have been working as scholar and activist on criminal justice issues since 1976 (first, when investigating prisoner complaints in the Virginia State Penitentiary, Richmond), the voices of the confined, crying out into a new millennium now as much as ever before, have enlivened the concerns treated in this volume. In many ways, without claiming to speak for them, I sense myself accountable to them.

Many of the imprisoned are some of those who have written letters to me about their struggle for life. I have not been able to respond adequately to them all. I have at times been overwhelmed by the numbers of those confined whose terror is clearly more than their error. The cynical among us will dismiss prisoners' laments as but the predictable complaining of violators who refuse to take personal responsibility for their actions, who blame the system. This dismissal overlooks the power of circumstances (pertaining to class and race, especially) that often lead to imprisonment, and slights the well-documented existence of political prisoners in the United States, those confined because of their political organizing against exploitative U.S. practices.[3] I have not been able to do enough for the numerous political prisoners in the United States, among them Sundiata Acoli, the MOVE 9, Leonard Peltier, Mutulu Shakur, and Assata Shakur in exile in Cuba. Their terror, if we rightly understand it, is a terror for all of us who, in different ways, inhabit this place called lockdown America. We must work and write because we share with them in the entire punitive order that characterizes this country today.

Several friends over the past years have quite literally helped keep me sane through the tumult of my political and personal life, especially James W. Jones, Kevin Reilly, and Susan Burnett (whom I remember as a sister in struggle for all political prisoners).

I have been enriched and strengthened by the people at the Imani Community Church, in Trenton, New Jersey, which was founded by friend and pastor, Rev. Jacqui Lewis-Tillman.

Within the growing movements for a death penalty moratorium and its abolition are many who have inspired me through their activism and example, most notably Jeff Garis of Pennsylvania Abolitionists United Against the Death Penalty, Lorry W. Post and friends of New Jerseyans for a Death Penalty Moratorium, Pat Clark and organizers of the American Friends Service Committee, and Sister Helen Prejean.

I have been enlivened, and instructed, by many activists who forge movements in the United States against seemingly insurmountable odds: Pam Africa, Ramona Africa, C. Clark Kissinger, Frances Goldin, Debra Sweet, Colleen Akai, Lee James, Miriam S. Goldberg, Harry Apple, Jason Corwin, Monica Moorhead, Rev. Lucius Walker, Leslie Jones, Suzanne Ross, Michael Yasutaki, Jeffrey Mackler, Safiya Bukhari, Bob Mandel, Robert Meeropol, Marpessa Kupendua, Tom Hansen, Bob Moore, Bob Witanek, and many more I should name but cannot do so here.

Deep appreciation goes out also to scholar-friends who dare also to be activists, especially to Elina Vuola, and also Marcus Rediker, Chung Hyun-kyung, Peter Linebaugh, Anna J. Brown, Farah Jasmine Griffin, Carolyn Birden, Robin D. G. Kelley, Martín Espada, Cornel West, Ched Myers, Robert Zaller, Dwight Hopkins, Lois Lorentzen, Richard Grounds, Carter Heyward, Eduardo Mendieta, George Tinker, Luis Rivera-Pagan, Anaida Pascual-Morán, David Batstone, Ann Farnsworth-Alvear, Will Coleman, Brett Greider, and all the many colleagues in the over one-thousand-member group, Academics for Mumia Abu-Jamal.

I also send out my gratitude to Princeton-area neighbors in the Coalition for Justice and Peace for Iraq, Ebtissam Ammar, Mike DeGregory, Matthias Gockel, Marietjie Odendaa, Mary Porter, Steve Slaby, Rima Taha, and others—all under the skillful direction of the Coalition's coordinator, Tamara Kohns.

Fortress Press, especially Michael West, saw the purpose and call for this book and helped make it better, as did others at Fortress to whom I am deeply grateful: Beth Wright, Tony Simon, Bob Todd, and Glendine Soiseth. Additionally, I thank Geneviève Duboscq for her excellent copyediting.

My community of employment, Princeton Theological Seminary, continues to provide generous support for research and writing each year. Three of my colleagues there, Professors Stacy Johnson, Sang Hyun Lee, and Brian K. Blount, took time to read portions or all of this book. Geddes and Carrie Hanson, Wentzel and Hester Van Huyssteen, Peter Paris—thank you for your friendship in this institution. Anita Kline, mother to my daughters, thank you for finding ways to make things work over the years.

Masters and doctoral students also continue to enliven and challenge my work—either by what they say, think, or write, or by how they forge their own activist lives for the justice we need to make. I am, therefore, deeply grateful to research assistant James Samuel Logan, who discussed portions of this book with me, and also to Giselle Remy, Ruth and Scotty De Jesus, Ryan Byers, Heather White, Omar Ortiz, Traci Franks, and Elizabeth Weill-Greenberg.

Music lovers will understand that I cannot survive a day without a song and music. I cannot omit, therefore, sending thanks out to friends Theodore ("Lôlô") and Mimerose Beaubrun of Boukman Eksperyans, as well as to daily friends to my ear, in no special order, such as Oscar Chávez, Bruce Springsteen, Ana Gabriel, Bob Dylan, Ruth Gerson, Ben Harper and the Innocent Criminals, Common, Lauryn Hill, Jimi Hendrix, Sweet Honey in the Rock, Ani DiFranco, Victor Jara, Mzwakhe Mbuli (may he soon be free!), Michael Franti of Spearhead, Luciano, Lucky Dube, Ozomatli, Paul Robeson, Cassandra Wilson, Bruce Cockburn, Dead Prez, Pablo Milanes, and the essential and irreplaceable Robert Nesta Marley. Would that I could write in a way that honored more the revelation worked by these musicians.

Grateful acknowledgment is also made to photographer David Michael Kennedy, for the arresting photo used on this book's cover. It depicts an eerie place of human killing, the gas chamber in the state of New Mexico. The picture may say more than my thousands of words. I will note, however, that its play with light and shadow well dramatizes the state's usurpation of godlike power over life and death, a usurpation that this book contests as illegitimate and destructive to us all. The photo also depicts the way executions today are situated in the built environment of prisons, full of the gadgetry and the clanking metal, pipes, and Plexiglas of an industrial material world, fueled by the exploitative capitalist and racist modes of production and punishment explored in this book.

While I am deeply grateful to all those named in these Acknowledgments, I do not presume that all would endorse what I have done in this book, and I know that many would not even agree with my attempt to offer a volume developing a Christian rhetoric for today's justice struggle. I surely hold none responsible for any flaws or missteps in this work. All of them, however, have formed the multiple, communal worlds of support and challenge within which my writing has emerged.

Finally, my work is part of the better future I dream for those to whom this book is dedicated, my daughters, Laura Kline-Taylor and Nadia Kline-Taylor.

index